Trading Miracles for Grace

Exploring Reality and the Collateral Damages of Miracle Claims

"I THINK YOU SHOULD BE MORE EXPLICIT HERE IN STEP TWO."

JEFF EDDINS

Trading Miracles for Grace

Exploring Reality and the Collateral
Damages of Miracle Claims

JEFF EDDINS

CONTENTS

Foreword

AT FIRST GLANCE THIS BOOK MIGHT APPEAR TO BE A skeptic's case against God and his power to intervene. Cynics may even look forward to reading this with an attuned sense of excitement as they hope to collect evidence against a supernatural being. But after reading *Trading Miracles for Grace*, I must say they will be disappointed.

I read this manuscript with a concerned eye on what the author, Jeff Eddins, was trying to accomplish. Fairly quickly it became apparent this book addresses one aspect of many people's faith that garners very little attention. For those who have been faithful, lived a difficult and seemingly unblessed life, and struggle with God's apparent absence, Eddins opens up a landscape for a new optimistic discussion.

As a practicing clinical psychologist for the last twenty-seven years, I have been privileged to counsel families and individuals in the wake of unspeakable tragedies. I have witnessed firsthand many Christians who walk away from God because he was not there for them in their greatest time of need. In my experience, this is the leading reason people leave the faith they once held dearly.

I have sat with countless grieving parents who've just lost a child, and they inevitably asked me, "Why would a God who loves us allow this to happen?" That is a very important question and one that Eddins tackles with a conscientious and thorough approach. I have heard many sermons over the years attempting to explain "why bad things happen to good people" and for those who find themselves in the throes of these tragedies, most of those explanations never seem adequate. Adding salt to their wounds, future exposure to others' claims of godly favor only adds greater angst and a sense of unfairness.

This book has the potential to help those who begin to have serious questions about their faith. Considering a different approach, even a different way of thinking about people who struggle with the incompatibility of a loving God who can but doesn't intervene is worthy of serious attention. *Trading Miracles for Grace* offers a deeply introspective and responsible exploration of these challenging questions.

This book is autobiographical, soul baring, and honestly risky for the author amongst many Christian communities because it can be easily misconstrued. But I believe this book needed to be written. Eddins successfully argues that: God exists, created our universe, Christ died for our sins, there is hope for everlasting life, and the fact that people do not receive miracles or experience Him as others claim is not evidence that God doesn't exist or that He does not love us. Eddins postulates a passive God is not an aloof God. *Trading Miracles for Grace* is a personal journey that can become your journey if you're willing to consider the author's case. I urge you to read it completely before judging it.

W. Rand Walker, Ph.D.

Educational & Psychological Services

Moscow, Idaho

Acknowledgements

FIRST, I WANT TO THANK ALL MY FRIENDS AND FAMILY who have spent their precious time over the years debating, tolerating, and offering input that has truly helped shape the content of this work. This includes two of my close friends and dedicated employees and the countless discussions they endured during our lunch breaks. To JR and Sergio, I'm not sure how much you really enjoyed our discussions on spirituality or how much you entertained my opinions only because you both wanted paychecks. I also want to thank the numerous people from the small group Bible studies I've participated in over so many years. They've suffered greatly listening to my doubts and challenging positions, and I want to acknowledge them here.

Secondly, many others have read early versions of this manuscript and offered credible pushback in specific areas—identifying blind spots I never considered. I'm grateful to everyone who read and offered feedback.

This has been a long and arduous journey, and I want to thank those who watched me struggle and never gave up on me. It's been hard to accept, but a few my friends have distanced themselves over our theological differences. But I will forever be indebted to those who continually encouraged me to seek the truth, even while disagreeing with some of my positions. You have all played a significant role in helping me find a path to reasonably reconcile the God I've been trying to honor with the God of reality and the universe in which I reside.

We must love them both, those whose opinions we share and those whose opinions we reject, for both have labored in the search for truth, and both have helped us in finding it.

—Thomas Aquinas

Introduction

SOMETHING WAS EATING AWAY AT ME AND HAD BEEN doing so for a very long time. Years of attendance and involvement with church left me with doubts regarding certain aspects of my Christian faith. I was certain that it was not some evil entity leading me away from God nor was it a lack of desire to humble myself and submit to what I thought God wanted from me. It couldn't have been a desire to distance myself from some of Christianity's traditional beliefs and practices because there was a time in my life when I would have been too afraid of segregating myself from my Christian family and friends.

I struggled for many years trying to make portions of the faith and God I desired to follow match with my observable reality. I could not make sense of some of God's biblical attributes and others' claims of God bestowing favor on them as well as some traditional practices of Christianity. To make matters worse, no one seemed to fully understand my struggles, and all I received from others were the "pat" Christian answers that never satisfied. Before I knew it, I was wandering alone in the middle of a vast desert, teetering on the edge of complete disbelief with no visible oasis on the horizon.

It's been more than two decades since I started to have a "crisis of faith." I wasn't doubting God's existence or my salvation through the gracious act of Jesus, but I began to feel inauthentic about other parts of my Christianity. I was in my late thirties and deeply struggling with what I perceived to be God's inactivity. It was becoming even more obvious that prayer seemed to be ineffective in seeing God move.

I would share my heart with God and pray on behalf of others, but the heavens always seemed to be silent. I just couldn't understand how to have a personal relationship with a God who didn't talk back let alone send some sort of a signal that I could interpret. Perhaps I wasn't qualified to hear or receive favor from God because my faith was insufficient. I thought, certainly, the reason behind God's refusal to communicate with me or provide relief to my prayers had to do with some insufficiency on my part because so many others claimed that God intervened and communicated with them. I just carried on like a good little soldier and stuffed that issue deep within until it didn't feel authentic anymore.

There are many like me who have or are currently struggling both emotionally and intellectually as they try to reconcile their reality with the Christian God they desperately want to honor. But most struggling Christians will never outwardly admit that. If you're able, please tell me where Christians turn after prayerfully calling on God to physically heal, protect, or provide peace and comfort, but never received anything? How do they reconcile these matters after always hearing and believing that God loves them and would be there in their greatest time of need?

Is the simple answer that they just need to accept those outcomes because, "God's ways are higher than our ways" or, it just wasn't in his plans or his will to help them? What is it like for a Christian parent who prayerfully begged God to heal their child from an unthinkable disease, yet God's apparent answer was, "No"? By what means do Christian parents put their worldview back together after losing their infant child who just didn't wake up from his afternoon nap? How does a husband who desperately pleaded for a miracle continue to trust in an active God after watching his wife succumb to cancer—leaving four young children motherless? Can Christian parents sincerely celebrate the birth of their physically or mentally disabled child after always believing God was involved in the fetal formation process?

What happens in the wake of atrocities like these when Christians ask God for peace and strength, but their anxiety, sorrow, and weakness never seem to subside? Tragedies like these—coupled with silence from the heavens and exposure to others' claims of godly favor—can lead many Christians to feel abandoned by God. In most instances, it disintegrates what seemed to be a concrete godly foundation into a vast sinkhole of quicksand.

In part, I'm writing this book for all hurting Christians like those mentioned above who love God deeply but are struggling to reconcile the God characterized in the Judeo-Christian Bible and portrayed by fellow Christians consistently with their reality. My intended audience includes devout evangelical Christians, Sunday-only Christians, and those considering God (seekers). Ironically, this book also invites non-believers to reconsider God in a way perhaps they never have. This is simply a call to logical reality, sincerity, and human kindness.

Attempting to address the ideologies of people who reside on opposite ends of the belief spectrum is a tall order, but I hope to offer everyone an alternate and perhaps a more authentic pathway to God for them. What you're about to read is my attempt to express my experience, strength, and the center of my hope.

I have deep empathy for believers who find it difficult to fit the pieces of their perception of God together in a way that meets with their reason, because I once sat there. I also have great sympathy for those who feel they have no choice but to reject the notion of the Christian God because they too find it difficult to reconcile with their own realities the God described in certain Scriptures and what I have found to be unreasonable "favor claims" made by today's Christians where he answers every prayer, even trivial ones.

Are you a Christian struggling with doubts because your faith posits that God cares enough about us to intervene on our behalf, yet you don't see that? Is your faith even in God's existence foundering because you see no real evidence of his activity? Are you struggling to reconcile what others claim God has actively provided them with the observations of horrific global suffering? Do you wonder at times why so many others claim to receive affirmative answers to prayer, godly communication, provisions of wisdom, peace, or strength, but you seem to be excluded from such favor? Do you have strong doubts regarding some of the biblical stories that do not seem believable to you? I've walked in your shoes.

Whether you're a Christian, an atheist, or anywhere in the spectrum between those two positions, are you able to entertain the possibility that the Bible contains *some* premises and claims that were simply man's attempt to describe the character and activities of God but were not always completely accurate? Is it possible for you to consider a Creator of this universe who has an immense, immeasurable love for you yet does not supernaturally alter the circumstances of your life to provide favor? Can you be open to accepting the sacrificial forgiving love of Jesus while simultaneously acknowledging that God's choice to provide your free will also means He will not be controlling or manipulating the events of your life?

If you're willing to take this journey with me, I'll do my best to convince you it's possible to live a full and abundant hope-filled life that does not require expectations or hope for godly intervention nor acceptance of others' claims of godly favor nor literal acceptance of every biblical story. I can assure you claiming to believe Jonah lived in the belly of a giant fish for three days or that Noah built an ark and loaded it with pairs of animals or that God is favorably altering anyone's circumstances today is not a requirement by God to live a life that honors him—irrespective of the validity of those biblical stories or miracle claims made by others today.

As you make your way through the following topics, I hope you'll be willing to seriously consider arguments that are contrary to what most of us have been taught about God and his purported current desire to intervene on our behalf. As troubling as this may initially appear to be, I'll be asking you to consider evidence that conflicts with what you may want to believe to be true and honestly weigh that evidence against the common realities of our world. You should also note that *everything* I will be arguing against regarding current godly intervention is something I once hoped for, claimed to believe, and runs contrary to everything I currently desire. Not to worry. You have a completely unbiased author here.

Here's a list of the signposts we'll be stopping at along our journey:

- The origin of the Bible and the known discrepancies, additions, and errors made by scribes who made copies as well as some of the embellished premises made by some of the unenlightened biblical authors
- The circumstantial evidence pointing to an Intelligent Designer while investigating the notion that God continues to create in a hands-on way every human after his initial creation
- The original sin and whether it's responsible for all current suffering
- Faith, hope, belief, and doubt, and their respective value-weighted applications
- "Theodicy," which simultaneously asserts that God is all powerful and all loving, yet he allows for suffering
- The biblical reasonings for suffering and contrasting current suffering with the legitimacy of current Christian miracle claims
- The efficacy of requesting prayers and whether the name-it-and-claim-it prayer promises of Jesus were meant to apply to anyone after his time on Earth
- Authentic prayer within the confines of non-supernatural reality
- Current blessing claims and how they sometimes conflict with Jesus's definition of them
- Purported miracle claims made by today's Christians
- Misapplication of Scripture
- Open Theism and its reflection of God's knowledge timetable

I sincerely hope you will see my humble hurting heart reflected in everything you'll encounter here. At times, it may not appear that way. I have no desire to hurt or mislead anyone. I want my words and expressions of hope to offer a pathway for emotional and intellectual equilibrium to those struggling in any way with their current perception of God. In places, the content you'll find here may be contrary to some of your current Christian beliefs, may be against what you want to believe to be true, and may create emotional distress for some. For those who find any of the content offensive or troubling, that is not my intention.

Throughout your read, I would like you to continually consider a quote from Steven R. Covey from the foreword of Alex Pattakos's book, *Prisoners of Our Thoughts*. Covey wrote, "Between stimulus and response there is a space. In that space is our power to choose our response. In our response lies our growth and our freedom."[1] Rather than initially reject something you disagree with here, I hope you'll use that "space" between any initial conflicting reaction you may have to critically think through the arguments posited.

I am fully aware that everyone brings their personal biases to the debate table as well as the many influences that have been ingrained in them from their education, upbringing, and life experiences. All of us seem to be guilty of defending our religiously biased truths to the bitter end. Our nature requires us to have a built-in defense mechanism that drives our unwillingness to consider opposing evidence or anyone else's worldview that conflicts with our own.

We're going on a journey, and I'm asking you to temporarily check any of your tightly held religious or even atheistic biases at the door and be open to what you may discover here. What makes being on a journey so potentially intriguing? You may not know what you'll discover along the way, what you'll do with what you find, or more importantly, *what you find will do to you.*

I'm not sure what brought you here, but I'm glad you showed up. I must forewarn you though; you've arrived at a place that may shake some foundational portions of your Christian belief system, but I mean that in a positive way. If you're a Christian who struggles to believe that God currently

---

1.   Steven Covey quoted by Alex Pattakos and Elaine Dundon, *Prisoners of Our Thoughts*, 3rd Ed. (Oakland, CA: Berrett-Koehler, 2017).

intervenes in our world or have doubts regarding the validity of portions of the Bible, you're in a safe place. If you're a Christian who believes God continues to be in the miracle business, I'll be providing some very important cautionary information that will identify potential risks and damages you may never have considered. If you're a seeker, a skeptic, or a non-believer and you have never been able to reconcile the biblically described God with the realities of this world, I'm hoping to provide a more reality-based pathway to do so.

Most of this book will focus on prayer, suffering, and current interventions commonly attributed to God. There are certainly diversions away from these topics which I felt were important to mention. I hope the reader will be able to identify with my thoughts and struggles. I doubt I'm the only one who thinks deeply about these matters.

You will also discover there are a few areas of redundancy. In part, this is due to the overlapping subject matter amongst the many topics. Rather than refer the reader to a previous chapter, I thought it better to briefly restate some of the previous arguments and how those arguments also relate to the current topic. I hope any redundancy will also serve as a reminder / refresher as well as help link the subject matter.

I'm aware it's impossible to have everyone agree with all my positions or to make anyone understand a message they're not ready to receive. Considering that, I think it's important we consider the quote from St. Augustine, who once said, "In essentials unity, in non-essentials liberty, in all things charity." It will be up to you to decide which portions of your faith are essential and if there are any portions that are not.

Although there are some references to biological terms and a few probability calculations, this book is not scientifically detailed and is certainly written in layman's terms. I've never tried to collect my thoughts in this way, but I hope the reader will gain something and maybe even be challenged for the better.

PART 1:

HOW I GOT HERE

---

[1] My Journey to Authenticity

As much as I'd rather not share my personal history with you, I think it's important to know something about me. The more you know about my life experiences, the better you'll be able to understand my reality and how those experiences have shaped my God worldview.

I was born in 1961 in Los Angeles and adopted by my parents in January of 1962 after spending my first eight months in foster care. My father was a good dad in the sense that I always knew he loved and cared about me. He was never abusive and always encouraged me to come to him no matter what problems I encountered in my life. He wasn't really involved in my life per se, as he rarely left our house after work and didn't attend all my athletic events. He did take me fishing from time to time, which I greatly appreciated.

When it came to the spiritual side of life, my dad was not present. His "holy roller" Southern Baptist experiences growing up in Mississippi discouraged him from ever wanting to have anything to do with church. I never discussed spirituality with him. I'm sure he thought religion could be a good thing to help someone follow moral rules and learn how to be a better person, but nothing past that. Ironically, my dad told me the two things one should never discuss are religion and politics. At least I'll be honoring half of his instructions here.

My loving mother was a "reformed" Christian who was raised in a Midwestern Lutheran church. She told me in her later years she struggled as a child with the "fire and brimstone" style of churches she attended. When I was younger, I remember her taking my sister and me to a non-denominational church that replaced its organs and hymnals with guitars, keyboards, and drums. This more modern style of church played worship songs (older hymns too) that were more in line with the kind of music I enjoyed. The pastor of that church always dressed in casual clothes and not the frilly garb of pastors or priests in more formal churches.

When I was seven, I recited Psalm 100 in front of a small church we attended. For accomplishing that task, I was given my own King James Bible. That Bible had a black cover and all the edges of the pages and the words of Jesus were colored in red. I can't seem to remember what I had for lunch yesterday, but I can still recite those verses from memory.

Justice and Grace

Perhaps my doubts about God's activities or even his biblical character representations started when I was in a fifth-grade Sunday school class. The teacher was trying to teach us about God's endless forgiveness and that no matter how many times we sinned, he would forgive us. So, in front of the entire class, I asked her, "If I murdered someone and asked for God's forgiveness, would he forgive me?"

She said, "Yes, of course."

I then asked, "What if I kill and repent again?" She again said God would forgive me.

After about three more iterations of the same questions and her affirmations, I simply stated in front of the class, "Well, I don't want to believe in a God like that." The teacher immediately escorted me back to the adult sanctuary and carefully seated me next to my mother. Since then, I've come to have a better understanding of sincere repentance, justice, and God's amazing forgiving grace.

During my youth, I remember having dinner at my grandmother's house many times on Sunday evenings and watching the Billy Graham crusades on TV. His delivery and his preaching methods were powerful and impacted me. I loved listening to the invitation song, *Just as I Am*, and seeing the people humbly come to the front of the stage to either accept the gift of grace for the first time or to rekindle their relationship with God. There seemed to be sincerity and heartfelt emotion displayed on the faces of the people who came forward. It wouldn't be until later in my life that I would deeply experience this same forgiving grace that greatly moved me closer to God.

Making Sense of My World

I remember always being afraid of dying. I recall our entire grade school being sent home near the end of our school year when Robert Kennedy was assassinated. They continually played the videos of the assassinations of both Kennedy and his older brother on TV, and it frightened me.

When I watched the movie *Brian's Song* about a professional football player who died of cancer, I became a hypochondriac. There was always a sense my time on this Earth would come to a premature end. I was diagnosed at forty with a bone-marrow disorder, a chronic form of blood cancer that will undoubtedly limit my time on this Earth. So, I'm no longer a hypochondriac. I've jokingly asked my wife to place the phrase, "I told you I was sick!" on my tombstone.

During my freshman year in high school, I watched one of my baseball teammates keel over on the field during a game and die from a heart attack right in front of me. His autopsy revealed he had the heart of an eighty-year-old man, and his death rocked my world. I can still clearly picture him lying in his casket, clothed in his green and gold–colored baseball uniform at his Catholic funeral. I remember thinking, "What was the purpose of his short life? If God loves and protects those of us who love him, or if Jesus loves all the little children as the Sunday school song suggested, why would he allow this boy to die at only fourteen?"

My mom bought me a special Bible in high school that had four different translations and showed all the same verses on the same page. I loved that

Bible, because if I couldn't understand the King James Version, I could easily look at another translation on the same page to gain a better understanding. It's funny to me now that I preferred trying to read the Shakespearean English of the old King James Version when I was younger. Perhaps I thought it better represented the exact words God wanted for us. I must have errantly thought Jesus originally spoke in Old English (thees and thous) during his days on Earth and it sounded different (smarter?) than the modern English I was used to. Today I find it strange there are Christians who continue to read and quote from the Old King James version.

Reading the words of Jesus really impacted me. He seemed like a quiet man who spoke with a calm wisdom. Even at an early age, I could see his parables and teachings were filled with power and wisdom for life application.

Choosing a Path in Life

I met my high school sweetheart and future wife when I was sixteen. She came from a stricter Lutheran background, but I watched her quickly move away from that denomination the more she was exposed to the informal non-denominational churches that were popping up around us. We read the Bible and prayed together, and I recall how good that made me feel. My mother and grandmother always encouraged me to find a Christian girl who loved God, and I was willing to take their advice. But I had a problem. I was too spiritually weak to overcome my own pleasure-seeking desires and was easily influenced by peer pressure. When I was with my girlfriend, I acted one way, but acted completely opposite around my friends. I truly was a chameleon. I claimed I was a Christian and tried to live that way as best I could but always had a sense of guilt when I was acting differently around my friends. I realized early it was extremely challenging to live up to the standards of Jesus and just how easy it was for me to choose wrong.

Playing football was my passion from the age of ten through my first two years in college. I studied very hard in math and science, but football was my life, and I desperately wanted to play in the NFL someday. In 1979,

I graduated from high school and went to college to play football and hopefully obtain a degree in physics. I played two years of college football (really played one year on the JV team and sat the varsity bench the next) before realizing I just didn't have the physical tools required to compete on that level, or certainly the next.

I was emotionally crushed the day I told my coach I was done. I can still picture the scene as I placed my white cleats on the top shelf of my closet with tears pouring down my cheeks, knowing my lifelong dream would never come to fruition.

My wife and I were married in 1983, and I finally graduated in 1985. We regularly attended a church in Davis, California, as well as a couples' small group Bible study. After graduating, we returned to Los Angeles where I went to work in the aerospace industry.

Within two years of returning to Southern California, we had two young children and attended a non-denominational church. Although I was sprinkled as a child, I decided to get baptized by immersion. I was ready to restart my life with a Christian belief system that seemed strong, and a young family I loved beyond measure.

Risky Business

In 1987, I left the aerospace industry to work for a friend in a small communications business before having to relocate for work in Las Vegas in 1990. It didn't take long for me to fall there. I started gambling, and video poker became my drug of choice. It was a lucky thing I didn't have a lot of money at that time because there's no telling how much I could have lost during those first two-and-a-half years we lived there.

I continued to attend church with my family, and nobody knew about my secret gambling habit. I regularly lied to my wife about having to meet with clients through the late-night hours, all while sitting in front of a poker machine until the wall-mounted ATM refused to give me another dime. Jeff the chameleon had reemerged in full force. One of my close friends suspected my gambling problem, but I was able to keep my secret from my immediate family.

Then, in 1993, our church on the east side of Las Vegas birthed a new church in the northwest and closer to our home. They hired a pastor from Kentucky and another from Ohio to lead it. We met in a local YMCA on a gym floor with the 350 people who left our parent church on the east side of town.

Our new pastor was an amazing speaker, and I was always fixated on his every word. I helped set up and tear down our makeshift church each Sunday, which included children's classrooms located in racquetball courts. We were as portable of a church as one could imagine. Since I was there before, during, and after our two services, I felt lucky that I had the opportunity to hear our pastor recite the same sermon twice each Sunday, giving me a better chance to retain his messages. It was incredible how he presented "the Word of God" and its life application.

Facing My Issues

In April of 1993, about four months after we started our new church, our pastor invited one of his friends from Kentucky to give his testimony at our Wednesday night service. This guest speaker spent four years in a Kentucky prison for embezzlement from the bank where he served as its vice president. Why did he embezzle? He needed to feed his gambling addiction.

He was an elder in my pastor's former church in Kentucky at the time of his arrest. He wrote over $250,000 in fraudulent loans at his bank to fuel his habit. He told us how he'd stuck a gun in his mouth and urinated on himself as he sat in his car in a vacant parking lot for eight hours, waiting for the authorities to show up. His wife found his suicide note but he didn't have the guts to pull the trigger while sitting in his car. I sat in that auditorium with tears streaming down my face as I listened to him give his gut-wrenching testimony. I realized I was just like him and related in so many ways to his suffering and addiction.

I could identify with so many of his struggles and the emotional toll gambling had on my own life. I remember on many occasions frantically running back to my car and desperately digging through my seats to find loose change, hoping to parlay that into winning some portion of my money back. I recall so many times crying out to God in my car after leaving the casino with not a penny to my name. I begged God to help me stop, and so many times I promised him I would.

Apparently, my addiction ran too deep—even for a supposed circumstance-altering God. My wife told me our seven-year-old daughter once asked her, "Is daddy's car going to be in the driveway tonight, or is it going to be out all night like it always is?" I would recall the goodness that came from the heartwarming Focus on the Family video series, *Turn Your Heart Toward Home*, that was shown at our church in California years before.

I was living in guilt and shame. My world was caving in, and I was completely lost as I sat in that church in my emotional "rock bottom". I was failing as a Christian husband and father, and hearing this guy from Kentucky tell his story literally brought me to my knees. As I sat there, I knew my life needed to change.

When my wife and I arrived at our house that night, I couldn't stop crying. After putting the kids to bed, we sat on our couch and I told her everything about my gambling and my lying and that I was sincerely ready to change. My lustful desires to have ongoing affairs with video poker machines had destroyed whatever trust my wife had for me and any measure of integrity I had for myself. She never deserved to be with someone like me, and I'll never understand why she chose to stay. I needed yet "another" second chance, and I was honestly ready to get right with God and her this time. Gambling led me to a place of quiet desperation, and I was ready to become the man I believed God wanted me to be.

I attended the first Gamblers Anonymous (GA) meetings at our small portable church. For the longest time it was just me and the guy who started it. His name was Luke, and he was a humble pillar of strength for me. He took me to local GA meetings around town, and then I found myself desiring to go to those meetings alone. I remember thinking, "How could a "good" guy like me end up in a room full of strangers, introducing myself with, 'My name is Jeff, and I'm a compulsive gambler'?" Gambling humbled me, and even today, I know I'm only one quarter and one video poker machine away from failing all over again.

I became very involved in our new church. It was starting to grow, and so was I. A friend of mine and I organized the first men's retreat that impacted the lives of many men in our church. I attended my first Promise Keepers event in Boulder, Colorado, and I'm getting chills as I type just reflecting on that event.

Turning Point

I remember walking into that stadium about fifteen minutes late with sixty men from my church. The worship band was playing a song I can't remember, but I remember hearing fifty thousand men singing in a deep tone. It still brings tears to my eyes when I reflect on it. I called my wife from my cell phone she could hear the music and singing I was experiencing.

I felt rescued from a life of deception and sin, and I was on a spiritual high. At that time, I felt God was actively involved in my life (rather than simply my engagement with God), and I was basking in his amazing forgiving grace. I had no concerns that God's continued active intervention in my life would ever fade.

I developed a servant's spirit and wanted others to know about the true freedom and salvation I had experienced. I gave my gambling testimony in front of our church and then later was invited to be interviewed by Dr. James Dobson on one of his *Focus on the Family* radio broadcasts. I began attending both a weekly men's and a couple's small group Bible study. As those groups expanded, we split them up to make room for others. As I became more experienced, I became the leader of some of those groups.

In our men's groups, we were deeply transparent with each other. We shared the details of our lives with each other and became close friends. We didn't sugarcoat life and held each other accountable to God's biblical standards. As the leader, I was taking prayer requests from the group members and praying for their needs in front of them.

I also began to step up in a spiritual way with my family. I didn't just thank God for the food before each meal or pray for safety when leaving in the car on a road trip. I sat on the edge of my children's beds on a nightly basis reading *Focus on the Family* devotionals and then kneeling and praying with them at their bedside. We talked about their concerns and fears. When they reached an appropriate age, we talked about God's expectations for their lives, his endless love, and his amazing grace. I wanted my children to know the depth of love I had for them as well as how much God loved them. I wanted them to feel secure in the arms of our protective "Heavenly Father" every night I tucked them into bed.

I had never been on fire for God like that. I wasn't much of a guitar player but got asked to play in the background during our smaller Wednesday night worship services. On occasion, when absolutely no one else was available, they let me play in the big service on Sundays. When I played my guitar and could hear the people of our church singing to God—all in the direction of the stage where I stood, it was another "spiritual" high for me.

On a side note, I had such horrible singing voice, the technical set-up guys for worship made sure there wasn't a microphone within a fifty-foot radius of where I was playing—just in case I started singing along. They wanted the church to have a chance to grow, and if anyone caught a note out of my voice box, things could go bad in the way of future attendance.

I loved the worship music we played at our church and the Christian artists that were on the scene at that time. I sat in my home and practiced those worship songs on my guitar for hours. My car was always loaded with Christian CDs, and I loved to worship God in that way. Listening to any other music genre at that time meant nothing to me. If I wasn't singing out to my God, I was only wasting my time.

Our church began to grow exponentially. We went from 350 people to 800 in about two years and from the YMCA gym floor to a large cafeteria in a local high school. We later bought property and built a very large auditorium of our own that we still call home. We're considered a mega-church now.

From 1993–2000, I attended at least one Promise Keepers' event per year, and it wasn't out of obligation. I truly wanted to learn and worship with a stadium full of like-minded fallible men who were also trying to honor God with their lives. I was amid 50,000 men who wanted to honor God by honoring their families. I will never forget the emotions I experienced at those events.

I remember breaking up into smaller groups at those events and listening to the other men share their struggles. I prayed for them in those groups and asked God to do something to help them, just as they prayed for me. In a similar way at our men's church retreats, we would find a place within the surrounding areas of the stadiums to sit alone and commune with God.

Are You There, God?

As I mentioned previously, I would share my heart with God during those "quiet times," but there never seemed to be any communication coming from God's end. I just couldn't understand how to have a personal relationship, one that had been encouraged by the Christian faith but never specifically mentioned in the Bible, with a God who never responded. I began to question whether others were being sincere when claiming God communicated with them or if my faith was insufficient in some way.

Sometime around 1998 (three years before my cancer diagnosis), problems began to mount. I mention the timing of my diagnosis because some may think my decision to refute godly intervention may have originated because I became angry or disgruntled with God for not healing me. There's no truth in that because I was clearly struggling with God's inactivity years before my diagnosis. I haven't thrown any celebratory parties over having cancer, but having a chronic disease has certainly made me appreciate life in a way I never could have. I'm basking in God's grace and plan to do so until I take my last breath.

I'm incredibly satisfied with the life I have lived and harbor no anger or bitterness towards my God because he has not shown specific special healing favor to me. As you will see going forward, I am convinced God has already shown his favor to all of us and his grace has completely satisfied the depths of my innermost soul. God's grace is *everything* to me, and *all* my hope is centered on that alone.

As I mentioned in the introduction, it was at this time I started to have a "crisis of faith" in a God who was actively involved in the events of this world. I wasn't doubting his existence or his love for me or others. But I'd had enough life experiences to see that prayer seemed to be ineffective in seeing God move. At times, I saw people move on God's behalf, but God seemed to be doing nothing.

My friends continued to claim specific life events were being controlled by God, but I could always formulate better reasonable and logical explanations that seemed much more plausible. As a small group leader, I continually led prayer for my fellow Christian group members, but that rarely seemed effective. If I prayed for someone's family member to be healed from a disease, they'd be dead within a week. If I prayed for someone to get a job they seemed to be on eternal unemployment. I lost count of how many of my friend's marriages ended in divorce after getting on my knees and asking God to intervene on their behalf.

When my prayers seemed to be effective, there was always a more logical and reasonable explanation than supernatural intervention. I started to wonder when my prayers appeared to have been answered favorably, if it was solely because my requests just happened to coincide with the natural events that would have occurred absent prayer. Were these God-incidences, or were they merely coincidences?

I specifically remember praying fervently for a sixteen-year-old girl in our church who loved God and was diagnosed with cancer. She was a high-school classmate of my daughter and came from a strong Christian family. Although our church was not a charismatic type of church and considered more watered-down compared to other more formal churches, our elders prayed and anointed her with oil as the biblical book of James suggests:

> Is anyone among you sick? Let them call the elders of the church to pray over them and anoint them with oil in the name of the Lord. And the prayer offered in faith will *make the sick person well*; the Lord will raise them up. If they have sinned, they will be forgiven. Therefore confess your sins to each other and pray for each other so that you may be healed. The prayer of a righteous person is powerful and effective. (James 5:14–16, emphasis mine)

Thousands in and out of our church were calling on God to do something, but she died after suffering for over a year. I remember her mother telling a group of us in the aftermath about the numerous times she went into her daughter's room at night, attempting to remove the fluid in her lungs that was nearly drowning her.

Did our prayers fail because our faith or the faith of our elders was insufficient, or were they lacking righteousness? Was adding oil to the equation some superstitious carryover from the people of the biblical era? Something was clearly faulty with this group of verses and I began to question their effectiveness and applicability for our era.

I prayerfully begged God to remove an anxiety and panic disorder from a close family member, but the heavens were silent. I was starting to feel guilty for my three daily pre-meal prayers—thanking God for the food he provided to me while fully aware millions of little children were succumbing to malnutrition on this globe. I felt embarrassed at times, as others observed me prayerfully plead to God for the relief of those who were suffering, only to have what felt like the "NO!" answer-door continually slammed in my face.

I was able to accept godly rejection, and I certainly wasn't requiring him to honor the name-it-and-claim-it promises many gather from the Gospels to always give us what we prayerfully asked for. I just couldn't reconcile a purported active, compassionate, and loving God ignoring the needs of innocent people who were suffering immeasurably while I was continuously being bombarded with favor claims from other Christian friends regarding how God had provided one seemingly petty thing after another.

[2] Facing Dis-Integration

FOR THOSE FIRST SEVEN YEARS OF MY REBIRTH INTO the Christian faith, I was able to stuff my doubts about others' claims regarding godly interventions. After that, my "doubt backpack" was overflowing, and it was becoming a heavy burden to carry. I was struggling intellectually and emotionally and realized my mental health was becoming compromised by the cognitive dissonance I was experiencing.

For me, our overall health is about more than what we're eating. It's also a function of what we're thinking, saying, and believing. I knew my mental health required a commitment to the common realities of our universe at all costs, even if it meant refuting others' current miracle claims or some generally accepted biblical positions held by the masses.

Rather than continuing to try to believe God would intervene out of his endless love for us or because I thought Jesus wanted to intervene to give his followers good gifts, I started to deeply doubt he intervened at all. Asking God for favorable intervention on behalf of my family or others seemed futile. I could keep on praying, but my prayers and meditations towards God were not going to be in the form of a request with expectations for anything, irrespective of what the generally accepted biblical interpretations or my "blessed" friends claimed.

I had to stop praying in the standard Christianese. I stopped using phrases such as "God help us to....," "God use us to...," "Guide us to...," "Watch over us," or "See that [a someone] would be healed." I concluded those prayers were only effective in reminding me or others around me of the difficult life concerns we were currently facing. I realized those types of requests were not going to cause God to act for anyone's favor. If they did, how could any of us sit at the top of our favored pedestal and accept that God was providing for our needs as he overlooked other Christians suffering without receiving any godly intervention.

My Christian friends continued to give God all the glory for the good things that happened in their lives. They continually claimed he moved and intervened on their behalf in every good circumstance of their lives. Somehow, they were able to discern when the mighty hands of God had moved favorably for them. If something unfavorable happened after praying in their family circle, their response was simply, "God's ways are higher than our ways," "everything happens for a reason," "it just wasn't in his plans," or "not his will," as if he manipulates and controls every action of every person or event for that matter.

It's as if we are to believe God constantly assesses and controls certain human circumstances and at times chooses to interfere with our personal free will, or the random events I am convinced are part of the chaotic universe we live in. I find it extremely disturbing when Christians give credit to God for favorable "answered prayer" and seem convinced he moved on their behalf yet throw their hands up in the air and declare "God's ways are higher than our ways" when their prayers seem to go unanswered or answered in the opposite of their request. They seem to know and understand everything about God's activity when the outcome of their prayerful request worked in their favor but claim it's a mystery no one will ever understand when it doesn't go their way.

Godly Intervention or Improvements in Medicine?

I just couldn't accept this way of thinking anymore. When a church member was declared in remission from cancer after receiving prayer, surgery, chemotherapy, and radiation, most if not all the praise and credit was given

TRADING MIRACLES FOR GRACE

to God. Was it a godly provision through prayer that healed the member, or was it more likely that only the medical procedures were responsible for their remission? If the family members would only have prayed and their loved one not sought medical attention, would that person's cancer have been remediated?

What about those with cancer 100 or even 50 years ago before the advent of so many medical advancements? What happened when the family members only prayed for their healing without the aid of today's medical procedures? One only needs to compare the morbidity rates for specific diseases over the last fifty (and more specifically the last thirty) years to know the advancement of medical science accounts for the diminishing rates of death by disease. Or should we consider prayer has become more effective over the last thirty years because humankind is more spiritually connected to God? I'm fairly certain that's not the reason. If our argument suggests that God is behind these declines, we'll have a lot of work ahead of us to explain why God didn't seem care for or intervene with the same frequency for those up to and before 1990.

The cancer death rate for both men and women in the United States has been trending downward since 1990. In men, the cancer death rate has dropped 1.8% per year over the last 30 years of available data. And in women, the death rate has dropped 1.4% per year during the same time period. Declines in death rates for female breast cancer, prostate, colorectal, and lung cancers are driving the overall decline in the cancer death rates in men and women.[2]

The statistics clearly show during the early 1990s through today, advancements in medical science are becoming more effective in remediating cancers. I think we can safely attribute these advancements to ongoing and accumulated knowledgeable research, the mapping of the human genome,

---

2.   "Cancer Mortality Continues Steady Decline, Driven by Progress against Lung Cancer," *Imaging Technology News,* January 13, 2020, https://www.itnon-line.com/content/cancer-mortality-continues-steady-decline-driven-prog-ress-against-lung-cancer.

computer science, as well our ability to share information quickly through the internet. It is blatantly obvious these death rates were not declining because God decided to become more active or that he decided in 1990 to start implanting disease-curing solutions into the minds of specific researchers.

Before the polio vaccine was invented and distributed in 1953, millions upon millions of expectant mothers prayed fervently to God that their unborn children would not be born with or later contract polio. I doubt any mother in the U.S. since the advent of that vaccine has spent any time worrying or calling on God to ensure her child does not contract polio. I'm not saying that medical science is the complete answer to ensuring our lives are not ridden with disease. I'm only pointing out what I think is improbable when it comes to divine healing.

I have never questioned the sovereignty of God (his supreme power). He's not powerless. He's simply established a position to allow us to experience the outcomes of our freewill choices, rogue cells to become cancerous within our bodies, drunk drivers and natural disasters to kill innocent people, and he does not favorably change our circumstances. Admittedly, it's not a "feel good" theology, but I'm convinced this is in line with our common realities. Accepting the fact that God has chosen to allow everything to run its course completely and reasonably explains the outcomes of the events occurring on this Earth. No mysterious explanations or apologetics are required here.

Today, I consider every miracle claim or "God-incidence" false—unless of course, the claimant can prove the God connection to their claim. To date, no one has ever been able to convince me their favor claim has been at the divine hands of God. Moreover, any human claim that God has performed a miracle on their behalf or by intercession on another's behalf, can only infer the Creator has shown them special favor—while others less fortunate continue to suffer and perish on this Earth.

Does God Play Favorites?

I cannot and do not consider myself so special in God's eyes that he would intervene on my behalf, and today I'm not sure I would want him to. After all, in multiple children's hospitals today, Christian parents will beg God through humble unselfish prayer to heal their child who will take their last breath as they suffer from some unthinkable disease. And other Christians will attempt to justify this using reasoning that the child is now in a better place while the surviving family lives the remainder of their lives in sorrow. They may also claim their prayers were not answered because God had a higher purposed reason to reject their humble request and their loved one is now safely home with God.

Considering that, should I ask God with any expectation for a promotion at my workplace? Should I thank him for the food I ate for lunch today because I believe he was responsible for providing it? What would a starving child think if he overheard me thanking God in prayer for providing my lunch today? Would I even have the courage to say a prayer of thanks like that in his presence? And if I wouldn't be willing to give thanks for my provisions in the presence of a starving child, why would I think it would be ok to do it anywhere or at any time?

I cannot reconcile selective interventive provisions without charging God with favoritism. It runs completely against my position that God is fair and just. If God is favoring the select few, perhaps he's not *actively* fair and just—at least from our perspective.

Facing Pushback

Meanwhile, some of my immediate family and friends started to look at me differently. It was as if I had gone to the dark side and now worshiped the pitchfork-wielding Satan. I think my friends felt threatened because, if I was right, it would mean they would only have medical science in their arsenal to combat their physical ailments—which is precisely my reality. It would also mean the biblically characterized God they've counted on for safety and security would not be there to physically protect them because they, too, would be subjected to the randomness of the events (both good and bad) of this chaotic world—just as I believe we all are.

Over the years I've had many people tell me, "You really don't even believe in God." They assume if I don't believe in an active, problem-solving, helping God, then I must not even believe in his existence. Nothing could be further from the truth for me. And to my surprise, some Christians have even asked me, "Why would you ever want to believe in a God like that?"

I've also had a few people tell me that I'm angry, and there is something deep within my heart that is driving me to think this way. They're right. I am angry, but certainly not with God. It should be very easy for you to ascertain during your read that justice is extremely important to me. I consider public miraculous claims of favor to be unjust to others who are suffering and receive nothing supernatural from God. These claims also paint God as a favorite player and is what has driven me to write here.

My Heart's Cry

I feel compelled to defend those who are doing without and continually hear others claim God's favor. My heart aches for those suffering, and I'm hoping to quell the desires of Christians who continue to, even if unintentionally, hurt others less fortunate with their unjust miracle claims. I'm pleading with Christians to consider the less fortunate and abandon any concern God will somehow be disappointed because they refused to make their apparent favor claim public.

After deep contemplation and emotional suffering, I needed to choose how I was going to perceive our all-powerful, loving and "active" God. I could just try to gut my way through and ignore the conflicts that were eating away at me. Or I could choose to walk away completely and reject the Christian faith, or even God.

My alternative was to modify what I thought I understood about God and try to find a way to reconcile Christianity and its biblical claims with my reality. There were some precepts / stories / promises in the Bible that I believe are not true or applicable for us today no matter how infallible or timeless Christians claimed they were.

Jesus claimed in John 14:6 that he was the way, the truth, and the life, and I was more than willing to believe that. For his statement to be true to me, I had to alter my way of interpreting what I believed was true for all of us today and what was applicable only to those in Jesus's era. I also needed to parse out some of the biblical authors' errant theories regarding how the universe operated as well as some of the unlikely representations of God's purported activities. I knew this also meant there were some complete stories in the Bible I would need to reject as actual events and try to glean as much as I could from a metaphoric perspective. I wanted to know how much of the Bible was "inspired" by God and just how much of it was only human thought, opinion, and positions on specific matters.

Looking for Answers

Where would I turn to for my answers? The Bible, of course. At that time, a friend and elder of our church held Precept Ministry Bible studies in his home every week. Those Bible studies were intense, and they examined every aspect of the written Word in detail. I thought, if I'm really going to know God and gain a better understanding of him, then I must dig deeper into his Word. I was hungry to know more and wanted to investigate every detail of the Scriptures I studied. I attended these studies on a weekly basis for over two years and invested at least eight hours per week dissecting and analyzing the Scriptures we studied. However, the deeper I researched within those studies, the more intense my internal struggles became. Exposing myself to this deeper form of study revealed even more conflicts with my reality. My questions and doubts became overwhelming.

When that didn't work, I turned to every Christian self-help book I could get my hands on to see if there were things I was missing. I emailed and briefly met with Lee Strobel, who is the author of *A Case for Christ* and many other Christian apologetics books. I wrote to the Dallas Theological Seminary multiple times to gain insight on the things that plagued me. I met with my pastor on a biweekly basis and probed his mind for the answers I so desperately needed. I exchanged many emails with Christian teachers I respected looking for help.

Unfortunately, it seemed their answers were never satisfactory to my soul or certainly my reason. Their answers never resolved my conflicts or reconciled some of the generally accepted biblical promises and God's biblical characterizations with my reality. The snowball started down the hill and there seemed to be no effective way to stop its momentum.

The term "deconstruction" is widely used in today's churches to describe the process I have been through. The older and more popular terms of similarity were either "backslidden" or "fallen away," but "fallen away" normally refers to one who has abandoned faith in God's existence. There are multiple ways one can deconstruct their faith. They can range from altering only a single position away from traditional Christian views, all the way to renouncing the Christian faith completely.

All or Nothing?

For many Christians, it's an all or nothing proposition, but I'm convinced it doesn't have to be that way. Unfortunately, it seems refuting the notion of an active God or only selectively accepting what I consider to be accurate accounts within the Bible for many conservative Christians is equivalent to renouncing the entirety of Christianity. This completely explains why it's difficult to have meaningful conversations with many evangelicals since they are steadfast in their positions that one must take the entire Bible in the way they think it should be interpreted, with no allowance to be selective about any of it. I saw a meme the other day that summed up that notion. It said, "God is not going to rewrite the Bible for your generation. Stop trying to remove portions, or change it, when it was written to change you." My response to that is simply, "Many of the portions of the Bible have changed me, and some portions are either false or were never meant to apply to us today."

I am at odds with many of my close friends, even some immediate family members over whether God is active. I'm convinced there will be many people attacking my positions on these issues and who will consider my positions heretical. I fully expect to be the target for a huge battery of arrows launched from conservative evangelical Christians whose positions are deeply entrenched in the rigid dogma of the church. And all I can say is, "Bring it!"

At this point in my life, I don't really care what people think about my theology. I'm interested in truth, even if it ends up only being my understanding of it. During some point in my journey, I lost my fear of a God who will eternally torture me for using my reasoning to try to understand who he really is and whether he currently intervenes. If there really is going to be a judgment day, I feel confident God will not accuse me of not paying attention to him or saying I wasn't seeking the truth about him with all my heart.

Review and Revamp

I have spent the last two decades reconsidering my God worldview. Who is this God and what is his true character? Is he the God of only the Jews? Is he the God of only the Jews and Christians, or is he also the Allah of Islam? Did he reveal his true character and desires to only one special faith-based group, and are there certain races or cohorts which have been shown favor and revelation over others throughout any time during mankind's existence?

Was Jesus really God in the flesh? Did God create the Earth and all its creatures, perform miracles on their behalf, and send Jesus to Earth 2000 years ago? Assuming Jesus was resurrected, was that the final miracle, or does he continue to intervene as many Christians claim? Does he actively communicate with his creation, provide wisdom, strength, or peace to certain favored people? Or is it more likely we knowledgeably gain wisdom, strength, and peace when we align ourselves and live within certain life-fulfilling instructions made by Jesus?

Do all the religious positions we hold by faith meet with the observable common realities within the universe we reside? Is God really working behind the scenes, manipulating people, their circumstances, or their consequences? Moreover, if the Bible and *all* the words of Jesus are true and applicable to us today, shouldn't they also be reflected in our com mon reality?

After nearly twenty-five years, I finally stopped attending my biweekly couple's small group Bible study. To say it was a struggle does not do justice. I loved the people in my group as if they were my own family, and I would still do anything to help them if or when they were in need. They are humble people who want to honor God with their lives.

The problem for me was I really couldn't contribute much in the way of petitionary prayer or agree with claims they made regarding God's current activity. Although I enjoyed the Bible studies that were centered on Jesus, it was very difficult to continue attending these sorts of groups because I didn't believe in the efficacy of prayer with respect to God supernaturally changing circumstances. I don't think my friends in my small group thought negatively about me. I think they wished I would just see the light and conform to their standard way of Christian thinking that I once held.

My small group was ok with me sharing my doubtful thoughts regarding requesting prayers and its ineffectiveness, but I didn't really want to spoil their party. They wanted to get together and confirm what they said they believed. They didn't want to hear from someone who was continually questioning something they desperately wanted to believe—even if at times, what they claimed to believe ran completely counter to the common realities of our world.

Defying Labels

Today, I find it difficult to precisely classify myself within one denominational church that describes what I believe. I seem to have belief systems that can be found in multiple sects of different Christian denominations as well as some that are outside of Christianity. I want to believe that Jesus was God in the flesh, and I hope with all my heart and soul that the Bible's characterization of Jesus is correct. I honestly don't know if any of the miracle stories outside of some sort of general creation story have any truth. Perhaps every biblical miracle story is true, but I don't believe God actively intervenes on this Earth today which partially places me in the deist, or maybe even the process theist camp. For deists, humans can know God only via reason and the observation of the natural world that God created but not by revelation or supernatural manifestations (such as godly instructions in written form or miracles)—phenomena which deists regard with caution if not skepticism.

Most deists claim the Bible is a human book that is false and stand firmly on the fact that God is not and has not intervened after establishing his creation. But being a deist would mean to throw out the possibility that Jesus was God and man, simply making him a wise historical man. It would certainly throw out the resurrection claim. That's a hard scenario for me to accept and admittedly, it's all because I was raised and indoctrinated in a God/Man Jesus who supposedly loved all of us enough to die for our transgressions.

I've worshiped Jesus for the greater part of my existence and it's a very difficult struggle to even consider moving away from the picture of a man performing a suffering sacrifice like that, if in fact Jesus was God in the flesh and his purpose was to offer forgiveness through that suffering. But deism makes sense to me and not just because it purports to be a religion of reason and not faith in godly activity. Deism also resonates with me because it has always been available in the same way and form to every human—not just some special sect of humans like the Jews and later the Christians. Deists love God as much as any Christian or Jew can claim they do, and they are thankful for God's initial creation.

Thomas Jefferson, one of our founding fathers, was a deist. He took multiple copies of the Bible and removed every miracle claim from both the Old Testament and the New Testament. He then pasted the remaining sections together to create his own Bible excluding all miraculous portions. He would later be labeled as a "Christian deist," an oxymoron to be sure. Jefferson was a follower of Jesus, although he considered Jesus only as an incredibly wise man and not a divine being. Thomas Paine was another founding father who authored the book, *The Age of Reason*, detailing his reasoning for accepting deism. I mention these two men because many Christians claim that all the founding fathers of the US were miracle-believing orthodox Christians. There were other founding fathers who also practiced other forms of unorthodox faith.

I have always struggled with any major religion that excludes people of other religions from the afterlife. If any one of the major religions is the one true religion of the God of this universe, then by default, the others are false. Deism states there is only one God and he is available to everyone—but not through a godly Jesus or any system of religion. Since I consider God fair and just, it's difficult for me to accept that God selected only one favored group of people (the nomadic people of the Jewish era or through Mohamed for the Muslims) to reveal himself to and left out the other groups of humankind. I'm not a complete deist by definition because I am a follower of Jesus, but I certainly agree with a portion of their premise that God is not intervening on this Earth today. And to be honest, I have no way of knowing if any of the biblical miracle stories were factual.

There is one very small sect of Christianity that resonates with me especially with respect to God's current lack of intervention. They call themselves the Berean Bible Society, and they have what I believe to be a very good explanation as to why the name-it-and-claim it prayer promises of Jesus and godly intervention are not applicable or available to us today. They observe and recognize God is not active today through those promises of Jesus and they claim God suspended miracles because the canonized Bible and grace through the sacrifice of Jesus have replaced the need for miracles. We'll discuss more of their reasoning and positions in a later chapter.

I agree there are many places within the Bible that have revelations of truth, especially the timeless life application parables Jesus taught his followers. I believe God knows the past and the present, but I'm not convinced he knows the outcomes to any future events, which places me in the open theism camp. But there are some (not all) open theists who believe God continues to interact with his creation today, albeit very infrequently, and I am unable to completely go there either. So, I'm not a complete open theist by definition. I'm certainly not a Calvinist who believes God has specific plans for each earthly event and manipulates us to do certain things or physically defies his own laws of nature to ensure the outcomes of his desires. I'm not saying he's incapable of intervening. I'm just observing our world and have concluded he does not intervene, and it's by his intention and obligation because it's clear to me he afforded us complete unmitigated free will.

I'm also not a complete process theist because even though they believe God does not intervene today or forcefully overrides the free will of his creatures, they believe God continues to persuade his creatures to take specific paths in their lives that will eventually be the best for everyone. I don't see God supernaturally persuading anyone.

I do, however, see people formulating their best understanding of God's character through, at times, a confusing collection of sixty-six books (the Bible) and then acting in a way they think God would want them to. That's a very different explanation than thinking God is actively persuading his creatures. And what kind of a Jewish or Christian God persuades only select favored humans, but not the vast majority of other humans on this planet? So, without trying to decipher exactly how to classify myself within the different sects of Christianity or even deism, I simply consider myself a Jesus-following Christian mutt.

[3] Foundational Positions

BEFORE WE GO ANY FURTHER, I WANT TO ESTABLISH A
few of my positions that will be the foundation of my arguments throughout
the remainder of this manuscript. As I do that, I have some other important
things for you to consider.

How can any of us conclude there is genuine godly love in the absence
of complete free will? If God is manipulating any of our intentions, choices,
or circumstances, then by default, he has not truly provided us complete
free will. Although I believe God is certainly capable of intervening, any
godly tinkering—whether solely by his own desire or in conjunction with
anyone's prayerful request—could have a favorable or unfavorable cascading ripple effect on the destinies of every other fellow human on this planet.
Those cascading events would also require infinite future godly managerial
interventions, forcing God to perpetually control the events on this Earth.
Without complete free will, we're merely robots or puppets at the end of a
string, carrying out his tasks as he manipulates us or our future circumstances. That wouldn't be genuine godly love any more than if human parents
were manipulating their adult children's lives.

> *God's love requires complete unabated*
> *free will for his human creation.*

It's also extremely clear to me that "God's will" is reflected by the outcomes of the freewill choices of humankind and his allowance of the random natural cause and effect events of our world. Contrary to my desires, I'm convinced his will does not include intervention today. He allows for prosperity and horrific suffering, and we know this because it's undeniably occurring in our midst. Going forward, it will be important for us to differentiate between God's will (our free will) and God's desires (what God wants) because they are not always synonymous. What God desires of us is not always in line with our choices (God's will), yet God's will (our free will) is to allow us to freely make those choices.

> *Mathematically, God's will = the outcomes of our free choices + the random natural cause and effect events occurring on this planet*

It's probably not God's desire for rapes, deadly hurricanes, fatal car accidents, cancers, or starvation to decimate so many, but it must be his will because he allows for their occurrences. Conversely, it is probably God's desire for us to care for the elderly, feed the poor, and love our neighbor, and we exercise our free will (God's will) to carry out those benevolent tasks. Our life's mission should be to identify God's desires and carry them to fruition using our freewill choices.

If you could be open to the premise that God is allowing this world to run its course, how might that alter how you've struggled to make sense of seemingly unselfish unanswered or rejected prayer? What would it be like to reconcile your realities with what many of the timeless Scriptures teach? This may require 1) ignoring some that were not written to or for us and 2) disregarding generally accepted but fallible biblical positions. That's right. You read that correctly.

I'll be directing you to some generally accepted life event interpretations made by both the biblical authors as well as the people who perpetuate them today that I believe are not accurate. My hope is that you will discover the same freedom that I have, by acknowledging that the Bible, written by well-intentioned but fallible men, does contain discrepancies and erroneous claims in certain places.

While I understand many people are deeply entrenched in their religious belief systems and seemingly immovable positions, I am very concerned many Christians as well as non-believers may find multiple off-ramps along the way to prematurely exit their read. As difficult as it may be for some, I'm asking you to muster up as much courage as possible and stay with me to the end. I want everyone, those who are certain of or those struggling with their current God worldview, to know there's more than one effective pathway to be a follower of Jesus.

On this journey, you'll be able to understand that God's love is real, even if it does not appear to be the same type of love good earthly parents provide to their children. It's not the same—it's so much better. I hope to point you in a direction that leads you to center your life in gratitude for what God has already accomplished and a good measure of hope for an afterlife, rather than false hope that God will make everything work out your way.

Christianity in a Nutshell

This life I'm referencing has only three components, and they encapsulate what Jesus claimed to be the greatest of all godly commandments.

1. Accepting God's sacrificial love through Jesus

    In gratitude for that,

2. Choosing to live by Jesus's life-enhancing principles (honoring / loving God)

    Out of gratitude from #1 above,

3. Loving the people in your sphere of influence with everything you
    have (honoring / loving people)

In doing so, you can live your life in authentic freedom, without hypoc-
risy (not having to pretend or declare you believe in certain things you cannot
reconcile) and draw yourself closer to God. There is a pathway to love God
and love people without invoking the supernatural today. But I need to be
very clear here. God is not currently chasing us down and seeking to gain
our interests in him. I'm not saying God is indifferent in desiring we align
ourselves with him. But if Christianity's main theme is correct, God has
already sought all of us, and he accomplished this by his sacrificial, loving
gift. It's up to us now to accept that gift, taking it to heart and applying the
known truthful and important portions of the Bible that lead to changing us
for the better and honoring God and those around us.

> *Gratitude alone for what God has already provided, rather*
> *than hope for current supernatural favor, will unlock the*
> *fullness of your life. Gratitude for God's grace (forgiveness)*
> *turns what you have into more than you'll ever need.*

There's a recurring series of TV commercials promoting a specific
credit card that always asks, "What's in your wallet?" Many of us carry credit
and debit cards as well as business and loyalty cards—not to mention store
membership cards. Most Christians also carry a "miracle card" somewhere
near the opening of their wallet for quick and easy accessibility. They also
have a "grace card" somewhere, but it's normally placed in an area that rarely
requires usage and probably won't be fully valued and played until right
before life's end.

Throughout this book, I'll be encouraging Christians to remove and
cut up their miracle cards, dust off and relocate their "grace cards" to the

forefront of their wallets. In doing so, their lives will be centered on life-enhancing gratitude that will never be dependent on their circumstances. We'll be exclusively playing the "grace card" here, eliminating the potential for faith-shattering disappointments that will surely occur after discovering miracle cards have always carried a zero balance after the era of Jesus.

Intervention = Immediate Gratification

For many, intervention has become a greater asset than God's eternal forgiveness because intervention could provide immediate gratification. For far too many, God's grace is something to cling to near life's end and cash in at the pearly gates. In my view, we have this backwards.

Grace (God's forgiveness) should always be valued over intervention because grace can be applied now and for eternity, whereas intervention would only be temporary. And where exactly did the apostle Paul tell us to direct our focus? "Since, then, you have been raised with Christ, set your hearts on things above, where Christ is seated at the right hand of God. Set your minds on things above, not on earthly things" (Colossians 3: 1–2). Correct me if I'm wrong, but wouldn't making requests with expectations for godly intervention be matters of earthly things? In line with that, I recall evangelist Billy Graham always saying, "Knowing we will be with Christ forever far outweighs our burdens today. Keep your eyes on eternity!"

I'm not a theologian and won't be formulating new ideas or introducing topics that have never been discussed by others more theologically qualified. I'm not claiming to have all the answers. However, if you're a follower of Jesus, I can promise you will be asked to put your "logic hat" on and seriously consider the questions posed. Your notion of "faith" as it relates to an active circumstance-altering God will probably be challenged here.

At times, you may be placed in a position which will certainly challenge you to lean on your own understanding, something Proverbs 3:5 suggests we *don't* do. Perhaps you'll refute your reasoning because any consideration to change your deeply ingrained beliefs could require an overwhelming internal and biblical investigative process. The thought of reconsidering the validity or applicability of each portion of the Bible seems like an impossible task for any of us.

Perhaps you'll also be resistant to changing your God worldview because you may be afraid of segregating yourself from what your friends and family claim to believe. At some point, everyone will have to decide for themselves. Is merely following others along the ruts in the road, absent deep contemplation, worth the cost of living in frustration when life's events do not coincide with one's expectations, especially if they are formulated by unfounded interpretations of portions of Scripture?

I also hope to draw nonbelievers towards God's love and help them realize they are not required to completely park their reasoning brains curbside. Many nonbelievers have accepted the theory of evolution and not solely because they are certain it's legitimate. There are many nonbelievers who would consider a divine Creator, yet completely reject God and the theory of creation because intervention believers are constantly bombarding them in person, on TV, and through social media with their claims that God is still working miracles for them today.

Nonbelievers would never be willing to accept the love of God if it meant they had to commit intellectual suicide and agree with such claims. And with all certainty, the major obstacle for nonbelievers to consider the Christian God is the notion that they must accept the validity of *every* miraculous story cited in the Bible. It should come as no surprise why our nonbelieving critical thinking friends refuse invitations to our churches.

Honest Evaluation

I want to challenge Christians to think about and honestly consider what they believe regarding current godly intervention—not simply what they wish for. You don't have to think like me. I'm just asking you to use your reasoning and draw your own conclusions. There's a meme I once saw of a horse standing with its head leaning over a fence in front of a watering hole, and the caption stated, "You can lead a human to knowledge, but you can't make him think." I'm not saying everything you're about to read is theologically correct. But I am saying, even if *everything* I have written in this book is *completely theologically wrong*, if you look at the world today, it's obvious God is not intervening or watching over and protecting anyone on this earth with the frequency attested by many. It is much more likely people are mistakenly associating what they errantly perceive to be godly activity to everyday events because it makes them feel better. If we say God is favorably intervening or offering protection, we've got a lot of work ahead of ourselves attempting to explain why there are so many people (God-loving Christians included) who are suffering immeasurably and doing without.

We'll have to explain why there are pediatric hospitals filled with cancer-stricken, suffering children and why a Christian mother of five young children was killed in a car accident today. I can think of no reasonable way to reconcile how 24,000 malnourished people (30% of them children) will die today while intervention believers prayerfully thank God for providing their dinner tonight. Unless of course, I'm wrong, and God plays favorites.

Although I am convinced prayer is an extremely important virtue, I do not communicate with others that God answers requesting prayer to favorably change their circumstances through miraculous intervention. Look around your local environment or watch the global news stations. Does our world appear improved by our requests for godly intervention or by God's own desire to make corrective earthly adjustments?

If we're honest with ourselves, this world looks exactly how we should expect it to look if free-willed, selfish, pleasure-seeking humans were controlling the outcomes of life's events. It should also be extremely obvious that God is allowing this world to run its course. If our God, in full or in part, is supernaturally intervening in the events of this planet today, should we be satisfied with his efficiency?

> *It's time we remove our training wheels (dependence on the errant premise that God will favorably alter our circumstances) and ride our bikes (our lives) only in gratitude for what Jesus did for us on that cross.*

During your read, I also hope you'll be willing to continually ask yourself the following questions: "Am I the type of person who claims to believe in something only because it's what I have been taught or because I want to believe it and it makes me feel good or because I actually believe it's true? And more importantly, can I continue to love and honor God with my life, live in accordance with the teachings of Jesus and bask in his amazing grace, if I knew with certainty God was not intervening in our world today?

Building on a Solid Foundation

This is not a Christian-bashing book, and I am not writing to change, weaken, or destroy anyone's faith in God's existence or his immeasurable love for creation. I'm not trying to dampen anyone's faith or hope, unless their faith or hope includes expectations for God to supernaturally alter their circumstances. What I'll have to say going forward is in no way a threat to the Christian faith. If you center your life on the principles of Jesus, it should not matter if my book stirs up some doubts for you. In fact, I hope to convince the reader that the Bible contains more than enough solid foundational information to build one's life on even with what I bring into question. I honestly want to encourage those who are struggling with doubts to not abandon their faith but consider a different pathway to accept the love of God.

Just so you're aware of who you'll be riding with, I want to establish three critical positions that I have staked my life on:

- I'm convinced (believe) there is a God who is the initiator of the original creation.

- I sincerely hope the story of Jesus is true and there really is forgiveness at the foot of the cross for all of mankind who would humbly and sincerely ask for it.

- As much as I desire the contrary, God is not currently active and does not supernaturally intervene on this Earth at the prayerful request of anyone.

Although I previously mentioned that I'm writing to help struggling Christians navigate a different pathway to God, that is not my sole purpose. I ultimately hope to caution fellow followers of Jesus to consider the potential damage they may inflict unintentionally on other believers, nonbelievers, and the reputation of our God, by publicly making claims he actively intervened on their behalf. I want to make it clear why I feel the need to share my thoughts regarding God's obvious inactivity and the difficult consequences that arise in the wake of those who continue to perpetuate his current acts of supernatural favor. The following four sections summarize the motivating factors that have driven me to pursue this endeavor.

1) Claims of Favor Create False Expectations for Others

Too many Christians are quick to publicly convey God was responsible for favorable events that occur on this Earth when it's impossible for them to know their claim is true. They are explicitly telling the world they have been shown God's favor by circumventing his own laws of nature or the God-given free will of humans. It's true, many well-intentioned Christians feel they are simply expressing their gratitude for favorable provisions they perceive to have received from God, honestly unaware of the damage they may be inflicting on others. But I am certain their claims are influencing other Christians to falsely believe that God has acted on their behalf—setting up other Christians to expect the same exchange when they need him.

Consider the following scenario: You and your friends from Bible study pray for Johnny in your group who's been desperately seeking employment for the past year. Three weeks later Johnny finds employment, and you, along with the others in your group, give praise to God for his provision. Every group member claims to be convinced God has acted.

Four months later, another member of your Bible study, Billy, requests prayer for his twelve-year-old daughter who was recently diagnosed with stage four terminal cancer. Shouldn't Billy have a reasonable expectation that he and your group's unselfish healing prayers for his daughter will be answered affirmatively? After all, if God provides jobs, shouldn't a fair, just, and compassionate God care at least as much about the life-threatening condition of a twelve-year-old girl? If Billy's daughter isn't healed, he will have a very difficult time understanding why God seemed more interested in Johnny's employment status four months earlier than he seemed to be with his daughter's well-being. I can assure you, claiming "God's ways are higher than our ways" or "It just wasn't in his plans" won't cut it for Billy.

Christians need to consider the potential damage they are causing other Christians with their conclusions regarding God's supposed activities. They are unknowingly misleading others to believe God operates this way. I'm not only referring to physical intervention claims like divine healing or employment provisions. I'm also referring to those who make public claims regarding how God actively communicates with them or favorably sends them wisdom, strength, or peace. Other Christians exposed to these claims will surely have expectations God will operate with them in the same manner. But what happens to the prayerful petitioner if they never receive supernatural godly communication, strength, peace, or miraculous healing after hearing others claim they do?

2) Claims of Favor Hurt the "Have Nots"

When we publicly make claims that God individually blessed us or provided a miracle specifically for us, we potentially crush the spirits of those who have not been recipients. Those who are doing without, even God-honoring Christians who love him deeply, must wonder why they are disqualified from God's favor when exposed to these claims. What must it be like for a struggling infertile couple in a Bible study to hear another couple in the group announce their latest pregnancy and that God is blessing them with their fourth child? Many Christians will become disheartened and question whether their faith is adequate when their prayers are not answered in the way that others claim theirs are. At some point, many will even consider abandoning their belief in the existence of God.

We can all claim we are legitimately blessed through the sacrifice of Jesus. But that is much different than saying God is directly giving to some, but not others. You may not agree with my theology or my assertions within the following chapters, but in the name of empathetic love, honor, humility, and Christian decency, we should always consider the less fortunate above our desire to think or publicly claim we have received special favor from our God.

3) Claims of Favor Impede the Great Commission

In Matthew 28:19, Jesus instructed his disciples (and it's assumed to include us) to "'Go and make disciples of all nations.'" But I contend current miracle claims by others are impeding our efforts to do so. Current miracle claims interfere with the possibility that many skeptics / seekers (our purported target audience) will ever consider God. When a skeptic / seeker hears a Christian claim that God was involved in healing their cancer or saving them in a car accident, the skeptic will consider them delusional and most likely never want anything to do with God. In fact, there's a better chance Christian miracle claims drive more skeptics and even seekers to atheism than those who might just run to the middle ground of agnosticism.

Critical thinking seekers will never accept the timeless wisdom of Jesus by hearing a Christian's miraculous favor claim. They're fully aware of the real suffering happening on this planet. If the Christian church really wants to reach nonbelievers, then we need to be careful about our miracle claims that might keep skeptics from accepting the Good News and minimize our vain desire to publicly proclaim God has somehow selectively shown us favor.

4) Claims of Favor Damage God's Reputation

Since it's impossible for any Christian to know with certainty that God has performed a miracle, they should never make public favor claims. If they were wrong and God had nothing to do with their alleged miracle, they would be standing on falsehood and also labeling him as a player of favorites. Since no one can ever know God intervened in any matter, no one should ever claim they do know. Notwithstanding one's desire to humbly give God his just due, anyone willing to credit God with providing specific favor is clearly putting God's reputation on the line.

PART 2:

HOW DID WE GET THE BIBLE?

[4] Those Sixty-Six Books

PERHAPS YOU'RE WONDERING WHY WE NEED TO INTRO-
duce the Bible (those sixty-six books) in a discussion regarding *current* godly
intervention. One reason is simply because we cannot and should not assume
that God is intervening today only because there were reports of him doing so
during the biblical era. Claiming the character of God is the same yesterday,
today, and forever in no way guarantees that God is active today. There are
many biblical principles that are not transferable outside of the context in
which they were written, thus we cannot assume that every biblical precept,
story, and premise from that era is applicable to us today. Yet Christians
errantly attempt to extend some of these biblical principles and examples to
their lives. What appears to many Christians to be on the biblical menu from
the past may not be what comes out of the reality kitchen today.

Another reason we need to investigate the Bible is because in places,
it contains fallible positions that conflict with our common realities. In this
chapter, I will point you to many biblical shortcomings and carefully lower
the Bible a few notches from its "perfection pedestal." It's critical for us to
understand, the Bible contains many important truths we should all seriously
consider applying to our lives, but it's not perfect. Moreover, I am certain we
do not need a perfect Bible to live a life that honors God.

When I was younger, I remember sitting next to my dad at our kitchen
table as we both read different sections of the newspaper. There were times
I would read an article that didn't seem to be factual, and I needed to ask for
my dad's opinion. On more than one occasion, I remember him tilting his

head downward, his eyes looking at me over the top of his reading glasses, and saying, "Son, you can't always believe everything you read." Little did I know at that time his statement might be applicable to portions of the Bible.

Most of us are doing it. We can deny that we are, but we're probably not being honest with ourselves. Contrary to claims regarding biblical inerrancy, many Christians treat the Bible as if it were a bag of trail mix, accepting certain portions and discarding or ignoring others that are just not palatable. I'm not solely referring to what can appear to some as mythical stories written by the biblical authors that we'll never be able to validate. I'm also referring to how some Christians claim God is active today only because there were biblical accounts of his interventions in the past.

Reality Rules

Some Christians are not simply rejecting some of these biblical miracle claims and today's current favor claims because they dislike them. They are rejecting them because they don't live in a world displaying miracles, yet they feel conflicted because of the pressure to believe the entirety of the Bible is the inerrant Word of God.

Many of us feel compelled to ignore or refute some of these matters because not doing so will require all of us to defend certain generally accepted biblical positions we cannot reconcile with our moral values or our common realities. Who can attempt to defend God's apparent acceptance of Jews possessing slaves from other nations and that it was ok to beat them if they didn't kill them? Who wants to defend the biblical reasoning that God always controlled when and where it rained, or that he "stopped the sun in the sky" to allow the Israelites to finish killing their enemy?

How can we accept current claims from people who have survived a disease after receiving prayer and medical treatment, giving credit to God for their recovery—while other disease-ridden Christians suffer and die despite prayer? Many of us stow away our doubts about these matters, never speaking about them publicly and simply do our best to sweep them under the rug or silently reject them. We try our best to carry on like good little Christian soldiers. However, if enough of those doubts begin to accumulate such that they become overwhelming and unmanageable, we become vulnerable to discarding everything contained within the Bible. At some point, we may even consider rejecting the notion of God, but we don't have to do that.

Aligning with Reality

I raised my children to know and love God and humanity in a way that the biblical Jesus called us to do. I have strong feelings that run very deep within the Christian faith. But what does one do when portions of their Christian belief system that were derived from the Bible, conflict with their observable reality? Should we dismiss the whole of that religion (throw the baby out with the bath water), or are we permitted to pick and choose from the "inerrant" word which supposedly comes directly from the Creator through man's transcriptions?

When we suffer cognitive dissonance (our realities don't meet our theological expectations), are we allowed to dismiss or alter the more popular and generally interpreted understandings of certain reality-conflicting Scriptures so they will align with our reality? How can any of us live with the internal conflicts which exist when our reality conflicts with what the Bible states, what we've been taught about it, or more importantly, how we've been interpreting and applying it? If we make alterations to the generally accepted interpretations of certain Scriptures or dismiss others, are we changing the text and declaring the Bible or the generally accepted interpretations of it errant? Does God really want us to live our lives in a confused state of mind and simply chalk up life's events we are unable to biblically account for to a God who is responsible for controlling those events behind the scenes?

I am fully aware we all have our own perception of certain realities, but there must be some common consensus regarding important matters of truth. Can different people perceive different realities? Certainly, and we observe these phenomena in courtrooms when multiple eyewitnesses to the same event all give testimonies that conflict with each other to some degree. But these are not the type of critical common reality conflicts I'll be addressing here.

Common realities (universal truths) are factual understandings that apply to everyone and cannot be refuted. None of us can refute the statistical data regarding the average number of people who will die from malnutrition, malaria, or cancer today. The force of gravity and the speed of light are common realities, and we all experience them in the same way.

When I point out some of the generally accepted Scriptural interpretations that conflict with our common realities, most Christians will support those Scriptures and interpretations to the bitter end. They will refute or ignore our common realities conflicting with Scripture because they have been taught and claim to believe the Bible is flawless. And once they have established that position, it's unlikely they will ever seriously consider any conflicting evidence.

Christians' biblical interpretations suggesting God is currently active cannot refute our common realities. When we use supporting Scriptures to indicate God actively prospers, provides sustenance, and shows his love for us today, it does not refute the statistical factual certainty that an average of 24,000 malnourished people will perish each and every day. The data indicating the number of prayerful Christian people killed last year by hurricanes, car accidents, and the flu trumps all premises that indicate God actively watches over and provides protection for us.

Our measuring standard for truth must be our common realities, and all Scriptures and our interpretations of them need to be measured against our common realities. *If we cannot trust the legitimacy of our common realities, then the logic and reasoning capabilities God instilled in his original human creation become meaningless. If God is illogical or he expects us to accept unreasonable and illogical positions, then he's left us all in a lurch.* The God who took our place on that cross and suffered for our transgressions cannot be a God who disrespects logic or desires that we all live in a conflicted or confused state of mind.

A God of Our Understanding

The conflicts I'm referring to come directly from certain Scriptures and from fellow Christians and their claims regarding God's current activity. They also come in explicit and subtle ways weekly from the pulpits of our churches. We hear pastors saying all the time that a certain current event was a "God thing," leading their parishioners to believe God was involved. Admittedly, there are times in my life I am embarrassed to call myself a Christian of any sort because of how God's present actions in the lives of believers are characterized and depicted by other Christians and certain Christian clergy.

I've heard many Christians say they are glad they can't completely understand God even with a canonized Bible. For them, God would be too simple of a being. I've also been told it's impossible to completely characterize, describe, or understand God because humans do not have the mental capacity for such a task. Any attempt to describe the attributes of God would only be anthropomorphism (attributing human traits, emotions, or intentions to non-human entities—God). And yet, I have a Bible written by men from antiquity who clearly tried to characterize God and describe his motives and activities.

I'm also faced with Christians who selectively tell me they do understand God and his intentions at certain times because of what they claim he's supernaturally accomplished for them. The biblical authors used their thoughts, observations, feelings, and words in the same way all of us do today when trying to describe the character and activities of God. Were those biblical authors, especially those who were not eyewitnesses to the events they wrote about, more qualified to describe God and his past activities any better than we are today? Were those fallible human authors supernaturally inspired (nudged) by God to write *everything* they wrote in each of their biblical books, or is the Bible also laced with opinions, laws, and commentary from the people of that era?

I hope that what I present will clearly convince you the Bible as we have it in certain places does contain discrepancies as well as some fallible precepts in both life application and factual science. You will also discover there are some stories that have been added to the Bible long after the original authors wrote their books. Feel free to slam the covers of this book together right now if you'd like, but if you stay with me, you should discover these discrepancies, additions, and errors, are in no way faith killers.

What you should come away with is a sense of freedom from the rigidity of the church that requires us to accept every portion of the Bible as God-ordained truth. I also think it's important for us to understand and acknowledge the known shortcomings of the Bible because doing so will enable all of us to have credible discussions with others who rigidly support biblical inerrancy. Disclaiming inerrancy also leaves room for those currently outside of the Christian faith to consider the wisdom of Jesus without having to accept every biblical precept or story as literal truth.

If one declares the Bible inerrant and is later faced with any irrefutable evidence to the contrary, it could destroy the credibility of the entire Bible for them. The Bible as we have it cannot and should not be placed on the "perfection pedestal" because it cannot, nor should it be required to live up to that standard. No Christian scholars are debating the fact that fallible humans wrote each of the sixty-six biblical books.

Love God, Love People

Irrespective of one's position on the validity of the entire Bible, we can still love and honor God and others without accepting the notion of complete biblical perfection. We all should cherish that common fertile ground. As I mentioned in the intro, "In essentials unity, in nonessentials liberty, in all things charity." It is not essential to have a flawless Bible to carry out Jesus's greatest commandment which requires us to love God and love people.

Inerrancy: Do You Bet Your Life on It?

The Bible is a collection of sixty-six individual books, written by forty different authors, over approximately 1,600 years. It's the most widely circulated and bestselling book of all time. I think it's prudent for us to discuss this popular collection of individual books since it is the foundation Christians base their lives on.

For most Christians, the entire canonized Bible (collection of sixty-six books) is a source of truth and serves as a road map of guidance for every part of their lives. They claim all the words contained within the Bible came directly from God through man's transcriptions. But many have not researched the Bible in painstaking detail to know whether it contains errors, discrepancies, and additions. Christians simply put their faith in their church's published statement of beliefs, which normally includes the statement that the Bible is the inspired word of God and is without error. Most Christian churches use the self-affirming Bible verse written by the Apostle Paul from 2 Timothy 3:16 that states, "All Scripture is God-breathed and is useful for teaching, rebuking, correcting and training in righteousness."

We should note, when Paul wrote that verse, there was not a formal New Testament (NT) collection of books. Therefore, the only Scriptures Paul could have been referencing were those of the Old Testament (OT) Jewish books and possibly the gospel book of Mark that may have been in circulation. There is no evidence that Paul or the other New Testament writers ever knew what they were writing would someday be added to the Hebrew Scriptures of the OT which would later form the complete canonized Bible we have today. Christians suggest if God was behind the authorship of these biblical books in any way and God is perfect, then all of what is written must be perfect/inerrant. Christians trustingly believe God divinely inspired these human authors to give an accurate account of who he was, how he operated during those times, and how he wanted his creation to live in the future. The problem is, most Christians don't really know how the Bible came to be and just how many known discrepancies and errors there are amongst the many ancient versions we have discovered or how many other books were disqualified from inclusion.

Bible Study Habits

To make matters worse, recent polls show that less than 20% of Christians read their Bibles on a regular basis.[3] Many who do read their Bibles regularly are not qualified to interpret it within its cultural context. It's also more likely they read and interpret the Bible in ways that make them feel better rather than ever attempting to assess its validity. If one always operates under the notion the Bible is without error, there would never be a reason to question any of its claims—even when at times, portions of Scripture conflict with their known reality. Fewer than half of all adults can name the four gospels. Many Christians cannot identify more than two or three of the apostles.

According to data from the Barna Research Group, 60% of Americans are unable to name five of the Ten Commandments. Multiple surveys reveal the problem in stark terms. According to 82% of Americans, "God helps those who help themselves" is a Bible verse—which it is not. Those identified as born-again Christians did better by a whopping one percent. A majority of adults errantly think the Bible teaches the most important purpose in life is to take care of one's family or to just be a good person.

Of over 2 billion Christians in the world, less than 30% will ever read through the entire Bible. The fact is, over 82% of Christian Americans only read their Bibles on Sundays while in church. A little over twenty years ago, Gallup released the results of a major study indicating that 86% of Americans claimed to be Christian, although only 70% of these admitted to being "born again" according to biblical measure.

---

3.   R. Albert Mohler, "The Scandal of Biblical Illiteracy: It's Our Problem," Albert Mohler, January 20, 2016, https://albertmohler.com/2016/01/20/the-scandal-of-bib-lical-illiteracy-its-our-problem-4/. Retrieved January 2019.

In recent studies, Pew Research indicates that only 25% of Americans now attend church (either physically or through a web broadcast) on any given Sunday, significantly down from 47% in 1990.[4] The study also shows that in evangelical churches throughout the United States, only 36% of those who attend church weekly indicate that believing in Jesus Christ is the only true way to heaven. A shocking (by Christian standards) 57% of American Christians believe other religions can lead to eternal life.

How can some of these statistics be like this? Shouldn't the historicity and authenticity of any collection of religious books be scrutinized from top to bottom by everyone who is willing to stake their life on it—especially for the Christian? I think so. But admittedly, I didn't do any research into the Bible during my early years prior to my conversion and baptism.

The Faith of Your Fathers

I did what most if not all people do with any written source of faith. I worshiped the God of my predecessors and trusted my teachers to have already completed the required research ensuring me that the Bible was correct in every word and deed. I relied on my mom, my youth pastors, and later the lead pastors of the churches I attended to give me the warm fuzzies that God was involved in the construction of the Bible. Surely all those people who came before me couldn't have been falsely led down the wrong path and simply assumed the entirety of the Bible was complete factual truth. When children are raised to believe what they are learning is truth, they usually accept it.

Later, when conflicts arise between what their reasoning tells them and what the Bible supposedly tells them, they're likely to continue to rely on the Bible or at least say they do. It's hard for most of us to turn 180 degrees and refute what we've been taught from an early age, especially if we've been

4.	Michael Lipka and Claire Gecewicz, "More Christians Now Say They're Spiritual but Not Religious," Pew Research Center, September 6, 2017, http://www.pewresearch.org/fact-tank/2017/09/06/more-americans-now-say-theyre-spiritual-but-not-religious/. Retrieved January 2019.

told and have simply accepted the inerrancy of the Bible. It could also make us look confused if we start to sway on biblical issues that conflict with our reasoning. No one wants to be confused or even appear to be in that state.

Hence, most people ignore their conflicts. For most, it's just a whole lot easier to hide one's head in the sand, go with the flow, and avoid the possible internal turmoil or conflicts with our Christian friends and family. But I contend that no one should be a follower of any religious system only because it's the faith they were indoctrinated into as a child. We all need to be critical thinkers and not blindly follow the paths of our forefathers. This type of critical thinking also needs to be applied to all the Judeo-Christian biblical stories as well as the life applications we attempt to derive from them.

Rightly Dividing the Word of Truth

It's one thing to trust that all the words contained within our sixty-six-book collection are the actual words and precepts God wanted in the Bible, and it's another thing to trust we can interpret them correctly. The Catholic fathers claimed the Earth was the center of the universe because the Bible seemed to have made such a claim. This popular medieval belief came from the writings of Ptolemy, a second century Greek astronomer. In his model, the Earth was at the center of the universe with the Sun, moon, and stars all orbiting us in perfect circles.

When his Earth-centered universe theory was rediscovered in medieval Europe, it was embraced by the Catholic church-sponsored scientists who believed that man was God's unique and special creation. They believed we were the center of the universe because we were special to God. The biblical passage they used as "proof" is found in Joshua 10, in which Joshua commands the sun to stand still in the sky to preserve daylight so the Jewish soldiers could finish slaughtering their enemy.

Later, after the scientist Galileo proved that the Earth revolved around the sun, the church initially imprisoned him for teaching otherwise during the Inquisition and forced him to recant his teachings about the universe. To be clear, I don't think science is at odds with God because I'm convinced God is the author of the universe that science attempts to quantify. However, I do believe some of the biblical author's misguided understandings or interpretations and descriptions of certain earthly events were not always in line with sound science. I'll present more of these false biblical premises as we go along.

Our biggest problem with the Bible may not be the entirety of the Bible itself. Don't get me wrong. You're about to discover there are some irreconcilable differences between the stories from the four gospel accounts (Matthew, Mark, Luke, and John) and some life event descriptions made by the biblical authors that are clearly not scientifically sound. Nearly every credible Christian theologian will tell us the Bible as we have it has discrepancies and contains errors. But what bothers those who have extensively studied the Bible is how the novice Christian incorrectly interprets portions of it and then perpetuates those falsehoods to others. Novice Christians think they can simply open the Bible to a specific chapter or verse and easily glean truth from it without being susceptible to false understandings. We don't need to look very hard to find biblically unqualified Christians because, as the statistics above reflect, they make up the largest portion of those who claim to be Christians.

We have countless small group Bible studies all over the world filled with those who are unqualified to teach, offer credible input, or understand the pitfalls of misinterpreting or misapplying specific biblical commentary. The greater the perpetuation of erroneous interpretations, the greater the masses will come to accept those interpretations as godly truths. One only needs to look at the countless false biblical interpretations and even false political commentary posted daily on social media.

I expect that those who are theologically competent will struggle with some of the examples of the false biblical interpretations provided here. I know they've heard some of them before, and I'm sure it will ruffle their feathers. But it's not just the novice Christian who perpetuates false biblical interpretations for life application. As you will see, prominent Christian pastors are also misinterpreting, misapplying, and embellishing Scriptures. This is how most of Christianity operates, and there seems to be no effective way to mitigate it.

[5] Biblical Textual Criticism

BIBLICAL TEXTUAL CRITICISM IS A METHOD OF STUDY used by scholars aimed at reconstructing the Bible to its original wording. Since we have many different copies of ancient versions of the same individual biblical books, all with differences when compared with each other, how are we to know which version of a specific book is more likely to contain the words that represent what the original author wrote? The word "criticism" appears to infer a negative connotation but that is not the case.

There are Christian, agnostic, and atheist scholars who historically critique the different ancient versions of each biblical book we have discovered. A biblical critic tries to determine which portions of the Bible are authentic and which parts have been altered or added to over time. For example, they try to determine which of the hundreds of ancient copies of the book of John is the earliest and more likely to be closer to the original. It is clearly known by Christian scholars that scribes who copied manuscripts (the books of the Bible) made many alterations over time. Some unintentional and some blatantly intentional.

Most of these mistakes are of no importance, but some have altered our understanding of what we think the original authors first wrote. There have been additions and omissions within the texts and certainly countless spelling errors over the time they were recopied. We have multiple sources of the same biblical books from antiquity that all contain differences when compared to each other. Biblical critics also seek to determine the identities of the original authors in biblical books that do not clearly identify who wrote it.

But why do we need this type of study? Isn't the Bible complete and true in the form we have it today? Don't the Bibles we have now reflect the exact words God spoke or what he conveyed to the biblical authors to write? The answers to these questions are, we don't know. And we don't know because we don't have the originals.

We don't have the originals?!!! The collection of sixty-six books that rest on our coffee tables most certainly do not have all the same words and phrases as the originals, and it's clear some later scribes have added additional stories to what the original authors wrote. Again, we know this because we have many old versions of the same individual books that all have textual variances as well as stories that were added or removed from them. But how could a God alleged to have inspired men to transcribe what he wanted in written form allow the originals to be altered or lost in antiquity? And secondly, if what we have today is not a complete duplicate of every written word supposedly spoken from the mouth of God from the Old Testament, and Jesus, Paul, and various other authors from the New Testament books, for that matter, how are we to know what we have is exactly what God or the original author intended for us? If anyone claims God was involved in the inspiration of the words in each biblical book, they'll have a lot of work ahead of themselves to explain why God would allow alterations to those books, or more importantly, the original manuscripts to be lost in antiquity.

Oral Tradition

As many people know, all the biblical books were transcriptions of oral traditions and stories that were circulating for many years before they were placed in writing. And, during both the OT and NT times, almost every living person was illiterate. They could neither read nor write and it was only the upper echelon who could afford to learn these skills. There certainly weren't scribes standing there as court reporters with stenotype machines recording each word as they were spoken by the biblical characters. Some of the original books (mostly from the NT) of the Bible were written only decades after their reported events took place. But the information contained within many of the biblical books, especially the Jewish Old Testament, was passed down orally from generation to generation over hundreds of years before they were put to parchment. This ought to give all of us at least some hesitation as to the accuracy and authenticity of the Bible as we have it today.

Have you ever played the telephone game? The game is played by having multiple people standing in line with each other. The person at the front of the line whispers a phrase into the ear of the second person, the second to the third, and so on, and so on. After the last person in the line receives the whispered message, he announces his version of the original phrase. Depending on the length of the phrase and the number of participants, the final phrase is rarely the same as the original phrase. But we're just discussing phrases in the telephone game and not the hundreds of biblical characters and stories that were passed on orally for decades or centuries, before being put in writing.

Think about it. I tell you thirty stories with each story containing hundreds of names and places. You sleep on these stories, and two weeks later, you try to retell them to your cousin and get all the names, places, and stories correct. Your cousin sleeps on your version of the stories and three months later he tells his version of them to a friend. Let this story passing go on for about 20–500 years before writing the final version, and what might you expect?

Then, let's consider the times and lower levels of enlightenment that were persistent when the Hebrew Scriptures were written. When I use terms such as, unenlightened, ignorant, uneducated, or uniformed throughout this book, I want to be clear I am not labeling the biblical authors stupid. I'm merely pointing out they did not possess the knowledge we have accumulated in our era. I am sure I would have viewed the world in the same way they did if I lived during their era.

What should we expect from the men of that era who thought that God was responsible for when and where it would rain, or that he was always responsible for selecting the leaders of each nation? They believed God was supernaturally controlling who the victor would be when they were in battle. Mix their simplistic understandings of reality with orally passing down complicated detailed stories that involve many names and places over a 20–500-year period, and I think you get my point. Not only do we not have the originals of each biblical book, but we also don't even have copies of the originals. To make matters worse, we don't even have copies of copies of copies of copies of the originals. What we have are copies that are in many cases, hundreds of years removed from the originals. Again, there are obvious textual differences between the oldest manuscripts we have discovered from antiquity and the Bibles we read today.

Discrepancies in the Bible

There is a world-renowned biblical textual criticist named Dr. Bart D. Ehrman. He is currently a professor of Religious Studies at the University of North Carolina at Chapel Hill and is one of the most distinguished within his field of study. He's appeared on many TV and radio talk shows as well as the History Channel. He's authored many books regarding his understanding of the books of the Bible and can be found online debating others in the same field as well as Christian theologians. If the reader wants to engage in Dr. Ehrman's work, I encourage the reader to watch his debates. I can assure you it will be worth your while. I also encourage anyone with an interest in truth and enlightenment to read two of my favorite Ehrman books titled, *Misquoting Jesus*, and *God's Problem*.

Dr. Ehrman's fascinating personal journey includes being raised in a conservative church in Kansas and accepting Jesus when he was in high school. After his heartfelt conversion to Christianity, he later attended Moody Bible College. He then went on to Wheaton Bible College before receiving his doctorate degree at Princeton Theological Seminary. He can read, write, and speak Hebrew and Greek fluently to ensure that he is able to decipher the biblical texts in their original written languages.

While attending Princeton Theological Seminary, Ehrman was asked to write a final term paper on a passage in Mark 2, where Jesus is confronted by the Pharisees (Jewish religious leaders) because his disciples were seen eating grain in a field on the Sabbath, which was forbidden. In that passage of Mark 2, Jesus reminds the Pharisees that even King David from the OT and his men went into the temple when "Abiathar" was the high priest and ate the show bread that was reserved only for the high priest. The problem with this is, according to the OT passage that Jesus was referencing (1 Samuel 21:1–6; Mark 2:23–27), Abiathar was not the high priest. At that time, Ahimelech was the high priest. Obviously, both Abiathar and Ahimelech could not simultaneously have been the high priest, and therefore, either the author of Samuel or the author of Mark, or even Jesus had the priest's name wrong.

Dr. Ehrman in his book, *Misquoting Jesus*, discusses how difficult it was to attempt to get around this problem in his term paper.[5] He came up with many convoluted explanations to possibly explain how a discrepancy like this in "God's word" could be. After all, Dr. Ehrman, like most of us, was taught in his youth that the Bible is inerrant. When he received his paper back, his professor commented, "Maybe the author of Mark just made a mistake." For Dr. Ehrman, this was the beginning of the erosion of his notion that the Bible was inerrant. He wanted to know if there were more biblical conflicts and just how many more.

Dr. Ehrman goes on to say, "And maybe these 'mistakes' apply to bigger issues. Maybe when Mark says that Jesus was crucified the day after the Passover meal was eaten (Mark 14:12; 15:25) and John says he died the day before it was eaten (John 19:14)—maybe that is a genuine difference. Or when Luke indicates in his account of Jesus's birth that Joseph and Mary returned to Nazareth just over a month after they had arrived in Bethlehem (and performed the rites of purification; Luke 2:39), whereas Matthew indicates they instead fled to Egypt (Matt. 2:19–22)—maybe that is a difference. Or when Paul says that after he converted on the road to Damascus, he did not go to Jerusalem to see those who were apostles before him (Gal. 1:16–17),

---

5.   Bart Ehrman, *Misquoting Jesus*, 20–22 (San Francisco: HarperOne 2005).

whereas the book of Acts says that was the first thing Paul did after leaving Damascus (Acts 9:26)—maybe that is a difference."[6]

According to Dr. Ehrman, there are between 300,000 and 400,000 known discrepancies between all the ancient manuscripts that we have today depending on who does it or how they are counted. In fact, there are more discrepancies between these texts than there are words in the New Testament itself.[7] Most of these variances are meaningless grammatical differences. For instance, one manuscript may use the phrase, "an apple" where another text might just say "apple." It's of no theological concern and can really have no effect on the meanings of the texts.

But there are a lot of other discrepancies within the four different Gospel accounts. And the best way to see these differences in the Gospels is to read them horizontally, rather than reading them vertically as an individual story or book. Read one story in Matthew, then read the same descriptive story in Mark, Luke, and John, and compare your stories and see what you come up with. You come up with major differences.

In a debate on this subject, Ehrman extrapolates,

> Just take the death of Jesus. Did Jesus carry his cross the entire way himself or did Simon of Cyrene carry his cross? It depends which Gospel you read. Did both robbers mock Jesus on the cross or did only one of them mock him and the other come to his defense? It depends which Gospel you read. Did the curtain in the temple rip in half before Jesus died or after he died? It depends which Gospel you read.
>
> Or take the accounts of the resurrection. Who went to the tomb on the third day? Was it Mary alone or was it Mary with other women? If it was Mary with other women, how many other women were there, which ones were they, and what were their names? Was

---

6.   Ehrman, 22.

7.   Ehrman, 132.

the stone rolled away before they got there or not? What did they see in the tomb? Did they see a man, did they see two men, or did they see an angel? It depends which account you read. What were they told to tell the disciples? Were the disciples supposed to stay in Jerusalem and see Jesus there or were they to go to Galilee and see Jesus there? Did the women tell anyone or not? It depends which Gospel you read. Did the disciples never leave Jerusalem, or did they immediately leave Jerusalem and go to Galilee? All of these depend on which account you read.[8]

Later Additions to "Scripture"

There are too many contradictions to list. Most of these are petty discrepancies that don't have much to do with anything, unless the discrepancies cause one to doubt the historicity of the whole collection of books. There have also been additions to certain books of the Bible after the originals were made. We know this because we have earlier (older) versions of the same biblical books that do not contain those stories or verses.

For example, consider the beautiful story of Jesus forgiving the adulteress. The Pharisees bring her before Jesus and tell him they have caught her in the act of adultery and Jewish law requires them to stone her to death. When they ask Jesus what he thinks they should do with her, Jesus challenges them and says, "'He who is without sin among you, let him be the first to throw a stone at her'" (John 8:7 NASB). The problem is that John 7:53–8:11 cannot be found in any of the older books of John that we have discovered to date. We know that the older books of any biblical manuscript would be closer to the original and likely to be more accurate and more like the original. The

8.   Ehrman, in The Craig-Ehrman Debate, "Is There Historical Evidence for the Resurrection of Jesus?" College of the Holy Cross, Worchester, MA, March 2006, https://www.reasonablefaith.org/media/debates/is-there-historical-evidence-for-the-resurrection-of-jesus-the-craig-ehrman.

story of the adulteress only shows up in the books of John copied hundreds of years after biblical scholars think the original was written.

We can also ascertain this story was an addition because it breaks the flow of John's narrative. If you remove that story from John's narrative, the flow of John's words comes together perfectly as it does in earlier versions of his books that we have found. One can also note there are words and sentence structures within the adulteress's story that are not found in any other part of the book of John.

The NIV and the ESV biblical translations note that the adulteress's story is not likely to have been written by the original author of John. This story being a late addition bothers me deeply because I love it and want it to be attributed to Jesus. It seems in line with the wisdom of Jesus and how he would have handled a situation like that. Another theory suggests that the story was factual and became an oral tradition that John either forgot or chose not to include in his original book. This theory suggests that a scribe who had heard the story later included it in a copy he was making hundreds of years after John composed his book. Unfortunately, unless we find the original book of John, we'll never know if that story was authentic. As of today, it's not likely to have been in John's original book.

Likewise, the following verses in the book of Mark were added at a later date since we have no older books of Mark that contain this passage: "'And these signs will accompany those who believe: In my name they will drive out demons; they will speak in new tongues; they will pick up snakes with their hands; and when they drink deadly poison, it will not hurt them at all; they will place their hands on sick people, and they will get well'" (Mark 16:17–18).

No current Christian theologians believe the final twelve verses were in the original book of Mark, and yet they are found in every Bible we have today. Many biblical translations have footnotes or italics indicating the last twelve verses of Mark were not in the original book of Mark. Simply comparing those verses from above to the common realities of today's world should also easily lead us to reject their validity. Any committed believer who drinks deadly poison today will not survive and laying hands on the sick will not heal anyone. Ironically, most US states have needed to enact laws prohibiting people in churches from handling venomous snakes while attempting to prove to their fellow parishioners they are authentic believers.

Advancing Discernment

Biblical scholars have made advancements over recent years critiquing portions of Scripture that were once considered authentic (written by the original author) but later turned out to be an addition. For example, let's say we have discovered 100 versions of the book of Matthew from antiquity, and after making comparisons, discover they have differences. Some versions may have simple differences where only sentences are included in one version but not another. And as we just discussed, there may be entire stories in one version but absent from another. Scholars are also able to approximate the age of these different books by the types of parchments used during different eras, as well as where they have discovered books from specific societies and the known times of their inhabitance.

When scholars discover that many older versions of the book of Matthew do not have either certain sentences or are missing complete stories but find books of Matthew copied hundreds of years later that do include certain sentences or complete stories, they are certain these differences were added by scribes that made copies in later years. These additions were most probably not what the original author of Matthew wrote.

For example, consider the King James Version of the Bible that was translated from Hebrew and Greek to English by forty-seven English scholars in 1611 under the direction of King James. These scholars did not have access to all the different versions of each biblical book from antiquity to sort through that we have collected today. In their version, Matthew 18:11 (KJV) states, "'For the Son of man is come to save that which was lost.'" Scholars today know this verse is not in any of the older books of Matthew that we have discovered and newer translations like the English Standard Version

(ESV) completely omit that verse. The KJV also included the verse from Luke 9:56 which states, "'For the Son of man is not come to destroy men's lives, but to save them.' And they went to another village." Newer translations like the NIV (New International Version) recognize a portion of that verse is not in the oldest books of Luke that we have uncovered. The NIV only has Luke 9:56 as, "Then he and his disciples went to another village." The ESV and NIV Bible translators made these corrections because it's obvious that scribes who made copies of Matthew and Luke long after the originals were written, made additions to what the original authors wrote.

But the most significant addition made to the KJV Bible with the greatest theological impact comes from 1 John 5:7–8. It states, "For there are three that bear record in heaven, the Father, the Word, and the Holy Ghost: and these three are one. And there are three that bear witness in earth, the Spirit, and the water, and the blood: and these three agree in one." These verses are the only verses in any Bible translation version that clearly define the triune nature of God. Without these KJV verses, there are no precise definitions of the trinity of God in any Bible translation. But like others, these verses are not present in any ancient Greek manuscript of the book of 1 John we've discovered. They are clearly late additions, and for that reason, they have been footnoted as such in nearly every modern Bible translation. The priests in England added verses 7–8 when they were compiling the KJV Bible in 1611, and they added them from a version copied 700–800 years after the oldest books of John's first epistle were discovered.

Faith or Denial?

I understand most of us don't have the patience, time, or wherewithal to extensively learn Hebrew and Greek or exhaustively examine and compare the manuscripts we do have. Some choose to not investigate the Bible's history and its intricacies with respect to its authenticity because they might discover something that could jeopardize their faith. Perhaps some of you are struggling to accept that there are discrepancies between and additions to some of the gospel accounts in our Bibles. It's mindfully less labor intensive to just apply the old bumper sticker motto: "God said it, I believe it, that settles it." But it does make me wonder about what most revere as God's inerrant word and in certain places, just how authentic it really is.

We know it was written and copied many times over by men, which certainly lends itself to mistakes. And again, we have ample evidence of these mistakes. The bigger question is: Are the known discrepancies critical to our understanding of what God or the original authors supposedly wanted? Even if God wasn't really coaxing / inspiring the biblical authors to write what he wanted them to write, can we have confidence that the texts we do have reflect exactly what the original authors wanted us to have?

The mistakes and additions listed above do not cause me to have concerns regarding what I believe about God's existence. As you will see in a later chapter, I don't even need a Bible to be sold on that. Clearly all the ancient manuscripts generally tell the same stories regarding creation through the time of Jesus and his resurrection, even if they have versions that don't completely agree with each other on what I consider to be minor issues. Notwithstanding our understanding that the three synoptic gospels (Mathew, Mark and Luke) clearly used a common source (referred to as Q) for some of their material, having some of these discrepancies in some ways adds credibility to the texts because we can know each biblical author has provided an independent account. In the same way courtroom witnesses have minor testimonial discrepancies, it's not surprising to see discrepancies between the biblical authors' accounts. But this is one of many reasons we cannot simply quote every Scripture word for word or claim the Bible as we have it is inerrant.

The Bottom Line

These biblical discrepancies also do not shake my confidence in the principles of loving my neighbor as myself or thinking the Golden Rule is somehow a questionable practice. Does it really matter if Jesus was crucified at 9 a.m. or at noon or before or after the Passover feast? Who cares how many women were at the tomb or whether the stone was rolled away when they arrived or not? The discrepancies mentioned above certainly do not refute the timeless truths that Jesus taught his followers or what he accomplished on that cross. More importantly, the Bible may not be completely inerrant in everything it actually reports but only in what it seeks to accomplish. And that's something for all of us to seriously consider because again, a Scripture-perfect Bible is not required to love God and love people.

But there is another underlying concern that may have an impact on the exact interpretations we hold dear in the Christian faith. This concern involves our translations from the original written languages. Have you ever spoken with someone whose primary language is something other than English who struggles to find the English words or phrases that would more accurately describe what they want to say? I have a friend who speaks Spanish and English fluently. Many times, during our discussions, he tells me that he cannot come up with an English word or phrase to precisely say what he wants to communicate in the exact way it would be said in Spanish.

The reason is because there are not exact translational words or phrases for every word or phrase in every language. There's an easy translation for the colors of the spectrum and for words like "chair" or "desk." But that's not the problem when it comes to the Bible. Some things are just not translatable, and using other words or phrases will not translate the intended meanings correctly. I have received emails in other languages and used an online translator to convert them to English. I am able to understand most of it, but there are some words and phrases within those translations that make no sense.

To complicate matters, Jesus and his disciples spoke the now defunct language of Aramaic. They certainly didn't speak Greek. All the oldest NT copies we have found were written in Greek, and therefore we're pretty sure the originals were written by highly literate people who spoke Greek. This means for the NT books, someone had to translate the decades-old oral stories of the ancient men who spoke Aramaic into Greek. Then in the

Western world, we've taken the Greek passages and translated them into English. The chance that it's *all* correct in grammar, meaning, or content as the biblical characters spoke is not very high. When I consider the process of oral traditions being passed down over many years through two translation iterations (Aramaic to Greek to English), recorded as thousands upon thousands of variances from the manuscripts we do have, as well as not having the originals, the telephone game looks like an easy game to get right on every occasion.

[6] Will the True Version Please Step Forward?

To make matters even more difficult, we currently have hundreds of different Bible translations from Hebrew (OT) and Greek (NT) translated to English. There isn't just one correct Bible version. We have versions such as the King James Version (KJV), New International Version (NIV), English Standard Version (ESV), Good News Translation (GNT), and the list goes on. Each of these translations is different in many ways when compared to others.

Depending on which versions one chooses to read and compare, they may or may not be able to find similarity in meaning when comparing two exact verses of each translation. This is yet another reason we can't simply quote a Bible verse and know with certainty it's exactly what the original author was trying to communicate. I have also noticed many Christians, including pastors, who search through different translations of a specific verse to find a translation that uses words that better support what they are trying to convey—even if it's not the translation version they normally use. It happens all the time even when the verse from the translation they select doesn't square up with more notable or popular and reliable translation versions of that specific verse.

For example, The Living Bible translates 1 Timothy 6:21 as, "Some of these people have missed the most important thing in life—they don't know God. May God's mercy be upon you." But the English Standard Version (ESV) translates it, "For by professing it some have swerved from the faith. Grace be with you." The phrase "not knowing God" can certainly be understood differently than "swerved from the faith."

Jeremiah 29:11 is translated in the KJV as "For I know the *thoughts* that I think toward you, saith the LORD, *thoughts* of peace, and not of evil, to give you an expected end." But the NIV translation says, "'For I know the *plans* I have for you,' declares the LORD, '*plans* to prosper you and not to harm you, *plans* to give you hope and a future.'" The KJV is referring to godly thoughts, yet the NIV translation, like most other translations, is referring to godly planning which is much different than merely what God thinks.

In another example, the ramifications of the first sin for the woman differ according to translation. The NIV translation, like most other translations, has the last part of Genesis 3:16 translated as "Your desire will be for your husband, and he will rule over you." But the ESV translation has, "Your desire shall be contrary to your husband, but he shall rule over you." Those two translations are not one and the same. They both declare the male will have authority over the female, but one version suggests the female desires will be contrary to the male, whereas the other does not. I tend to agree with the ESV translation since this is how most men experience marriage. (I'll need a place to hide for writing that previous sentence.)

Why do translation differences matter? They matter because everyone who studies the Bible scrutinizes each word and phrase and looks for meaning and life application from those words and phrases. Different words or phrases in one translation can lead one person to a disparate understanding than someone else reading another translation of the same exact verse.

I've participated in many Bible studies and have observed people scrutinize every word or phrase of a specific verse attempting to gain better understanding. And yet, often the translation version they use may lead them to conclude something different than someone else reading from a different translation. This helps to explain why so many people have different interpretations of the same passage and why we have so many different Christian faith denominations.

Then we need to deal with if or how we're going to apply a specific biblical verse to our lives. We are all susceptible to errantly pulling one verse from the Bible and using it as evidence to prove something we're argumentatively standing on is true or moral. We do this without considering the context of that verse or the entirety of the book in which it comes from. It's certainly done by many of us without any reference to the historical time it was written or who the author's intended audience was.

We errantly think, "If it's in the Bible and was said to one man or all the people of that time, it must be applicable to us in the twenty-first century." Again, consider Jerimiah 29:11. The most popular translations of this verse (unlike the KJV) states that God has *plans* to prosper "the recipient" and not to harm them. We'll need to answer if the intended recipient of that verse was only the people of Israel thousands of years ago during their captivity, or if we're to be included as recipients of that favor today. Did God have plans to prosper the Jewish people at that time, and if so, does that mean he's planning to prosper us now? I doubt any Holocaust survivor believed that verse applied to them. Certainly, many of the biblical stories, precepts, and laws are applicable to us today, but not all of them. The parables of Jesus are timeless and are as relevant to us today as they were when he spoke them. But there are also many Scriptures that were only applicable to the people of that era.

Divinely Inspired or Colored by Personal Opinion?

Additionally, how do we know when a point made by a biblical author is exactly what God would have wanted him to write down or if it was just the author's or his society's interjected personal opinions about a certain topic? Isn't it possible some portions of the texts from each of the biblical authors are what the author thought God would have wanted written (inspired), and some parts simply reflected the cultural beliefs of the author and his society but may not have been consistent with godly inspiration? Moreover, since we know we only have the copies of the originals in the NT, where it is known it has been altered by a scribe, don't we need to be concerned that some of what the scribe has added is just his opinion and not that of the original author or even from godly inspiration? Should we feel compelled to consider all later scriptural additions to the biblical books to also have been inspired by God?

Or, what if the entirety of the Bible is only man's attempt (without godly inspiration or assistance) to describe the events that took place during the biblical eras of both the OT and the NT? If that were the case, it could account for some of the Bible being correct regarding godly characterizations and explanations of life events and other biblical portions being incorrect. I doubt most of us believe God instructed the Jews it was ok to make salves of people from other nations as the OT clearly states.

I lean heavily towards the notion that the biblical authors wrote a mixture of what they thought God would have wanted them to put to parchment and what those authors personally thought about life events, including some of the laws they provided in writing. There are just too many biblical positions that do not meet our moral standards and reason to be attributed to a perfect God we claim inspired all of the authors to describe. I don't know how to ally myself with a God who condoned slavery and inspired the OT authors to put that in writing. I'm hoping that law was man-made, otherwise we'll be forced to believe in a pro-slavery God.

Consider the following: What if Moses, the author attributed to the book of Leviticus, was just providing his or his society's general position on homo sexuality when he wrote in Leviticus 20:13, "If a man lies with a male as with a woman, both of them have committed an abomination; they shall surely be put to death; their blood is upon them" (ESV). What if the thought of two men having homosexual relations was so difficult to consider for Moses and most of the Israelites at that time, as it has been for many heterosexuals today, and Moses was only giving his / their positions about that subject? What if these were not God's instructions through inspiration warranting capital punishment for homosexual behavior?

Similarly, what about some of the other Hebrew tribal laws that very few, including many Jews, adhere to today? Did God inspire Moses to write that eating a ham sandwich (Deuteronomy 14:8) or working on Saturday (the Sabbath, Exodus 35:2), or wearing a garment made from two different materials (Leviticus 19:19) warranted being stoned to death? Or were those just Moses's or his society's general thoughts and practices?

Did our God instruct or inspire Moses to write that if a bride is discovered to not be a virgin on her wedding night, she should be brought back to her father's house and stoned to death by her father and her groom (Deuteronomy 22:13–21)? Or was that just a man-made law and punishment the Israelites came up with at that time to keep women in line? Are we to believe God instructed Moses that rebellious children who curse their parents should be stoned to death (Deuteronomy 21:18–21)? Isn't it possible some of these tribal laws and subsequent punishments are just human laws and opinions (not from God) regarding how people should behave?

Jesus claimed he did not come to abolish the OT Jewish laws but to fulfill them. But was Jesus referring only to the greater laws of the ten commandments or every one of the 613 tribal / scribal laws provided in the OT by the Jewish authors? Did Jesus condone capital punishment for violating those laws?

To be extremely clear, I'm not trying to minimize the importance of the Jewish laws whether or not some or all were orchestrated or written by men. Absent laws, no society can function with order. Following some of those laws would certainly minimize the natural consequences for violating them. Although today we would consider killing someone for eating pork or wearing a garment made from two different materials barbaric, perhaps God through the OT was informing the people of that time that there wasn't a point scale assigned to specific sins. The judicial systems of today assign different penalties that seem to us to be proportionate to their respective crime. Stealing a candy bar today does not carry the same judicial punishment as murder.

Perhaps to God, sin was sin, and violating any law, even what today looks like a trivial tribal law, was justification for capital punishment. What we see here just makes the God of the OT to appear as a God of wrath, while Jesus seemed to be the God who promoted compassionate love. Jesus didn't promote stoning people to death for violating the laws from the OT. Jesus labored to explain the spirit of the Law and encouraged compassion and forgiveness to anyone willing to repent.

I'm fairly certain the Bible is loaded with the author's personal opinions. If I'm wrong, we would need to believe, at times, God manipulated each of the author's minds or hands and forced them to write only everything he wanted—leaving little or no room for personal thoughts or positions. You will find it difficult to find a Christian theologian who believes God forced the biblical authors to write only what he wanted.

The Loaded Questions

The God described in the Old Testament was recorded to have encouraged the Israelites to keep the spoils of their victory, which included their rival's livestock and their women. Notwithstanding the extent to which God hates sin, stoning people for violating trivial tribal laws or wiping mankind from the planet with a global flood seems a bit contrary to a God who has immeasurable love for all his creation. The Bible's condoning of slavery doesn't sit well with most of us today, and yet we are told that God was behind the acceptance of such practices.

The Promise Keepers founder and former University of Colorado football coach, Bill McCartney, spoke at the second conference I attended. He was encouraging improving race relationships because it seemed as if the stadiums were filled predominantly by white men. There were Latinos, Asians, and other races in proportion to the numbers in our society, but the Black community was not attending these events in the same proportion. I embraced this whole-heartedly.

I have a soft spot in my heart for all races that have been mistreated over history, but for some reason, it is the African American and their sufferings at the hands of whites throughout our nation's history that continues to affect me deeply. Perhaps it's because I watched the made-for-TV series *Roots* when I was an early teen. I remember when that first aired and how ashamed I was to be Caucasian and how it completely crushed my heart. I have also watched many documentaries that showed the horror that went on in the South before and during the 1960s and felt very sad for the Blacks of our country. Although it's nowhere near what it was in the past, racism is still a problem in our society.

No, I didn't have anything to do with what happened 400 years ago. But I still feel burdened knowing people with my skin color kidnapped black men from Africa and brutally used them to toil under slavery—while the southern whites used the Bible's slavery examples to justify their mistreatment.

After all, the Hebrew Scriptures (under the first covenant written by and for the Jewish nation) clearly teach in the books of Leviticus and Exodus that the Jews could possess slaves from other nations, but not fellow Jews. In fact, the Jewish people could pass their slaves and the children of those slaves down to their own children after the slave owner died.

> As for your male and female slaves whom you may have: you may buy male and female slaves from among the nations that are around you. You may also buy from among the strangers who sojourn with you and their clans that are with you, who have been born in your land, and they may be your property. You may bequeath them to your sons after you to inherit as a possession forever. You may make slaves of them, but over your brothers the people of Israel you shall not rule, one over another ruthlessly. (Leviticus 25:44–46 ESV)

Another passage on slaves in Exodus 21:20–21 (ESV), says "'When a man strikes his slave, male or female, with a rod and the slave dies under his hand, he (the slave) shall be avenged. But if the slave survives a day or two, he is not to be avenged, for the slave is his money.'"

Do you find it interesting the God of the Jews allegedly gave instructions to the Jews allowing for the ownership of slaves from surrounding nations, as long as they were not fellow Jews? Did our Judeo-Christian God really instruct the Jews they could beat their non-Jewish slaves as long as they didn't kill them? Did that God (our God) actually equate the value of those salves to the currency of that era? Or is it more likely the Jewish people alone created this self serving law? So, I do understand why the southern whites in our country used "God's Word" to justify slavery before the civil war, but you and I know it's an immoral practice.

If God did not accept the trivial Jewish tribal laws that required the death penalty, or even slavery, then where are his corrective instructions to them to cease and desist from carrying them out? I have a difficult time reconciling the God of the OT with the God of the NT, and yet, we are taught in the NT Scriptures that they are one and the same. Perhaps Jesus also came to clean up the portions of some of the tribal laws that may never have really been endorsed by God, but only by man. He certainly refuted the way the Jewish Pharisees were practicing their faith (through the Jewish law) and continually challenged their interpretations and practices to such an extent they had the Romans crucify him.

Many Christians say we just need to trust that all the words, practices, and precepts contained within the Bible are directly from God because they are all his positions and all of them are true. If you have convinced yourself that all one needs to do is trust that every word, concept, or deed contained within the Bible is truth, I hope you're willing to reconsider your position.

[7] God's Truth or Man's Opinion?

I WILL PRESENT JUST A FEW BIBLICAL EXAMPLES OF THE many that exist, which should lead us to conclude that *all* the words or supposed conceptual "truths" from the biblical authors cannot be from godly inspiration, unless we're to conclude that God was wrong.

Governing Authorities

> Let everyone be subject to the governing authorities, for there is no authority except that which God has established. The authorities that exist have been established by God. Consequently, whoever rebels against the authority is rebelling against what God has instituted, and those who do so will bring judgment on themselves. (Romans 13:1–2)

Are we to believe that God selects / establishes our leaders? If so, what are we to say about Adolf Hitler, Joseph Stalin, and the leader of Cambodia, Pol Pot—all of whom are known to have been responsible for horrific genocides? Did God really establish those leaders, and would the people of those nations have brought godly judgment upon themselves for rebelling against those evil leaders mentioned above? I hope not.

Isn't this passage more likely to be a false theory from a man from antiquity who believed God was controlling everything? Many Christians believe this principle to be true for us today and explains why they may be willing to accept certain shenanigans from their current leaders. They believe they must accept and tolerate everything from their leaders because the Bible tells them their leaders have been appointed by God. If true, I'm not sure why they continue to vote.

Women Silent in Church

Paul "allegedly" wrote by the inspiration of the Spirit, "Women should remain silent in the churches. They are not allowed to speak, but must be in submission, as the law says. If they want to inquire about something, they should ask their own husbands at home; for it is disgraceful for a woman to speak in the church" (1 Corinthians 14:34–35). Are we to believe these are inspired godly instructions given to Paul through the NT to be relayed to other followers of Jesus? Or are they simply man's words, consistent with their cultural positions regarding the inferiority of women from that era?

Perhaps I shouldn't have included these verses because this is yet another group of biblical verses that cannot be found in any of our oldest letters / books of First Corinthians written by Paul. These verses are clearly an addition made by a scribe who made a copy of First Corinthians hundreds of years later, and most likely were not in Paul's original letter / book to the people of Corinth. We should reject these verses on their merit and not solely because we believe they are inauthentic. But like others, they remain in all our Bible's today.

Ironically, many Christian churches today allow women to speak and even teach in their churches. They are clearly ignoring the verses attributed to Paul mentioned above, and I doubt it's because they believe those verses are inauthentic.

The Source of Physical Disabilities

A few different stories in the New Testament attribute physical disabilities such as muteness and physical deformities to spiritual sources.

> While they were going out, a man who was demon-possessed and could not talk was brought to Jesus. And when the demon was driven

out, the man who had been mute spoke. The crowd was amazed and said, "Nothing like this has ever been seen in Israel." (Matthew 9:32–33)

A woman was there who had been crippled by a spirit for eighteen years. She was bent over and could not straighten up at all. (Luke 13:11)

The people of that era falsely believed epilepsy was caused by evil spirits / demons. Today, we don't call on exorcists to cure these ailments. We rely on medical science to treat those afflicted with these disorders.

This is not just a matter of semantics where the biblical authors were using the word "spirit" to replace the term disorder or physical ailment. Those last two biblical claims mentioned above and others like them led the early church leaders to claim that demonic activity was the primary cause of disease. St. Augustine, the Christian Roman church father who ordered the canonization (assembly) of the Bible, declared in the late fourth century, "All diseases of Christians are to be ascribed to these demons." And through errant extension of those positions, many Christians today continue to believe physical disorders and diseases are in some way the works of the devil.

Jumps in Logic

I could go on and on with examples like these, but I'd end up with carpal tunnel syndrome. From what I've presented, can you honestly claim the Bible is correct in every premise and deed or that *all* its contents come directly from God through the men who wrote it? If we claim God was involved in the inspiration of every biblical scripture, then we'll have no choice other than to conclude at times that God was wrong. I won't go there—which can only lead me to conclude at minimum, *some* biblical Scriptures were not God ordained and were only at the hands of man. This is another important reason why we cannot simply claim the truth in all Scriptures or accept and apply everything we read in the Bible to our lives.

I cannot claim the Bible is completely inerrant without defying logic, morality, and sound evidence to the contrary. If one suggests my interpretations of any of the above-mentioned Scriptures are wrong, I'll simply state that most Christians interpret and perpetuate them exactly the way I've presented them. If their biblical interpretation is in line with what the author was trying to convey, then they and the author are wrong.

And what about all the generations that have existed between the NT biblical era and today? Why have we / they only been left with unoriginal documents and fragments that are not dated close to the originals? Have those past generations of people after Jesus ascended not needed or qualified to hear more clear and additional direct revelations from our Creator? Why is it that our active living God, who supposedly intervened in the affairs of his creation and provided scribal revelations thousands of years ago, shows no signs of doing so today?

With all the issues that seem to cause so much conflict in this current age, for example, homosexuality, gender identity, abortion, and eating pork, why doesn't God intervene today to make his revelations about these matters so clear to us that there can be no ambiguity? All we have today are biblical interpretations of the evangelical Christian right, interpreting the copies of copies of copies of copies of books that were handed down thousands of years ago. I'm not God, but if I was, I would unambiguously let my creation know what is and what is not acceptable to me.

The sixty-six books that make up the Christian Bible have flaws, and those flaws were caused by the fallible men who wrote them and by the many scribes long after who tried to make copies of them. The biblical authors and the people of that era did not always understand or interpret life events consistently with the reality of their world.

I'm certain some of the life events they reported did not have the actual supernatural causation they claimed as their reasoning. Scribes have clearly added, removed, or altered some of the passages, albeit most are of no theological significance. There's more to the story about this collection of sixty-six books that is beyond the scope of this book. There were a lot more books about God from antiquity than the sixty-six assembled in our Bibles today, and again, it would be fallible men (not God) who would do the sorting of those books to determine which ones qualified to be included in the biblical canon.

What Cannot Be Refuted

Let me establish something of great importance to me. As much as I am a skeptic and have been providing evidence indicating that the Bible, constructed by fallible men, has some deficiencies, there is one thing that I cannot refute. It's Jesus.

I can't ignore Jesus's words and his parables nor how he turned the world upside down with his wisdom. I cannot refute his truths. In so many situations described in confrontations with policy leaders of the day or depicted in his parables, he asked us to resist our human instincts and act in such a way that could bring about what is good and right. He asked us to continually examine the condition of our hearts.

The words of Jesus simply stop me in my tracks and force me to constantly reassess my attitudes and my positions in all matters of my life. His words do make me consider the log in my own eye before I judge someone else who has a very small splinter in their eye. The words of Jesus have forced me to consider the hearts and life circumstances of others before immediately condemning them for how they live their lives. His principles have driven me to offer forgiveness to others because he has promised to forgive me for the countless times I've chosen to do wrong.

He's asked all of us to care for the foreigner, orphan, and those who are suffering, and I can find no way to escape those truths. Treating others in the same way I wish to be treated is a timeless, universal truth that we should all follow. These life application principles resonate with me to such an extent, I am convinced the biblically attributed principles of Jesus to be authentic when understood in the proper context.

Irrespective of the doubts I have as to whether everything in every biblical book is accurate or not, or even if the Bible is incorrect and Jesus was not divine, I willingly choose to follow him. The risks to myself and others in doing so is hardly measurable, and yet the potential for living a freedom-filled, full, and abundant life is extraordinary.

If you're currently not a follower of Jesus and not ready to step over the line and place your trust in who the NT authors claimed Jesus was, I'd like to encourage you to read his words and tell me why you couldn't or wouldn't want to align your life in the ways he asked us to. If you are not a Jesus follower, I'm asking you to temporarily ignore what you've heard about him from others, including the purported mysterious miracle claims of today, and read the words attributed to him. Let Jesus do the talking, not some of the imperfect people of today who continue to misconstrue and misapply his foundational truths. This is clear to me: we do not need a perfect Bible, and the shortcomings I've mentioned in this chapter will never refute or negate the life-enhancing principles of Jesus.

There is complete freedom when one chooses to that accept the Bible, based on copies of the biblical books as we have them long separated from the original writings, does have flaws. I know this sounds scary to many, but there's nothing but trouble lying ahead for those who hold on to the premise or requirement that the Bibles we possess are completely inerrant. The general theme of the Bible and what it tried to convey from a macro perspective may very well be truth. But from my research and understandings, some of its stories and life event interpretations are not full proof. And we shouldn't expect it to be because it was created and altered over time by fallible men. I'm also asking the reader to let go of the notion that *every* word, concept, or story contained within the biblical cannon is the absolute truth. I'm encouraging you to cling to the life-enhancing principles of Jesus that are clearly true and right for all. When you do that, you will never be required to defend the known biblical positions that are indefensible.

PART 3:
RANDOM CHANCE, DIVINE DESIGN, OR BOTH?

---

[8] In the Beginning . . .

For you created my inmost being; | *you knit me together in my mother's womb*

Psalm 139:13, emphasis mine

Your hands shaped me and made me. | Will you now turn and destroy me?

Remember that you molded me like clay. | Will you now turn me to dust again?"

Job 10:8–9, emphasis mine

But who are you, a human being, to talk back to God? *"Shall what is formed say to the one who formed it, 'Why did you make me like this?'"* Does not the potter have the right to make out of the same lump of clay some pottery for special purposes and some for common use?

Romans 9:20–21, emphasis mine

IN THIS CHAPTER, WE'LL BE EXAMINING WHAT I AM CON-vinced are errant Christian positions regarding reproduction and the faulty reasoning regarding current consequences of "the original sin." I'll provide circumstantial evidence pointing to an Intelligent Designer, and in doing so, simultaneously dispel the commonly held Judeo-Christian position that God continues to be involved in the reproductive processes that create life today.

Christians continue to claim God fabricates in a hands-on way every human that has ever been conceived. They do this because of the errant antiquated Scriptures regarding this matter. They also desire to make this claim because:

- It reassures them God continues to be supernaturally involved in this world.

- It allows them to believe they are more special to a God who wanted and intended to create them, thus there is a divine reason and purpose for their personal existence.

I am convinced there is a Creator of the universe, and therefore the original Creator of everything it contains. I use the term "original" to refer to my belief that God put everything into place in the beginning, including humans with their reproductive system, plants and trees with their biological systems, an atmospheric system capable of providing both a soft steady rain, or a powerful tornado or hurricane. But I am convinced he does not continue to manipulate the intricacies of those systems. These systems are autonomous and self-sustaining, not requiring continual intervention by the hand of God because he designed them that way. God does not coerce us to marry a specific person, nor does he arrange the meeting between a specific sperm and egg to produce the unique person he desires to exist. He does not select or manipulate the genetic codes to determine the physical traits of each fetus as it develops in the womb. He is not controlling the electrical stimuli that cause our hearts to beat nor is he causing certain people to "wake up" each day.

Likewise, and contrary to another commonly held Christian position, I'll provide opposing arguments against the position that the original sin is responsible for *all* human suffering today. A violent lethal storm that devastates a specific community in Kansas may contain remnants which hydrate a farmer's crops somewhere down the road. The original or even current sin does not cause God to punish us with pestilence, drought, famine, violent storms, earthquakes, car accidents, birth defects, cancer, or lethal viruses today—irrespective of what the ancient biblical authors claimed. Neither is a Satan-like spirit (assuming there is one) invisibly roaming this Earth responsible for the above-mentioned events. God did not design humankind to physically live forever, and the original sin does not explain why we die.

Creation

Most of us are somewhat familiar with the theory of evolution and how it conflicts with the biblical creation story. I'm certainly not the sharpest tool in the shed, but I do have an extensive degree in the sciences. I understand the different theories, for example, abiogenesis which suggests that given enough time and the proper conditions, the probability increases that life in one form or another could have been accidentally created. However, that probability is immeasurably low notwithstanding the time allowed, and I completely reject these theories from a macro perspective. For clarification, evolution is not a theory that attempts explain the origin of the first living creature. The crux of evolution assumes that the first living creature was randomly created, and only attempts to explain the incremental processes that caused the progressive changes in all forms of life.

Paul wrote in Romans, "For since the creation of the world God's invisible qualities—his eternal power and divine nature—have been clearly seen, being understood from what has been made, so that people are without excuse" (1:20). Also, in Psalm 19:1 from the Hebrew Scriptures, "The heavens declare the glory of God; | the skies proclaim the work of his hands." Nothing could be truer to me than these two Bible verses. I don't agree with them solely because they come from the Bible but rather because they are my truth and my reality. Making the same observations within the world and universe I live that the biblical authors made thousands of years ago, my conclusion is the same.

Many of us look at the detailed intricacies of our universe and conclude that something planned for and initiated all of it. I am unable, not unwilling, to attribute the origin and intricacies of humankind to accident. However, proponents of accidental creation (abiogenesis) argue, if given enough time, it is more probable that an energy source (lightening or geothermal processes have been postulated) interacted with a random sequence of molecules in a warm pond (primordial soup), and a simple life form randomly came into being. After that, this simple life form has evolved over time to represent all the creatures that now exist or have ever existed on our planet. I've honestly been willing to give the evolutionists my attention during my lifetime. I've thoroughly read their positions and have seriously considered their arguments. As you'll discover, I'm not one to just throw my hands up in the air and accept certain Christian or other systems of belief because it could make my life easier. Many choose the path of least resistance during their lifetime, but when it comes to truth, that doesn't work for me. For me, it's the complicated details and functionality of our universe and the earthly creatures that provide strong circumstantial evidence that we were designed, not created from primordial soup and random evolutionary processes.

The Anthropic Principle

My first reason for rejecting the evolution theory comes from my observation of this planet and the conditions necessary to sustain life. Scientists have developed what is commonly known as the anthropic principle to justify the creation theory and how our universe is too intricate to have been randomly assembled. Evolutionists counterargue that it is exactly these conditions that allowed the first simple life forms to evolve and explain why other observable planets are unable to create or sustain life in the way that we observe on Earth. In other words, they argue, if the earthly conditions (Earth's tilt, water content, atmospheric properties etc.), were not the way they are or have been, nothing could have come into existence. But I observe it differently. I appreciate the anthropic principle because for me it points to the Designer/

Creator whom I call God. But that's just my conclusion. Here are just a few of that principle's assertions.

The anthropic principle is merely a list of finely tuned conditions required to sustain life as we know it on Earth. For example, we have a moon that is so large and so close that it moderates any large shifts in the tilt of the Earth's axis. Without this, the planet's climate would fluctuate dramatically, making it exceedingly difficult for most living creatures to survive. If the gravitational force were altered by only 0.000000000000000000000000000 0000000001 (1.0×10^{-36}) percent, our sun would not exist, and neither would we. Talk about precision! The 23-degree axis tilt of the Earth is exactly right. If the tilt were altered slightly, surface temperatures would be too extreme on Earth. I have concluded that a designer put our environment together with precision. I urge the reader to further investigate the anthropic principle to see just how much more finely tuned our planet and universe are.

Amazing Complexity

My second reason for believing in a Creator is the complexity of the human eye and the amazing calculating ability of the human brain. The intricacy of the eye and brain have been discussed many times before, so I will only briefly discuss them here.

The computer chip, which runs a computer, is a small silicon wafer with a marvelously intricate connection of parts, all a fraction of an inch in size. It has been deliberately designed and created. I know of no evolutionist who claims that any computer chip was formed by a series of accidents involving lightning, water, gravity, or randomness. So, there is no doubt even among the most doctrinaire evolutionists that silicon computer chips were designed and created by a higher intelligence.

On the other hand, the human retina is far more complex than any computer chip. Yet an evolutionist examining the human retina might suggest that developing creatures required sight for survival and therefore simply developed a retina out of necessity—providing no developmental method for this intricate body part. I think this points out the curious double standard concerning the subject of origins that is present among otherwise good scientists. The computer-retina analogy is very useful for demonstrating this double standard.

The retina lining in the back of the eye is a very thin membrane, thinner than Saran Wrap. Compare this with a computer chip. The May 1985 issue of *High Technology*[9] showed computer silicon chips that were about 7 millimeters across and had a capacity for 100,000 transistors. Today's silicon chips have the capacity of 19.2 billion transistors and the increase is solely due to better design and not random evolutionary processes. The retina contains photoreceptors that may be compared to transistors. However, a photoreceptor is a very efficient, high gain amplifier immensely more complex than a transistor. The retina has 200,000 photoreceptors per square millimeter. That's phenomenal! High technology computer chips don't even come near the complexity of the retina. And yet, we are asked to consider randomness and necessity as the causation behind the inherent sophisticated functionality of the human eye.

The brain is the center of a complex human computer system more wonderful than the greatest computer ever built by man. The body's computer system computes and sends throughout the body billions of bits of information per minute—information controlling every action and reflex, including the flicker of an eyelid. In computer systems, information is carried by wires and electronic parts. In the body, nerves are the wires carrying the information back and forth from the central nervous system. And in just one human brain there is probably more wiring and electrical circuitry than in all the computer systems of the world combined.

---

9.   Joseph Calkins, "Design in the Human Eye," Creation Moments, *Bible Science Newsletter*, March 1986, https://creationmoments.com/article/design-in-the-human-eye/. Retrieved June 2015.

Reproduction from Evolution?

My third reason for rejecting evolution comes from my observation of the amazing complicated reproductive system of mammals. Assume for the moment that the origin of the first living cell was created from molecules colliding in some way with an energy source. How is it that this newly created life form could think or desire its way into needing the correct reproductive parts, and then actually form those functioning body parts to accomplish reproduction? Are we to assume that when an energy source interacted with the primordial molecules, it didn't just create a living creature, but also simultaneously created some sort of reproductive system allowing itself to replicate? Or how long would it take for a reproductive system to formulate within an evolving creature? Certainly, it couldn't happen within the lifetime of one of these primitive primordial creatures. Thus, its likelihood of quickly becoming extinct would be very high.

There are life forms (some plants and other organisms) observed today which are asexual and do not need a partner to reproduce. Are we to believe that even they were accidentally created with this type of reproductive system by an energy source interacting with some primordial collection of random molecules? To me, this type of speculation is equivalent to having a tornado go through a junkyard, and when it has left the area, we find a brand new completely painted and functional Boeing 747 airplane laying in its wake.

Where did the erogenous zones come from that are located on the sexual organs of both male and females? It's already beyond imaginable that the reproductive body parts could have come into existence randomly, but how did humans generate these erogenous areas on those parts which cause a physical stimulus in them driving the desire to reproduce? I need to keep this book G rated, but you know exactly what I'm talking about.

How does a simple life form develop a penis or a vagina or the required reproductive components such as sperm, eggs, ovaries, or fallopian tubes? How is it that there are two different life forms for mammals (male and female) that have one or the other body types that match perfectly to each other and are able to reproduce? How did females develop milk producing breasts that were required to feed their infant child after birth? It would be beyond miraculous for just one creature to morph into a male version with a capable reproducing body, but how would the counterpart female version of the same creature originate? That female creature would have needed to develop over time with completely opposite reciprocating body parts and do that simultaneously with its male counterpart. If not, that species would be wiped from existence.

I saw a funny cartoon refuting the notion that snowmen are evolved entities. The cartoon depicts a male and female snowman, both wearing scarves and hats, each with facial features made from coal, with carrots for noses and tree branches for arms. The background shows snowflakes falling all around them. The caption has the male snowman saying to the female, "Don't be absurd! Nobody made us! We evolved by chance from snowflakes." How many trillions of years would we need to wait to observe two simple randomly and accidentally created snowmen standing next to each other with facial features made from coal and carrots, wearing scarfs and hats—all from random snowflakes falling from the sky? To my knowledge, snowmen are unable reproduce. Are there any evolutionists who would deny that simple snowmen are designed and created?

How did our taste buds randomly show up within an evolutionary being? Or why would we need them if they weren't designed by a Creator to be on the tongue for our pleasure? What mechanism could cause evolving creatures to have them? Accident, desire, or an elongated time period couldn't explain the origin of taste buds, and they are not a necessity for a mammal's survival.

It's beyond my ability to give credence to humankind evolving from a simple cell over time. Something, a Supreme Being / Designer, had to be responsible for creating the amazing intricacies of all living species.

But please don't confuse my firm belief in God as the original creator of human life with a God who has been and continues to be involved in the fabrication of every human after his two original masterpieces. In the following sections, I hope to convince you there is no need for God to coerce the courtship of lovers or to manipulate the conception and fetal formation processes by purposefully selecting individual human traits after his initial creation. Contrary to what the Bible suggests and most Christians claim to believe, God is not actively creating / fabricating human beings today. His autonomous random reproduction system is responsible for that.

The First Humans

The Book of Genesis tells us God created Adam and Eve and they were the first human inhabitants of this Earth. Did it happen the way the Genesis author describes it with man being created from dust and then the woman by way of Adam's rib? I can't be certain of that, but the "how" part of that story is irrelevant for our discussion. I'm also not completely certain God didn't create multiple races of humans simultaneously, but that subject is also far from the scope of this book. Once one is convinced that a Designer laid out the universe, it doesn't really matter how he created any of it.

Considering the writings of men from nearly 4,000 years ago who observed the world they lived in, they tried their best to describe how mankind and their environment came into being. The author of Genesis (Moses) was not present to witness any of it. I agree with their general theory of creation because, 4,000 years later, I am faced with the same observations and have come to the same conclusion. In saying that, the biblical story regarding the method and material God used to fabricate mankind is probably not accurate.

Most Christians believe, and the biblical authors and clergy teach, that God is actively responsible for creating each of us as individuals even after he created the first two humans. But I'm certain this position is completely errant. This theory refutes not only logic and reason but also clear and sound scientific evidence.

When I say God created humankind, I mean God is the creator of the "original" humans, Adam and Eve, if you like. I can take it a step further and say that you and I are part of that creation as we are descendants of the first humans. However, it would be false to think that we (you and I in the physical bodies we possess) were planned for and intentionally created by God with our exact unique genetic features. We are all indirectly part of his overall creation, but everyone after his original creation was not directly created by God. We were created by our free-willed forefathers who carried an amazing autonomous reproductive system from their forefathers that was instilled in the first two humans in tandem with the random genetic processes that take place before, during, and after conception.

Each person comprises a collection of genes passed down through generations and *random genetic processes* occurring through reproduction, beginning with the first humans. I know this might sound cold or harsh, and at first glance, this type of thinking doesn't promote a God who really cares for us individually or is interested in his *de facto*—but not literal—handywork, but I strongly disagree. Even through the genetic randomness after Adam and Eve, I'm convinced our God loves his creation irrespective of their pathway into existence. Think about it. If he made the reproductive system random, how could God not be in love with the outcomes of all creation? Sure, it sounds much better if we want to believe God was actively involved in the creation of every human after the first two, but do we want to look at facts, or do we just want to feel better about who we are and how we arrived here? If your answer is "to feel better," the next chapter will certainly challenge you to reconsider your position regarding this matter.

[9] The "Purpose-Driven" Fallacy

MY POSITION THAT GOD IS NOT INVOLVED IN MANIPU-
lating the creation of each human runs contrary to the closely held beliefs of
many Christians and Christian clergy, particularly Rick Warren of Saddleback
Christian Church. I have great respect for Pastor Warren as a speaker and for
his philanthropic work, but some of his biblical interpretations are fallible.
I find his interpretations of passages from uninformed biblical authors that
God involves himself in every detail of our existence misleading.

He writes a daily column I receive by email called, "Purpose Driven
Connection," or a later version called "Daily Hope." He is also the author of
the incredibly successful book, *The Purpose Driven Life*. I'll be discussing
some of Pastor Warren's claims throughout this book. His positions are
upheld and taught in many churches every Sunday, but at times, they conflict
with our known common reality.

Pastor Warren states in *The Purpose Driven Life*, "Each and every one of
us was created on purpose, for a purpose," and "God selectively manufactured
every one of our physical traits (hair and eye color, height, etc.)." He goes on
to say, "You are who you are for a reason," and "You exist only because God
wills that you exist." His term "reason" is not by the randomness of the autonomous genetic reproduction system I'm convinced exists within humankind.
Pastor Warren wants us to believe we are all created individually by intent
and manufactured by the manipulating hands of God.

As Warren introduces *The Purpose Driven Life*, he cites a poem by Russell Kelfer titled, "You Are Who You Are for A Reason."[10]

> You are who you are for a reason.
> You're part of an intricate design.
> You're a precious and unique design,
> Called God's special Woman or Man.
> You look like you look for a reason.
> Our God made no mistake.
> *He Knit you together in the womb,*
> You're just what he wanted to make.
> *The parents you had were the ones that he chose,*
> And no matter how you may feel,
> They were *custom designed* with God's plan in mind,
> And they bear the Master's seal. (emphasis mine)

Confusingly, Pastor Warren cites the above listed poem, stating, "The parents you had were the ones that he (God) chose." Yet on August 1, 2014, his "Daily Hope" email broadcast clearly states the following: "The Bible teaches us that we are to choose our friends carefully" and adds, "You should be even more careful about who is going to be your life partner. Notice it is a choice. God doesn't do this for you. God says you make the choice".[11]

So, which one is it? Does God choose our parents as stated in the poem Pastor Warren advocates in *The Purpose Driven Life*, or did our parents freely choose each other as he states in his daily devotional? Seems to me that Pastor Warren is advocating two opposing positions that cannot both be simultaneously true.

---

10. Russell Kelfer, "You Are Who You Are for a Reason," quoted by Rick Warren, *The Purpose Driven Life*, 6–7 (Grand Rapids, MI: Zondervan, 2002).

11. Rick Warren, Daily Hope email broadcast, August 1, 2014.

The foundation of Pastor Warren's claim regarding our specific individual genetic features comes from a few biblical Scriptures.

> For you created my inmost being;
>> you knit me together in my mother's womb. (Psalm 139:13)

> "Your hands shaped me and made me.
>> Will you now turn and destroy me?
> Remember that you molded me like clay.
>> Will you now turn me to dust again?" (Job 10:8–9).

> But who are you, a human being, to talk back to God? "Shall what is formed say to the one who formed it, 'Why did you make me like this?'" Does not the potter have the right to make out of the same lump of clay some pottery for special purposes and some for common use? (Romans 9:20–21)

Many might like to believe that God had his hand in either choosing our parents or was involved in every cell division that resulted in our specific being. All of us would like to believe there was a divine reason and purpose behind our individual characteristics and our personal existences—all the way down to the selection of our eye color. For Pastor Warren and the people living during the biblical era, it wasn't God's autonomous random reproductive design he instilled in his first two humans that caused our existence and physical characteristics. It was an active God who manipulated the actual DNA strands and genes for each of us upon conception, which created the exact child he desired.

Pastor Warren's biblical interpretation makes us feel good, and I think this explains, in part, why his *Purpose Driven Life* book has become so popular. At times, he tells us what we'd like to hear, not what is more likely to be true. He's using the reasoning from men living 3,000 years ago who had no clue regarding the process of reproduction.

"Intentional Design" Vs. Free Will

If Warren and the biblical authors' positions are correct, it can only mean God has been manipulating not only the courtship between lovers as the poem above suggests, but also the desires of rapists, fornicators, and the timing of birth control users. It would also require God to manipulate the hands of the doctors selecting specific sperm cells and eggs during in vitro fertilization as well as the conception and cell divisions that take place within the womb. Are we really to believe God is forcing or even directing males and females to each other, selecting which sperm meets which egg, or manipulating the genetic embryotic codes so the exact child that God wants will be conceived? Whether God is directing the paths of potential lovers or not, should we believe that God is selecting each person's eye and hair color or whether they will be born with some debilitating ailment?

Let's look at this from an unsophisticated scientific position. To be clear, science is mankind's attempt to interrogate and understand the physical laws of God's creation. Science is not necessarily at odds with the Bible, unless in certain places science either refutes the biblical authors' claims or our attempts to interpret their claims. What I'm about to argue is from a scientific perspective, not against God. It's against people like Rick Warren who accept and validate Scriptures written by unenlightened men—and then claim they are accurate godly truths that are reflected in our common reality. And as I mentioned in the previously, when one takes the position that the Bible is inerrant, they feel compelled to ignore or reject any evidence refuting biblical claims.

There was only one possible way to make you in the physical form you exist in. First, your biological parents needed to have intercourse (assuming you're not a product of in vitro fertilization). Second, males ejaculate approximately 250 million sperm cells during intercourse with each cell carrying different genetic information. No two sperm cells are alike and therefore no two humans can ever be genetically the same. Twins and triplets can be nearly "identical" but that occurs because of egg splitting, not because there are identical sperm cells. The strongest, best swimming sperm cell is the one that has the greatest chance of reaching the egg with no guarantee the fittest sperm will achieve its goal. The sperm in the back of the pack are also less likely to reach the egg first. It's completely random and impossible to predict which of the 250 million unique sperm will arrive and penetrate the female egg first, locking out all other genotypical possibilities. It's clear to me that God designed males to ejaculate enormous quantities of sperm cells to increase the probability of one of them reaching the female egg—absent any preference as to which one arrives first.

Why don't you have genetically induced purple hair with pink polka dots? Why are your hands and feet shaped in some similar form to that of your parents? The simple scientific answer is that we all carry certain traits of our parents because that is the gene pool from which we originate. Our genetic make-up is not the result of God selecting specific genetic traits from our parents as we are formed in the womb. God is not playing Mr. Potato Head by fabricating embryos to be short or choosing the shape or size of their noses. Those traits are also random, with some increased probability of occurring because of dominant over recessive genes. It would also be false to think God is nudging one unique desired sperm cell ahead of all the other sperm cells to see that he gets his desired fetus. To further ensure that the reader fully understands the intent of Pastor Warren's claims, here's an excerpt I received from his "Purpose Driven Connection" newsletter[12]:

When You Reject Yourself, You're Rejecting God's Design

My friend, I ask, "Who do you think you are to question God? 'Does the clay have the right to ask the potter why he shaped it the way he did?'" (Romans 9:20 CEV).

---

12.   Warren, Purpose Driven Connection email, "When You Reject Yourself, You're Rejecting God's Design," April 22, 2021.

Spiritual gifts,

Heart,

Abilities,

Personality,

Experiences

These are the five things that make you, you. I call them your SHAPE.

Accepting your SHAPE—the unique way that God made you that brings glory to him—means to believe that God knows best. It all comes down to the matter of trust. Do you believe that God made a mistake when he made you? Or do you trust him, knowing that he has a plan for your life?

Do you believe it?

When you say, "God, there are things I don't like about myself. I wish I had different hair or a different color of skin. I wish I were taller, shorter, skinnier. I wish I had more talent. I wish I could do 'that.' I wish I looked like him. I wish I had her smarts" and on and on. This kind of thinking is basically telling God, "You blew it! Everybody else is OK. But you goofed up big when you made me."

When you reject yourself, you are in essence rejecting God, because he's your Creator. When you don't accept yourself, it's rebellion against God. You're saying, "God, I know better than you. You should have made me different, with a different set of strengths and a different set of weaknesses."

But God says, "No, I made you exactly to be you because I want you to be you—with your strengths and your weaknesses. Both of them can give me glory—if you'll just start doing what I made you to do instead of trying to be like everybody else." It's actually quite arrogant to reject yourself. The Bible says in Romans 9:20 (CEV),

"My friend, I ask, 'Who do you think you are to question God? Does the clay have the right to ask the potter why he shaped it the way he did?'"

Whenever we doubt God's love and wisdom, we always get into trouble. The root behind all of your problems is that you don't trust God. You don't believe God really loves you. You don't believe that he really has your best interest at heart. You wish he had made you something different. As a result, there's a spirit of bitterness in you that keeps you frustrated and keeps you from being the person God wants you to be. Job 10:10 says, "You guided my conception and formed me in the womb" (NLT). God wanted you, and he loves you. Believe it, and then trust it!

Do you see the errant way of thinking here? To believe what Pastor Warren is promoting above, you're required to believe that God purposely directed the unique sperm cell that represented you from the 250 million ejaculated sperm and selected every physical trait that you received during your fetal formation. If a different sperm cell would have penetrated your mother's egg, you would be a completely different brother or sister to your siblings. You may also have been born with a debilitating birth defect. If you believe in science as I do, namely that we are randomly given the traits we have during the process of conception and those traits come from our parents, then all of what Rick Warren says about this subject is nonsense.

Applying "Intentional Design" Equally

If God is in the business of manipulating each of our traits during our formation, then isn't he also accountable for stillbirths, birth defects, or other fatal diseases that befall fetuses or infants? Why would any of us want to hold God accountable for the random processes that occur during and after the conception phase? Would we be willing to tell the parents of a child born with Down syndrome, autism, or muscular dystrophy that God has purposely, and in a "hands on" way, made their child with those disorders? We cannot hold God accountable for the random outcomes occurring in the reproductive process because he was not involved in that process. He made the reproductive system autonomous and random by the original design he instilled in the first two humans.

I also find it nonsensical to believe God instills specific "abilities" in each of us as Pastor Warren suggests. If God is monkeying around in the formation process, then he's obviously playing favorites. Many Christians claim, as Pastor Warren suggests, that not only does God select our individual physical traits, but he also instills specific unique gifts in each of us as we form in the womb. For example, Christians errantly suggest that God selectively provides certain people a spirit of humility, the gift of discernment, or a specific gift of higher intelligence. Ironically, we never hear Christians claim God was the provider of mental traits in children born with autism, or those who suffer with other types of mental disorders.

Pastor Warren also suggests our level of trust and our perception of God's love for us is somehow tied to our belief that he's the one that created us: "You don't believe God really loves you." These are clearly false premises. We can certainly believe and trust that God loves all his creation without believing he's involved in manipulating the reproductive processes to see that each of us exists with our exact genetic traits.

When I was very young, my parents told me they handpicked me from all the children that were available at the adoption agency. They claimed I was special to them because after perusing all the other children at the orphanage, they only wanted me. Did that make me feel special? Absolutely, and I remember telling all my friends that I was more special than they were because I was chosen (adopted).

But my parents weren't being truthful with me. The adoption agency simply assigned me to my parents who never saw me until the agency presented me to them on the same day they took me home. When I discovered in my early teens that I wasn't chosen but assigned, in no way did that affect my relationship with my parents or the love we shared. I was living on a false premise that made me feel more special as a child, which is exactly what is happening with those who believe God intended for each of us to exist and fabricated each of us as a special creation with a special purpose.

My parents had nothing to do with my creation, yet they loved me as if I was their biological child. We should all feel that same kind of godly love—understanding our existences originate by random processes. It shouldn't matter that we were created by God's random reproduction processes nor how we got here. Again, if God made the reproductive system random as science confirms, what would make us ever consider that he does not love the entirety of that creation?

These conception and formation processes are scientific facts and really not up for debate. And every time a critical thinking non-believer or skeptic who understands the scientific processes of reproduction hears a Christian claim that God desired and designed each of us by intent, it becomes yet another reason to reject Christianity. These microscopic processes are known to us now, unlike what was unknown by the biblical authors David, Paul, or Job thousands of years ago. For the people of their era, a child developing in the womb must have seemed like magic, and the only way for them to explain life forming in the womb was by the active hands of the Almighty.

We need to stop perpetuating these false biblical theories. God's miraculous random reproductive system instilled in his first creation is amazing, but it says nothing about his involvement anywhere before, during, or after the conception phase of reproduction. That system has been passed down throughout the generations and is random by design. It carries with it the beauty of perfection, and the risks of random genetic process that can go wrong from time to time. Medical statistics suggest the number of miscarriages occurring for pregnant women who are at twenty weeks or less, are between 15–20%. Are we to believe God's hands were in the initial conception phase of those pregnancies, but he took his hands off that process and sat idle while the fetus died in the womb?

God's reproductive system is not flawless, but it is amazing. It does not require godly intervention, and we shouldn't hold him liable when the system fails from time to time or we don't care for portions of our physicality. We certainly shouldn't say that miscarriages or birth defects occur because they are all part of God's active, mysterious fetus-forming activities. Rick Warren and the biblical author's theories are incorrect, and I believe God values all of us independent of our pathway into existence or the outcomes of those random processes.

The Real Probability You Exist

Since we have just established that God does not need to be nor does he involve himself in the process of reproduction, just how improbable is it that you exist? We'll need to approach this topic from a probabilistic perspective since we've established that the genealogical and reproduction processes are random events. The question we should be asking here is not whether God selected our parents, physical traits, or any of our inherent attributes, but rather, what are the odds of you becoming exactly you after God created the first two humans?

We'll need to do a little math here, but I want the reader to go through the process with me for two reasons. First, it will give you a sense of reality when you realize just how improbable it is for you to exist in the exact physical form you possess today. It would have taken only a slight deviation in our ancestry to change everything about who each of us are phenotypically or whether we would exist at all. Secondly, I hope the reader will appreciate the miraculous reproductive system that God placed within his first human creation. This system allows for the random diversity of our inherited traits and solidifies our uniqueness.

Dr. Ali Binazir, a medical doctor, author, and speaker, compiled an interesting calculation to show just how improbable it is that each of us exists in our exact physical forms. He titled his article, "Are You a Miracle?"[13] His calculation, however, includes an evolutionary view that I will replace with a more Judeo-Christian view—specifically that the generally accepted biblical position is correct and humans have only existed about 6,000 years.

If you're not aware, Christians have used the specific genealogical lineages listed in the Bible to come up with that 6,000-year figure. Some Christian thinkers seem to finally be moving away from the hard-held position, and we can thank scientific methods for that. Archeology suggests humans (in our current form) have been around much longer (about 100,000 years), but to appeal to Christians, my calculation below will use the generally accepted biblical view of the 6,000-year lineage. Dr. Binazir's calculation presumes a 300-million-year existence of evolutionary humanoid creatures (the original creature(s) from primordial soup that evolved into humans over time) which makes the final probability that each of us exist beyond astronomical. My calculation using only the biblical timeline will be astronomical enough.

Are You a Miracle?

If you're not interested in following the assumptions or math here, please feel free to simply review the *bold font* portions. I will be presenting the facts of Dr. Ali Binazir's calculations from his article, "Are You a Miracle" adjusted to fit the biblical timeline of roughly 6,000 years for the existence of man.

First, let's talk about the probability of your parents meeting each other. If they met one new person of the opposite sex every day from age fifteen to forty, that would be about 10,000 (10^4) people. Let's confine the pool of possible people they could meet to one-tenth of the world's population twenty years ago (one tenth of 4 billion = 400 million) to consider not just the population of the US but all the places they could have visited. Half of those people, or 200 million (2×10^8), will be of the opposite sex. So, let's say

13.   Ali Binazir, "Are You a Miracle? On the Probability of Your Being Born," HuffPost, June 16, 2011, https://www.huffpost.com/entry/probability-being-born_b_877853. Retrieved March 2014.

the probability of your parents ever meeting is 10,000 divided by 200 million: $(10^4/(2\times10^8)) = 5\times10^{-5}$, or one in 20,000.

Probability of boy meeting girl: 1 in 20,000

So far, it's pretty unlikely that your mother and father meet.

Now let's say the chance of them talking to one another is one in ten. And the chance of that turning into another meeting is also about one in ten. And the chance of that turning into a long-term relationship is also one in ten. And the chance of that lasting long enough to result in offspring is one in two. By the way, I consider all these chance assumptions extremely conservative. This calculation will also not consider the number of times your parents used contraception or when your mother had intercourse with your father when she was not ovulating, therefore eliminating the chance to produce children. So, the probability of your parents' chance meeting resulting in children is (10 x 10 x 10 x 2), or one in 2,000.

Probability of same boy impregnating same girl: one in 2,000

So, the combined probability that our parents meet and have children is already around one in 40 million (20,000 x 2,000)—long but not insurmountable odds. Now things start getting interesting. Why? Because we're about to consider the volume of sperm cells, which come in very large numbers.

Each sperm and egg are genetically unique because of the process of meiosis; you are the result of the fusion of one unique egg with one unique sperm. A fertile woman has on average 100,000 viable eggs during her lifetime. A man will produce about 12 trillion sperm over the course of his reproductive lifetime. Let's conservatively say a third of those (4 trillion) are relevant to our calculation, since the sperm created after your mom enters menopause become irrelevant. So, the probability of that one sperm with half your name on it connecting with that one egg with the other half of your name is:

$$1/[(100,000)(4\text{ trillion})]= 1/(10^5)(4\times10^{12}) = 1 \text{ in } 4 \text{ x } 10^{17},$$

or one in 400 quadrillion.

> *Probability of right sperm meeting right egg from*
> *your parents to make you: one in 400 quadrillion*

But we're just getting started… because the existence of you here now on planet Earth presupposes another supremely unlikely and utterly undeniable chain of events. Every one of your ancestors must have lived to a reproductive age—going all the way back to the first humans. You are a representative of an unbroken lineage of the first two humans.

Let's give the Bible some credence and say the first humans were on this planet only six thousand years ago. Again, this is in direct conflict with what most scientists believe, that humans (in the physical form we all carry today) have existed for at least the last 100,000 years. If humans have only been around six thousand years, and an average generation is about 20 years, that's 300 generations. Let's also conservatively assume over the course of all human existence, the likelihood of any one human offspring surviving childhood and living to a reproductive age and having at least one child is 50:50—1 in 2. Then what would be the chance of your lineage remaining unbroken for 300 generations?

Well, that would be 1 in 2^{300} which is about 1×10^{90}

> *Probability of every one of your ancestors*
> *reproducing successfully: 1 in 10^{90}*

But let's think about this more deeply. Remember the sperm-meeting-egg argument for the creation of you, since each gamete (the reproductive cell that carries half of each of your parent's genetic traits) is unique? Well, the correct sperm (the one that created each of your forefathers which will in turn create you) also had to meet the correct egg to create your grandparents. Otherwise, they'd be different people, and so would their children, who would have produced children who were like you, but not quite you. This is also true of your grandparents' parents, and their grandparents, and so on, back to the original creation. If only once, a different sperm cell met a different egg in your lineage, you might not be sitting here trying to follow this calculation. You might be more like your cousin Kevin, and you never really liked him anyway.

So now we must account for that for 300 generations by raising 400 quadrillion (probability your parents created you) to the 300th power:

> *Probability of the right sperm meeting the right*
> *egg for 300 generations $[4x10^{17}]^{300} \approx 10^{5100}$*

That's 1 chance in 10 followed by 5,100 zeros

To get the final answer, we'll need to multiply 10^{5100} (probability of the right sperm meeting the right egg for 300 generations) by 10^{90} (probability all of your ancestors reproducing successfully), and by 2,000 (probability of boy impregnating same girl from above), and by 20,000 (probability of boy meeting girl from above). For the sake of completeness:

> *$(10^{5100})(10^{90})(2x10^{3})(2x10^{4}) \approx 4x10^{5197}$*
> *Final probability of your existence: 1 chance*
> *in 4x10 followed by 5,197 zeros*

For comparison, Dr. Binazir's calculation that includes humanoid existence (the initial life form randomly created from primordial soup) for the past 300 million years, unlike my biblical human timeline of 6,000 years, calculates the probability of each of our existences would be $10x^{2,685,000}$. That would equate to 1 chance in 10, to the power of 2.68 million. In either case, the Christian 6,000-year human existence or Dr. Binazir's, the numbers are overwhelmingly improbable.

To get some perspective about the probability that you exist as you are, consider the following:

- 10^{27} is the approximate number of atoms in an average sized adult male.
- 10^{50} is the approximate number of atoms that make up the Earth.
- 10^{80} is the approximate number of atoms in the known universe.

Our individual existence based only on the biblical timeline is *1 chance in $4x10^{5197}$*!

I wanted the reader to go through these calculations to show the improbability of your physical existence as you are, and to highlight *miracles were not required after God created the first two humans*. No godly planning or intervention by genetic manipulation is needed to explain our specific height, hair color, birth defects, or our existence. One chance in four times ten followed by 5,197 zeros that we exist in our specific form is improbably amazing. Humankind was generally planned to exist in the future by our God because he created the miraculous reproductive system, but certainly not with the exact specific genetic traits that each of us carry. He made it random to ensure our uniqueness, but we cannot confuse that with his active involvement of individual creation for each of us to exist with the exact specific genetic codes we uniquely carry.

The calculations from above do not provide all the reasons why we are here but only help us understand how unlikely it is for each of us to exist. The probability calculations I provided do not explain all the intricacies of the amazing reproductive system instilled in the first humans that we all carry as their descendants. But the processes and intricacies of that system do not require, nor do they involve godly manipulation.

Why does any of this matter? It matters because many Christians believe, as Rick Warren advocates, that God orchestrates or manipulates: the meeting of sexual partners, the conception processes, and the fabrication of each person in our mother's womb. They believe God is actively responsible in a hands-on way (like a potter forms clay) for our individual physicality as well as any deficiencies we carry. In that way, Christians believe they are even more special to God rather than accepting that each of us exists only because of the free will of our forefathers and the genetic randomness occurring in the reproductive process. All these beliefs are grounded in the false premise made by some of the biblical authors from antiquity. As I will further demonstrate with the following examples, the biblical authors, or Christian interpretations of their claims regarding reproduction, are false.

[10] God's Handiwork?

As I mentioned earlier, I landed in the arms of two parents who adopted me at the age of eight months and loved me as a son. I spent over twenty years searching to identify both of my biological parents. I discovered that my birth resulted from a mother who was very promiscuous meeting my birth father from another country when he was randomly vacationing in Las Vegas in August of 1960. My existence can be clearly traced to the freewilled "sinful" choices of my unmarried birth father and birth mother and to all the previous random freewilled choices of all my forefathers.

If Rick Warren is correct, and God intervened to see that I was created, he had to manipulate and override the free will of my biological parents to go against his own moral laws to achieve my conception. After their encounter, did God's divine hand reach down into my mother's reproductive canal and push the sperm cell that represented me, and only me, ahead of all the other ejaculated sperm to ensure it reached its destination first? Did he see to it my hair and eye color were brown?

If you're in the camp that believes God intentionally created you in your exact form, then you are required to believe that randomness in sperm migration and the free will of humans are nonexistent. Following Rick Warren's theory, and the poem he opens his book with, God would have needed to preordain fornication for me to exist. Does God cause people to sin?

Does God manipulate the minds of rapists to commit violent crimes against women to ensure that a specific and unique person is created? Don't forget, Pastor Warren claims all humans were planned and created by God. We all know planning requires intent to act.

How are we to perceive God's supposed "hand" on the in vitro fertilization process? Millions of sperm are ejaculated by the potential father and placed in a petri dish. Then the doctor selects a few of them and has one and only one matched to the egg from the female. If you were a product of this process, would you say the doctor is partially responsible for your genetic outcome, or would you say that God manipulated the doctor's hands and made him select the one sperm out of the 250 million that represented only you to meet with one specific egg from your mother?

Is God in the business of planning or manipulating sexually active couples (married or not) and the use, absence, or ineffectiveness of birth control in precise timing to determine the conception of the child he desires? Or is it determined by an individual's free will when or if they use birth control? Does God see that condoms malfunction at certain times, or does he purposely manipulate certain females to forget to take their birth control pills on certain days to ensure he gets his "planned child" to exist?

Unfortunately, if you take the theories recorded in the Bible by uneducated men, you will arrive at such a conclusion. The clergy of our day accept some of those theories as truth, and they influence their parishioners to believe them—even when science and sound reasoning clearly conflict with such interpretations.

Homosexuality

You might be asking yourself why I'm including the topic of homosexuality in this chapter. The simple answer is because I am convinced that homosexuals are genetically born with their sexual preferences. I want to dispel the notion that God has made them that way on purpose, for a purpose, or that homosexuality is a simple choice. This seems to be a subject most Christians do not like to discuss in detail.

With people like Rick Warren advocating the position that God created every detail (evidently excluding one's sexual orientation) of every human that has ever lived, it's inconceivable for Christians to consider God making anyone to desire the same sex. So, the only option for Christians who believe this reasoning is to claim desiring the same sex can only be a choice. "God couldn't have created them that way." They're right. God did not make them that way, and I will seek to dismantle their "choice" argument in the following paragraphs.

I'm aware there's an ongoing debate amongst many people regarding whether the root desire for one to be homosexual comes from a genetic trait or whether that desire only comes by choice or even from how a child is raised by his or her parents during their formative years. Does homosexuality originate from "nature," "nurture," or simply free choice?

I'm convinced genetics are at the root of homosexuality in the same way we randomly receive our other physical traits upon conception or in the same way that a child would be born with an abnormality like Down syndrome. I don't mean to liken a disorder like Down syndrome to homosexuality, but homosexuality is not the "norm" nor is Down syndrome. Both are considered statistical aberrations.

We are all genetically either male or female, and that was certainly determined by the presence or absence of our father's sperm cell that carried either an XX or XY chromosome pair. For brevity, we'll leave the subject of hermaphrodites out of our discussion. The chromosomes from our father determined whether we had male or female reproductive organs, but they did not determine our hair or eye color, sexual identity, or orientation. Just because one has male reproductive parts does not guarantee that he will be attracted to women.

It is estimated that 5% of humans are genetically wired with the desire for the same sex. Using genetic reasoning to explain sexuality also helps to explain why there are masculine women (bodies more like a male) who were born with a genetic trait that makes them desire women. In essence, they are men in women's bodies yet possessing female reproductive parts. Likewise, there are feminine men whose genetic preference marker is bent towards desiring men. They are mostly feminine and yet they possess male reproductive organs. Each of us received a genetic trait during our formation in the womb that gives us all our sexual orientation or identity, irrespective of the sexual reproductive organs we received at that time.

This also explains the existence of those we refer to as transgender. Transgenders seem to have the "wrong" body parts for their sexual identity just as homosexuals have a different sexual orientation for their reproductive parts. Rather than live in internal conflict and risk societal damnation, some transgenders choose to do something about what they know they can change. For the transgender, it's better to chemically alter, or surgically change their body parts, rather than try to force or attempt to change their inner sexual identity, enabling them to be in line with society's norm. If the desire to change one's sexual identity was only a simple choice, I doubt there would be anyone who would spend the money and go through the agony of reconstructive surgery.

It should come as no surprise that homosexuals and transgenders have chosen to live in the closet for all these years. Honestly, who would want to expose themselves to the torment of society for something that was simply a "choice"? Who would want to be denied medical or tax benefits and be publicly labeled a fag or lesbian if it was merely a simple choice to be heterosexual? Who would put themselves through hell if choosing a sexual preference was just that easy? The genetic wiring / sexual preference / desire / identity is not about a choice any more than your skin or eye color. Our sexual orientation and identity are what we received during our conception. Nobody is pretending to desire intimacy with the same sex. The societal and interfamilial consequences have always been too high to fake something like that.

What are we to make of all of this? Conservative Christians say even if homosexuality is a genetic trait, homosexuals should choose a life of celibacy and not be in same sex relationships. They liken this "disorder" to someone who might be predisposed to alcoholism or drug addiction. But I propose that being predisposed to alcohol or drugs is not a good analogy. Children before or during puberty do not desire drugs or alcohol like a child who is born with the desire for the same sex or a child identifying as the opposite sex. This seems to be an easy thing to say for Christian heterosexuals. They are not the ones who will be living a life of celibacy and loneliness. They are also not the ones who will have to suppress their true inherent sexual desires for the remainder of their lives.

We all desire to love and be loved in deep meaningful relationships. I believe God wired his first creation with this desire and it is written in the fabric of each person's DNA. If God actually does construct each of us on an individual basis as we are formed in the womb, and if I'm correct that homosexuality is a genetic trait, then it follows he has actually intentionally made about 5% of us with the desire for the same sex. In the same way, he must be purposely designing and creating 1 in 700 people with Down syndrome[14] or 1 in 68 with autism as reported in 2012.[15] This is not the way it works, and the days of refuting the origin of homosexuality as genetic are over. Although medical research has yet to determine the genetic pathways explaining our sexual identities or orientations, I am confident that will be forthcoming.

Birth Defects

If God is involved in the reproductive process and intervenes to make each of us on an individual basis, then what is to be said about his workmanship or his intent for those who are born with physical or mental disabilities? What about children who are born with lethal ailments and won't survive their next birthday? If one claims God is the hands-on fabricator of unfortunate

14. "How Many People Are Living with Down Syndrome in the United States?" CDC Birth Defects Data and Statistics, June 27, 2017, https://www.cdc.gov/ncbddd/birth-defects/downsyndrome/data.html. Retrieved January 2019.

15. Autism and Developmental Disabilities Monitoring Network, "Community Report on Autism 2016," CDC, from https://www.cdc.gov/ncbddd/autism/documents/community_report_autism.pdf, link downloads report.

children like this, I'm not sure how they'll be able reconcile this without charging him with the liability.

My wife and are very good friends with a couple from our church who have a son with Down syndrome. His parents love him as much as they love their other three children. He may have special needs, but his value to their family is no less than any of his siblings. The night he was born, I sat with the pastor of my church and the boy's father, and although it was hard for everyone, we celebrated his son's birth. I remember my friend quietly smoking a celebratory cigar and coming to the realization that his son would, in some way, probably live with a reduced quality of life. His son would most probably not be able to marry and have children of his own.

Of course, I had heard of Down syndrome before, but that was the first time I was up close and personal with someone whose family had been affected by it. I remember at that time reviewing what I had learned about that "disorder" and how the embryo, when formed, had an extra chromosome twenty-one—giving the child forty-seven chromosomes rather than the normal forty-six. I remember asking myself, "How did this happen?" Was this just a random mutation that occurs for one in 700 children born here in the US, or was this the handiwork of God? Did God mess things up, or did he intentionally design my friend's son so he would not be able to live the same quality of life as most other children? Did God make this child with this disorder, as Pastor Rick Warren states, "on purpose for a purpose"?

I wondered if God intentionally gave him that extra chromosome to teach the rest of us not directly affected to appreciate life because we were "blessed" our children were not born with this disorder. But that didn't sit well with my soul. There was no way I was going to attribute a child's disorder to the Creator, and I certainly wasn't going to "count my blessings," as if to infer my family was somehow shown God's favor over my friend's family.

I started thinking about other children who were born with heart defects and other lethal ailments which could not be corrected by medical science. I wondered if or where God's hands were during the conception and embryo-forming processes for them. It became beyond me to accept Rick Warren's concurrence with the biblical author David's theory that God made each of us specifically as we are. Do you and I want to believe in a God who is forming children with lethal forms of cancer or irreversible brain damage? Does he intentionally give them defects that will cause them to die during a premature birth? Perhaps we should forget about what we "want" to believe. Do we actually think this is how God operates?

Our True Purpose

If we are not individually intentionally created by God, we (as specific individuals) cannot be created for a specific purpose as individuals. However, as I've already proposed, we (humankind as a whole) could all have been created from the randomness of the genes of our forefathers to have a collective general purpose. For me, that purpose for all of us is twofold and it comes straight from the biblical claims of Jesus. I am convinced that these two commandments are the specific desires and purposes that God wants for all mankind.

> One of the teachers of the law. . . asked [Jesus], "Of all the commandments, which is the most important?"

> "The most important one," answered Jesus, "is this: 'Hear, O Israel: The Lord our God, the Lord is one. Love the Lord your God with all your heart and with all your soul and with all your mind and with all your strength.' The second is this: 'Love your neighbor as yourself.' *There is no commandment greater than these.*" (Mark 12:28–31, emphasis mine)

So, what does it boil down to for all of us? What's the actual general purpose for all the randomly created descendants of Adam and Eve? It's simply to:

1. Love God
2. Love people

When we refute the notion that God is responsible for the specific physical traits of each of our bodies (both healthy or disabled, heterosexual or homosexual), then we remove him from any liabilities for any of our perceived shortcomings. We don't need to be angry at God because we're too short or have a big nose. We can't be frustrated with God because we were born with a club foot or even as a carrier of a lethal disease. God is not creating homosexuals, heterosexuals, or children born with Down syndrome.

It's only when we allow ourselves to think along the lines of people like Pastor Warren and David in the Old Testament, namely that God orchestrates each of our physical traits as we form in our mother's womb, that we feel the need to hold him accountable for our unwanted traits. We are who we are for a reason, and that reason was the free will of our forefathers and most importantly, the randomness that God instilled in the amazing autonomous reproductive system of the first two humans.

Original Sin

Christians assert sin has been passed down as a curse to every generation of humans only because Adam and Eve disobeyed God by freely choosing to eat the forbidden fruit. They claim their sin sent the entire Earth on a course for chaos, suffering, and death. Offering counter reasoning, I hope to convince you that our desire to sin is not a mysterious curse that resulted from their mistake but rather part of God's initial design for mankind. Our desire to sin is simply the result of God originally wiring his first creation to be seekers of pleasure, and we're all genetically tied to them. Death, suffering, and a chaotic world would have all come to fruition in the absence of anyone's sin.

There cannot be any truth that we are sinners because of Adam and Eve's initial fruit selection. Sin originates from our pleasure-seeking thoughts and desires and is carried to fruition with our selfish actions. When God created Adam and Eve, didn't they carry the general genetic traits that craved pleasure just as we do today?

Moses wrote in Genesis 3:16–19 after Adam and Eve screwed up:

To the woman he said,

"I will make your pains in childbearing very severe;
   with painful labor you will give birth to children.
Your desire will be for your husband,
   and he will rule over you."

To Adam he said, "Because you listened to your wife and ate fruit from the tree about which I commanded you, 'You must not eat from it,'

"Cursed is the ground because of you;
   through painful toil you will eat food from it
   all the days of your life.
It will produce thorns and thistles for you,
   and you will eat the plants of the field.
By the sweat of your brow
   you will eat your food
until you return to the ground,
   since from it you were taken;
for dust you are
   and to dust you will return."

The author Moses tells us God needed to implement some consequential physical changes to the female DNA structure by causing all women from that point forward to experience pain during childbirth. As we've discussed, it was also at that time that God supposedly established the hierarchy of the family structure and that the man would be running the show from that point forward. I'm going to forward that verse via email (not in person) to my wife right now to ensure she gets the message! I think she needs a reminder, and I'll probably need a bodyguard.

God also decided that man would now have to work much harder by toiling in the fields to obtain sustenance. It's as if all generations following

Adam and Eve were destined for an easier life in their fabulous garden and be subject to painless childbirth if they had not chosen wrong. Apparently, the author of Genesis (supposedly Moses and male) decided to use this reasoning to ensure the woman would always be subordinate to her husband. I appreciate your efforts, Moses, but she's just not accepting that.

It makes me wonder what Eve's nerve structures were like before she sinned. Were there no nerves connected to her birth canal prior to her sin, and God changed her nerve endings or DNA to make sure that pain would occur during childbirth? As much as it pains me to say this, I know it's possible that God could have made these changes. But I don't think it's probable that God altered the woman's DNA the way the story goes.

I think it's more probable that the author made this up to explain why women experience pain during childbirth. For the author, childbirth should have been a natural event that God ordained, and yet the author needed to find a way to explain why there would be so much pain associated with that process. The reality has always been that Adam and Eve had the same genetic makeup as we do, and all women from the beginning of God's design were always going to suffer through childbirth.

Freewilled and Pleasure-Seeking

God created humankind with the desire to seek pleasure and has allowed us to make wrong choices. All humans (beginning with Adam and Eve) are pleasure seekers because God made Adam and Eve with human bodies that crave things outside of what is best for us. As their descendants, we all have nerve endings in our bodies that crave pleasure. Many of us want to eat more than we should. Some choose to drink in excess or use drugs to numb and minimize their emotional pain. Some chose to live promiscuous lifestyles to satisfy their sexual desires. Others seek to steal rather than work to minimize their labor. We were wired to desire taking the path of least resistance and minimize our labor and suffering. We were originally designed to have bodies that desire the fulfillment of our pleasures and selfishly care about ourselves more than others. We are not that way because of Adam and Eve's original sin.

The next illogical step made by Christians is to suggest that *all* the world's suffering occurs only because of the first sin committed by our devious first couple. In chapter 13, I'll be introducing a photo of a starving child who represents one of the *24,000* people who will *expire today* from malnutrition. I have named this child Haji, and my hope is that you will never forget him. I will cite many examples of intervention-believing favor-claiming Christians throughout this book, and I will continually be asking you to compare the plight of Haji against those same claims of favor. If you get nothing else out of this book, my desire is that you will always consider the Hajis of this world before you consider making your next public claim of favor or specific godly blessing. But for now, I want to briefly approach the topic of suffering from the common Christian perspective as it relates to the original sin.

Disasters and Sin

Suffering on this Earth occurs in various ways. The most obvious suffering occurs when one person sins against another. There's a cause-and-effect relationship when a man harms a fellow human. Adolph Hitler was a perfect example of that. Out of his hatred for the Jewish people, and his lust for power, he was responsible for the suffering deaths of millions of people. These types of sins have a moral component and can be directly tied to human causation. Freely choosing to do anything immoral can certainly cause suffering.

There's also earthly suffering that cannot be attributable to sin and therefore has no moral component. For example, can you tell me what current or former sin anyone has ever committed that could be linked to Earth's crust slipping, causing deadly earthquakes and tsunamis? Can you possibly tell me what current or former sin anyone has ever committed that would cause famines in certain African regions that have wiped billions from this Earth for thousands of years? What possible current or former sin causes violent tornadoes or hurricanes or even volcanoes that kill so many every year and have since the beginning of time?

I know there are examples of these types of disasters in the Bible, and many were reportedly caused by God as forms of punishment. The prophet Isaiah from the Old Testament claimed that God said, "'I form the light and create darkness, | I bring prosperity and create disaster; | I, the LORD, do all these things'" (Isaiah 45:7). Are there people today who really believe God is actively behind the timing and location of such natural disasters that have been killing people from the beginning of time all because of the original sin?

Well, I'm glad I asked that question because once again, Pastor Rick Warren is one such person who believes that current natural disasters are a direct result of past and current sin. In yet another Daily Hope devotional, Pastor Warren quotes Romans 8:22, "We know that the whole creation has been groaning as in the pains of childbirth right up to the present time" to support this claim.[16]

He goes on to say:

> Nothing works perfectly. Because the entire human race has made poor choices. *Everything is broken, and nothing on this planet works perfectly. Sin has damaged everything.*
>
> ... Sin has ruined. . . destroyed, corrupted, and spoiled . . . and injured everything. . . every relationship, idea, dream, and human body.

I think I can agree with Pastor Warren's claim, except the use of the word, "everything." Our sins and the sins of those before us have certainly caused a lot of suffering, but sin has not corrupted everything. Trees don't naturally get diseases because of sin. Children are not born with terminal diseases because of Adam and Eve's fruit selection. Our DNA has not been

---

16. Warren, "Sin Has Damaged Everything," reprinted at Salt + Pepper, November 6, 2014, https://40daysjourneywithchrist.blogspot.com/2014/11/sin-has-damaged-everything.html. Retrieved May 6, 2021.

changed from the original creation to be susceptible to diseases like cancer or heart attacks solely because of sin.

One can credibly argue that environmental conditions may play a role in those disorders, but they are not necessarily sin driven. We have the same arms and legs, internal organs, and reproductive parts that are exactly like that of the first two humans. Despite Pastor Warren's arguments, sin has done nothing to generally change our overall physical attributes. Past or present sin does not cause genetic heart disorders in children.

But here's the kicker: Pastor Warren wants us to believe that all natural disasters are the direct result of the original sin. He states the first result of sin is natural disasters and deformities, and "We're not living in Eden anymore." Pastor Warren agrees with the English Poet John Milton that paradise is lost. Thus, Warren explains disasters in that light:

> We live on a broken planet. And as a result, we have hurricanes, typhoons, wacky weather, earthquakes, droughts and floods.
>
> It's amazing to me that insurance companies call all these things acts of God but doesn't call the birth of a baby an act of God. In other words, an act of God is only the negative stuff that happens. *God does not want these things happening in the world. And he is as upset by natural disasters as we are.* The world was broken when sin damaged everything.
>
> The Bible says in Romans 8:20, "Creation is confused" (CEV). Everything on this planet has lost its original purpose. Everything in the world was damaged including your DNA, your parents' DNA, and their parents' DNA. Have you figured out yet that your body doesn't work right? If everybody's body worked perfectly, there would be no need for doctors. (Emphasis mine.)[17]

---

17.   Warren, "Sin Has Damaged Everything."

Should we believe when God created the Earth there was no need for an atmosphere that contained the necessary elements like oxygen, nitrogen, and water vapor to sustain Adam and Eve? Or perhaps we should believe those elements were present in the atmosphere, but before the original sin, God was manipulating the water vapor laced clouds and the sun in such a way that no violent storms (hurricanes or tornadoes) were ever produced anywhere on our Earth. Should we believe that after Adam and Eve committed their sin, God altered the Earth's composition and structure such that we now have tectonic plates shifting causing catastrophic earthquakes? And if God made any alterations to the Earth after the first sin, is he responsible for when and where these natural disasters occur today or is it more likely they are simple random natural events that have occurred in specific geographic regions since he created this planet?

What's very interesting to me is the Bible states in many places, as I just referenced in Isaiah, that God is the one who causes natural disasters. Then, Warren suggests that God is as upset about their occurrences as much as we are. So, using this type of logic, God creates disasters and then feels bad about them afterwards. Does that make any sense? I've searched for biblical verses that state that the original sin is the causation behind natural disasters, but I've never found any. The only biblical commentary that I have found referencing natural disasters are always at the hands of the Almighty as a form of supernatural punishment.

Does God Intervene?

I believe this is what we should expect from unenlightened biblical authors who believed God was behind those events. And this certainly explains why there are Christians and some Christian pastors who continue to perpetuate that current natural disasters are at the hands of an active God who causes them to punish current sin. And here's something else to consider: when Warren suggests that God doesn't want natural disasters to occur and he feels bad about them, is that not another clear indicator that God has allowed this Earth to run its course without intervening? If Warren is correct, then God must also feel bad about people suffering with cancer or killed in car accidents. But apparently, he has relinquished his right to do anything about it because of the free will he has extended to us. Unlike Pastor Warren, I don't claim to know what God feels, but I am convinced he is not interfering with the events or circumstances of this world, and he certainly has no liability in any of it.

I believe God set this planet in motion and created natural consequences for our desires to choose wrong (sin). Those non-supernatural consequences are mostly tied to violating God's laws. However, "natural" disasters do not occur because the first two humans made a selfish bad choice. The Earth and its physical properties are generally the same as they were at creation. Hurricanes, tornadoes, volcanoes, famines, and earthquakes were all possible the day God created our planet.

If I accidentally kill someone by failing to see a stop sign in an intersection and there was no alcohol or driver distraction, the victim and or their family would suffer. I didn't do it intentionally, and that's why we call it an accident. This is simple cause and effect. The victim didn't suffer and die because of any past or present sin on my or their part. They certainly weren't killed because of Adam and Eve's sin.

If Adam and Eve had not sinned, would we be exempt from fatal car accidents today? Would the Newtonian laws addressing force, mass, and acceleration have been null and void in the absence of the original sin? Would gravity have been negated in such a way that no one would ever accidently fall from a ladder and not be harmed? Does a toddler quickly learn that pulling on a dog's fur usually returns a row of teeth marks across its knuckles? Do employees learn over some period that being continually late for work usually ends in their termination? Do people who contract viral diseases suffer? These are simple cause and effect events and the suffering caused by those events are not sin related.

Christians feel compelled to sum it up and use the original sin argument as the causation of all suffering. You hear it all the time. "We live in a fallen world because of the first sin, and that explains why people suffer and die." As we will discuss in a later chapter, this is a common justification Christians need to employ since they are unable to reconcile an all-loving, active, and powerful God who could but doesn't stop atrocities from happening. Again, they will always tell us that bad things are a mystery we'll never understand, but that's not what we hear when favorable events occur in their lives.

Some may disagree, but I believe sin is never by accident. It's always planned, and it can cause very serious consequences. When we sin, we consciously choose it. Can't we see this for what it really is? Moses, a man living in antiquity, was trying to explain his version of how things came into being. His version of the creation and sin stories come 2,500 years after events he never witnessed and lacked the knowledge we possess today.

Moses was using the limited knowledge he had at that time, and again, I don't fault him for that. He attempted to find an explanation as to how life started and the consequences for people's bad decisions. He was trying to tell us that God's original design for females included painless childbirth and that God needed to change her genetic makeup as a form of punishment. He tried to tell us that God's initial design for us would be that we would never die. Our bones, joints and internal organs are no different than his first two humans, and we all know these body parts decay over time. That's how it was always going to be and is how God created his first two humans. I don't think God ever wanted man to physically live forever on this globe, and it's clear we were not designed to. Otherwise, how would we be able to appreciate our physical lives today if there wasn't going to be an end?

If God really wanted us to be looking to eternity as the Bible says, how could death have not been an option for Adam and Eve before their sin? In summary, the "original sin" is not the reason that people suffer on this Earth today. Suffering occurs either by the natural consequences of current intentional sin or by the accidental hand of man, by natural environmental disasters, or by the random events of the chaotic world we live in.

PART 4:
OUR
FOUNDATIONS

[11] Ya Gotta Have Faith

I WOULD LIKE TO TURN OUR ATTENTION TO THE SUB-
jects of faith, hope, belief, and doubt. These subjects are important to all
Christians, but each term can carry a different weight depending on their
specific applications. Overextending these terms past the probabilities of
our common realities can create devastating emotional consequences. We
should consider exactly which ideologies and life circumstances they apply
to as well as their relative magnitude.

What is faith, and exactly what matters should we place our faith in?
What is hope and how can that influence our ability to make reasonable
assessments of the events that occur in our lives? What role does doubt play
in our overall ability to establish our beliefs? I think it's best to start with
defining these terms to minimize potential misinterpretations. I'll begin each
subtitle with its corresponding definition.

Faith

1. confidence or trust in a person or thing: faith in another's ability.

2. belief that is not based on proof.

3. belief in God or in the doctrines or teachings of religion: the firm
    faith of the Pilgrims. . . .

8. *Christian Theology*: the trust in God and in his promises as made through Christ and the Scriptures by which humans are justified or saved. [18]

One exercises faith when moving from the position of the unknown to a position of confidence, having some measure of supporting evidence but not absolute knowledge. We all can have knowledge regarding certain matters where faith is not required. For example, it doesn't take much faith to state that the color of my car is red. The only assumption I would need to invoke for this claim is that I'm not colorblind.

The apostle Paul gave us his definition: "Now faith is confidence in what we hope for and assurance about what we do not see" (Hebrews 11:1). For me, exercising faith is taking steps in the same direction any supporting evidence points to without complete certainty that I'm going in the right direction.

Reasonable Faith

We have biblical books that say Jesus died and was resurrected, and I do my best to live as if it were true. Those who honestly live their life as if something is true must have a reasonable faith in that something. I willingly choose to place my hope in the biblical claims of Jesus (even in the absence of first-hand knowledge) and not because I'm afraid of eternal torture.

My following Christ has nothing to do with Pascal's wager. This wager encourages people to bet on Jesus to avoid eternal torment. My motive is not that I don't want to be wrong and go to hell. Rather, I am a follower of Jesus because aligning my life according to his principles is the only certain way, to me, to experience life more abundantly. The wisdom of Jesus provides confidence (faith) in the hope I have in him, assurance of his divinity without witnessing him or his miracles.

I've also had to ask myself, is it probable or even reasonable for the Creator of this universe to want his human creation to continually live their

---

18. "Faith," Random House Unabridged Dictionary (2021), dictionary.com.

lives in the bondage of guilt and shame created by their own selfish human desires—providing no way out? Is it possible for God to have created his first humans as pleasure seekers, knowing they and their descendants would, at times, choose wrongly, yet offer no remedy for them? What would life be like if there was no way to remove the guilt and shame from our past transgressions? To date, I have found no other logical or reasonable way to rid myself of the stains of sin that once encapsulated the entirety of my being.

For me, faith is an assurance in God's existence, and a confident trust that is not based on my ability to have ever seen, heard, or knowingly experienced him. With complete knowledge, we would not be exercising faith. If I ever do observe godly activity or "experience" him in the way we are examining here, I will not need faith to believe in his existence because I would have complete knowledge that he exists.

If God ever spoke to me audibly or sent a mysterious sign, why would I ever need faith? The Apostle Paul told us that we must have faith, not complete knowledge, to enter God's kingdom. Is it possible that Paul knew God would not be revealing himself or actively intervening on this planet after the era of Jesus, and we would never have complete knowledge—even of God's existence?

Paul wrote, "For we live by faith and not by sight" (2 Corinthians 5:7). He also clarified our source of salvation: "For by grace you have been saved through *faith*, and that not of yourselves; it is the gift of God: not of works, lest any man should boast." (Ephesians 2:8–9 NKJV, emphasis mine).

I know the second verse is mainly instructing us that salvation is not attained by our works, but I think there's something else to glean from it. Notice we are *not* saved by grace through complete knowledge. And, if it takes faith to have a confident assurance of God's existence or in the biblical claims of Jesus, enabling us to enter his eternal kingdom, none of us can ever have such knowledge. We cannot get to the heavenly realm with complete knowledge. According to 2 Corinthians 5:7, we also can't be saved by observing ("by sight") God or his activities because that would also eliminate the need for faith. If Paul was correct about this, salvation can only be attained by faith.

If miracles were occurring with the frequency that many allege today, then we would certainly have knowledge that God exists. But Paul said we must exercise faith, not knowledge. So how can miracles be going on in the world we live in? Perhaps this little fragment of understanding also indicates that God is not active on this Earth today. If God is healing cancers or changing people's circumstances for the better, then who would need to exercise faith to simply believe in his existence—let alone the resurrection of Jesus?

None of the biblical books remotely suggest we are required to believe or have faith that God is currently intervening today. Faith in the existence of Jesus, acknowledging we have separated ourselves from God with sin, and his promise to forgive us are the only requirements—not current miraculous intervention. I've had people tell me, "You may be right about that, Jeff, but you're missing out on a lot of blessings because you don't ask for them. God wants to give you more, but he won't do it unless you have faith he can and will."

My faith in God's existence is not based on my eyewitness accounts of God's actions or acceptance of other's current miraculous claims. Those are unreasonable positions to hold because they require God to play favorites and refute our God-given free will. As we've already discussed, my faith in his existence comes from the reasonable, observable circumstantial evidence (the anthropic principle and the complicated intricacies of human creation) and the wisdom of Jesus that leads me to extend my faith in God. It's not an unreasonable blind faith.

Likewise, another kind of reasonable, subjective evidence has driven me to exercise my faith and hope that Jesus is real and his death and resurrection have set me free. He seems to be the only perfect "round peg" solution that fits the round hole in my guilt-ridden heart resulting from my choices to do wrong.

One may argue that I choose to accept and have faith in the existence of Jesus and his sacrifice because it's just a crutch I use to make myself feel better. One might say, "Jeff, you're like the rest of the Christians who need and want it to be true to relieve your guilt and shame." I'm not completely denying or refuting that this argument might be valid. But I cannot come up with any other earthly or religious-system solution to my sin problem that makes better sense.

Since I'm reasonably willing to credit God with all of creation, it's a small and reasonable step for me to accept a sacrificial solution to my sin problem. There is no doubt I'm a pleasure-seeking sinner, and I'm certain I would have come to that conclusion without exposure to the Bible. Every other method I know of to rid myself of the anvil that used to rest on my shoulders turns out to be a square-shaped peg that never seemed to fit the round sin-shaped hole in my heart.

This isn't just a feel-good answer that came as a result of youthful training. For many years, I questioned the validity of Jesus as the sin offering of the world. After years of contemplation, I have faithfully and reasonably accepted this amazing, grace-filled gift because I am convinced it has set me free.

The Truth of Grace

While we're here, I want to express some of my views on God's grace and how it has deeply impacted my life. I have committed some pretty horrible sins during my life, causing devastating consequences for both those I have harmed as well as my own psychological well-being. All of my offenses may not have been illegal, but they certainly crossed moral thresholds. When you have perpetrated any sin and possess even a moderately compassionate disposition, you will undoubtedly feel a sense of guilt. That guilt will surely fester within you until you express your sorrow to those you've hurt.

For those of us who believe there is a higher standard of accountability, we become desperate to be reconciled with that standard. The guilt or concern I'm referencing is not motivated by fear of eternal punishment but rather a deep understanding that we have failed the God who took our place on that cross.

We cannot undo our past injustices without a godly remedy. There's no other way to escape the full effects of our sin. And for people like me who have committed what seems to be unthinkable harm to others, we find ourselves like a deer panting for water. We desperately and humbly seek to have the shackles of guilt removed by the one who suffered a miserable death and promised he would clean our sin-stained slates.

As I mentioned earlier, I raised my children in the Christian church. They were certainly taught about God's amazing grace and they would always have an outlet to remedy their sin with him. But because of their constant exposure to that message, I remember always being concerned they would just be lulled into accepting that option without much thought. Unless they did something horrific by our human standards, they may never deeply appreciate that godly promise the way others who have been desperate for it. I was worried that God's "amazing" grace may eventually turn into simply God's "good ole" grace to them. Perhaps my kids are both serial killers and I'm just not privy to it. I'm kidding, but I know it's not likely one can deeply appreciate the sacrifice of Jesus like those who've crossed "serious" moral lines. Having head knowledge about God's grace could never be appreciated like those who have experienced the deep sense of rescue from the emotionally tormenting despair of guilt and shame.

During my journey to authenticity, I concluded if given a choice, I would never be willing to exchange my freedom through God's amazing grace for any supernatural intervention. If forced to choose, I would always take eternal forgiveness and a chronic form of cancer over perfect health and lifelong guilt / shame. I am certain most imprisoned convicted murderers or rapists who've later sincerely accepted God's grace would never trade that for their physical freedom. His grace is that important, and is why I'm directing people to place their hope and trust in God's promise to forgive rather than in miraculous intervention to remedy their difficult circumstances.

Here's what I've discovered for myself and what I'm encouraging others to consider. There really is only one main thing for those who follow Jesus. That "one thing" for all of us should be God's forgiving, gracious love. That one thing is not answered prayers for healing or material possessions. That one thing is not supernatural relief for our personal problems. And once we figure that out and faithfully center our lives only on that, the need for godly intervention or anything else for that matter becomes meaningless. When one feels secure in believing their tarnished past has been removed, there is nothing more freeing in life. There are no earthly substitutes for that kind of freedom, and the gratitude that flows within us will greatly motivate us to honor God and love others for the rest of our life.

The Consequences of Faith

But what if my faith in Jesus is false? If I'm wrong about Jesus and it turns out he was a fictional character or maybe just a wise man and not a part of God himself, it won't do any damage to me or others. Accepting it will have allowed us to live a life that is guilt and shame free. It will allow others like me with grateful hearts to honor him with their lives. It will also convict us to love and offer forgiveness to others here in this world as Jesus asked us to do.

Our faithful acceptance and acknowledgement of Jesus's loving sacrifice (whether he existed at all) or our hope he was God in the flesh cannot do damage to anyone like those who make miracle claims today. If we end up as spiritless worm dirt with no consciousness in the afterlife, then we will certainly not face any disappointment from the false faith we placed in Jesus's sacrifice while we were alive because no one will know with certainty about the validity of Jesus until they have passed on. It's impossible for a spiritless fleshly dead body to become disappointed. And the most important part about his sacrifice is that it is available to everyone.

It's not the same as the tornado or cancer survivor's specific favored blessing claim by supernatural means. I feel that those false claims can lead others to a place of false expectation, disappointment, or never considering

God on this side of eternity. Trusting (extending my faith) that Jesus has forgiven my sins will never negatively mislead anyone.

I am trying to clearly present that having a reasonable faith that Jesus died for our salvation but is not active in our world should not lead anyone astray. It should lead others to want to follow Jesus for the right reasons, namely a life filled with gratitude for forgiveness and freedom from guilt, which in turn should motivate us to love and forgive others. My argument is against unreasonably perpetuating the notion God is actively doling out miracles to the select few. Such faith can certainly lead to frustration and disappointment for others whose unselfish prayers are rejected.

Most Christians do not really live their lives extending faith in an active God who protects or favors them. They might tell you they do, but in most cases, it's not true. I think many have hopes God would help them here on Earth, but that's much different than counting on him (extending faith to belief) to act on their behalf.

We live our lives with our eyes wide open, and we use our reasoning and experienced brains to make decisions that promote our own and others' welfare. We all rely (place our faith) on medical science to remedy our infirmities, and we do so because we know it's the most effective method. We wear our seatbelts because we have a reasonable faith they will offer more protection than an active God.

None of us use faith in an active God when we approach an intersection when the light is green. We have faith in our traffic systems, and we use our rational thinking minds to assess the probability that we will get through an intersection unharmed. We don't close our eyes as we approach an intersection, ignoring the color of the light, having faith that God will protect us. Most of us don't construct plans to rectify certain problems in our lives by just having a blind faith that God will take care of them. The common saying "Let go and let God" has no effectiveness in solving our earthly problems. The longer one chooses to approach life problems assuming through faith that God will solve them, the more intense those unattended problems become.

But what if the actual traffic statistics indicated 50% of all cars crossing an intersection resulted in an accident? If that was the actual probability, most would abandon faith in our traffic systems and slow down to a crawl every time we entered an intersection, causing horrific traffic jams.

What if the actual statistics indicated 10% of all commercial flights ended with a deadly crash? Our faith in that industry would vanish, and the airline industry would quickly be out of business.

What if the actual cure rate for cancer was 90% when the patient only prayed and never sought medical attention? Cancer research would be minimal and oncology departments would be nearly nonexistent.

We all know these scenarios do not have those outcome probabilities, and we use our reasoning minds to determine the reasonable course. We don't use faith in godly protection or intervention in these scenarios. We use our sight and our reasoning minds, the same type of sight and minds that God instilled in his first two human creations.

Faith as a Feeling

Many Christians claim God is active because they say they have "experienced" him. These claims also serve to bolster one's faith that God could or would help them with any future interventive need. They believe if he's providing these types of experiences, then he must be active.

This is certainly a subjective claim that cannot be disproven by any scientific method. Nor can I prove to anyone Jesus is factually the answer to relieving my guilt and shame with his selfless sacrifice. The obvious difference between these two types of claims is: (1) The experiential claim uses feelings, and (2) my Jesus claim is based on reasoning.

Some claim that when they pray / meditate with God, he actively communicates with them. Many Christians also say they can feel God's presence or his hand reaching down into their hearts as he comforts them. For those who make these claims, they seem convinced this is not a self-generated "feeling" during their quiet prayer time as they consider God's goodness.

According to them, it's also not a psychological phenomenon causing these feelings. They claim it is a gift that comes directly from the Creator.

Of course, none of us can know with any certainty if what they are telling us is true. But isn't it more probable that the person praying is erroneously concluding that God is actively providing either peace, strength, or comfort? Isn't it more likely that when someone focuses (prays or meditates) on how they perceive the love of God, they simply *feel* good because during their prayer session they are aligning themselves with what is good and right (God)? These feelings they claim to receive don't seem to just randomly happen throughout their day without any attention towards God. They only seem to occur when they focus on God while in prayer or singing worship songs.

If God is providing these types of spiritually favored experiences to some, how are we to explain or compare those sorts of purported godly favored actions to the experience of those who are horrifically suffering and receive nothing from God? Are we to believe them and conclude there's a God who telepathically sends invisible miraculous wave-packets of comfort, peace, and strength, or even informative guidance, but allowed fifty toddlers to die from leukemia today?

Here's the problem for me personally. I've never been able to experience God in that way. I've never knowingly had God communicate with me or provide strength or peace in a way that is knowable to me, unlike the claims of so many. I've tried every prayer and meditation technique known to man to tune in to God's channel, but for me, the heavens have always been silent. I'm unable (not unwilling) to extend the faith I have in Jesus to a God who communicates with us or sends peace or strength. We'll discuss this in further detail in a later chapter titled "The Personal Relationship."

I equate my inactive God experience with some of the lyrics of the song, *Smell the Color Nine*, written by the Christian musician, Chris Rice. His song summarizes just how seemingly impossible it is for him to find God by hearing him speak, observing miraculous signs, or receiving any of the revelations so many others claim to receive. He goes on to say that he keeps his faith intact, yet for him, finding God is like trying to smell a number's color. And since a number (in this case the number nine) is not a color and because it's impossible to smell a color, his song depicts his frustration to experience God in a way knowable to him.

His song clearly reflects my frustration and experiences when trying to find this elusive, active, peace-providing, communicating, and involved God. I have concluded it would be cognitively and emotionally safer for me to either abandon all faith or stop carrying any expectations that God acts in the way others claim he continues to today. Unfortunately, many other people are unable hold on to their faith and completely abandon their belief in God because they can't find a way to experience God in these ways. This is how public favor claims can create problems for other people's faith.

Music-Enhancing Faith

Music is another method Christians use to bolster their faith. As I mentioned previously, when I played guitar at my church, it was an incredible rush for me. There really isn't a way to describe what I was *feeling* when the band was playing and the people in the church were singing. I would get this charge of emotions and chills running up and down my arms when certain songs were being played. I would also get those same feelings when worshiping at the Promise Keeper's events and at men's retreats. I wasn't in a trance of some sort, but those feelings / experiences were real to me, and I felt them.

I remember wondering if those feelings were the Holy Spirit giving me a charge of emotions, even though at the time I really wasn't sure what the Holy Spirit was. The problem with that way of thinking: I could experience those same feelings when listening to secular songs that touched my heart. Since I was able to have the same experiences with both genres, I concluded that these feelings were probably human generated. I doubt God was involved as the "feeling" provider when I was listening to secular music.

I love a lot of Christian music. But there are biblical lyrics in many of the songs I disagree with. These lyrics reference God's active physical healing, his attention to our individual lives, and his comforting, protective, miraculous hands. So, even though I refute the truth to some of the lyrics, I love the sound of the music and how it still allows me to focus my attention to loving God back in my own personal way. I essentially try to ignore portions of the lyrics I disagree with, which is not an easy task.

But why was I experiencing chills and feelings when the music was playing even when I clearly was conflicted with the reality of some of the lyrics? Was it the music that affected me emotionally or was it the meaning of the lyrics I did agree with? And how could I listen to other soft secular music and have the same kind of feelings when the rhythm and lyrics touched me emotionally?

We ought to ask ourselves if the meaning of the lyrics alone is enough to give us our high. The truth about God cannot be found in the beats, tones, and rhythms of worship music. Why don't we get the same kind of high when we read biblical passages without the music? And what happens if we connect our "God experience" and our emotional responses with a specific song and then we no longer "feel it"? Some people even look for their church homes by qualifying and selecting the praise band that suits their musical desires. But we must ask ourselves if we should establish or extend our faith based on our subjective experiential feelings or solely on our hope in Jesus? When we attend a church service that does not play our favorite worship songs or the songs that particular Sunday are not the kind that fit our style, are we less likely to "experience" God in the same way that we want to? If so, it appears the worship band is the responsible party for increasing our faith and bringing us closer to God.

Evidentiary Faith

As we've discussed, faith cannot have a component of absolute evidence. Yet, it doesn't stop the Christian community from seeking that kind of evidence. Years back, when carbon dating was completed on the shroud of Turin (the supposed blood-soaked cloak that Jesus was buried in outlining a human body, which also revealed detailed facial features), Christians were hoping it would scientifically date back to a year close to the time of Jesus. Turns out the cloak was dated to at least 1,200 years after Jesus's death. Can you imagine the enormous bolstering of "faith" that would have been poured out if, in fact, the dates matched to the era of Jesus? If the dating matched, the followers of Jesus would not have needed faith in the reality of Jesus because they would have claimed to have had evidence the cloth was Jesus's burial cloak.

We also have the infamous discovery on a mountain in Turkey that some Christians hope or believe is Noah's Ark. Christians everywhere are clinging to new updates because they want physical evidence to confirm that the biblical story of Noah was true. It seems odd to me that Christians will refute reason and evidence against some of the biblical claims and certainly evidence against their current miracle claims, but they thirst for supportive evidence that would validate biblical stories. Some Christians seem to need strong evidence just like many others before they can sincerely feel confident about some of the Bible's claims.

[12] More Than Feelings

AS WE'VE ESTABLISHED, FAITH SHOULD NOT BE BASED on feelings. Next, we will move on to hope, which gives us a reason to keep going. Then I will explain how when we ascribe faith and hope to beliefs that conflict with our common reality, it leads to doubt and cognitive dissonance.

Hope[19]

noun

> 1. the feeling that what is wanted can be had or that events will turn out for the best. . . .

> 3. grounds for this feeling in a particular instance: "There is little or no hope of his recovery." . . .

verb

> 6. to look forward to with desire and some reasonable confidence.

Hope is a desire. It's an internal feeling in conjunction with thought that normally causes one to desire something good for themselves or others regarding a future event. Hope is normally a desire for gain and most of us consider it more than a "wish." It can be used as a subject, but normally it's used as a verb. When we hope for something, we anticipate an outcome that is in line with our desires. Hope is a "want" that many times can be a

---

19.   "Hope," Random House Unabridged Dictionary (2021), dictionary.com.

"need." However, with hope, comes the opportunity for Christians to formulate false conclusions to certain life events because their wants or needs override their reasoning. More importantly, false hope can also lead us to grave disappointments.

In a previous chapter, I stated that I sincerely hope the story of Jesus is true. I used the word "hope" rather than "believe" or "know" because no modern Christian was an eyewitness to the life, death, and resurrection of Jesus. We do not have firsthand knowledge that Jesus was who the Bible said he was nor do any of us know with certainty that he died and rose again to forgive any of us from our transgressions.

Are we willing to admit that? We don't have firsthand knowledge of the life of Jesus. What we do have, however, is hope derived from circumstantial evidence (copies of biblical books) which originated from oral traditions but can be transformed into a reasonable faith for lives lived in accord with that hope. We also have many irrefutable timeless truths contained within the Bible that can lead one to experience life in a more abundant way. And for me, that lends credence to who the NT authors claimed Jesus to be.

With that said, I'm pretty sure there was a historical man named Jesus who roamed this Earth 2,000 years ago, but that doesn't necessarily make him God. I hope the story of a godly Jesus to be true, but that doesn't mean it is true. If it is true, and 20% of the world claims to be followers of Jesus today, then it appears more than 80% of the earth's population since the resurrection of Jesus is either in hell or swiftly on their way, as Christianity requires the acceptance of Jesus to avoid eternal torment. It's also obvious God is allowing people of other non-Christian faiths to continue to influence their innocent children to accept other faith-based religions, supposedly providing them a one-way ticket to Satan's fiery pit. Admittedly, that is a tough pill for me to swallow. Although justice is very important to me, I do struggle with the concept and validity of a place like hell.

I think we all need to decide at some point in our lives what things we're willing to hope for. We can all hope to hit the lottery (which may or may not be a good thing), but since we know the real probabilities of winning, our hopes are more like a wish. For reasonable hope to have any merit, it should carry with it some statistically weighted probabilistic chance of coming to fruition. We shouldn't place a great deal of hope in matters where the probabilities are extremely low. There's a big difference between future events that are probable and those that are only possible. Yes, long shots come in from time to time, but they are not matters in which we should invoke hope. If I received a terminal diagnosis from three different doctors, hoping to be cured is probably false hope.

We can hope for our children to live full, productive, moral lives. We can hope that our legacy will be looked at by God and others to be something of value to future generations. We can all hope that the Jesus story is true, and our sin slate has been erased. We can all hope that we will be reunited with our loved ones in the afterlife. But I will continue to argue that anyone willing to place their hope in an active problem-solving God merely lives in false hope. That's a very dangerous and risky place to live.

I've been asking you to consider moving any current and future investments in hope for godly miracles to whatever measure you have already invested in hope for God's promise to forgive and provide you with an afterlife. Placing all your hope poker chips in gratitude for God's grace will avoid faith-crushing disappointments that will surely occur when your unselfish prayers go unanswered. Hope for that will unlock the fullness of your life, ensuring you'll never need to contemplate why God didn't help in your greatest time of need. It's hard to ever become disappointed with God when you don't hope for earthly intervention. But unfortunately, it's not until the aftermath of a difficult life circumstance that many discover hopeful expectations were just premeditated resentments.

The level of your hope for a miracle will be the same measure of disappointment you will experience when God doesn't provide help. When it comes to earthly matters, line up your hopes with what is probable not what is merely possible.

If you center your hope solely in God's grace, something independent of your circumstances that can never fade away, you will never feel abandoned by God because of unfavorable circumstances. We can either chose to live this way now or wait until we're near the end of life (given the opportunity). If you're a Christian, eventually you'll be forced to comply with centering your hope only in God's grace because near the end of your life, that's all you'll have left to hope for. Why not consider doing that now?

When a Christian prays and hopes for the results of a CT scan of their brain to be negative and cancer free, and it is negative, they're apt to give God the credit for the good news. This validation of their hope leads them to believe that God has come through for them, maybe even because of their merit. To these people, God is certainly active. People like this never seem to consider there never was a tumor in their brain. For them, there might have been a tumor before the test and God may have miraculously removed it after they or their loved ones prayed for the results to be negative.

If the results were positive for a tumor, their hope moves on to the next stage of treatment. They now hope that with prayer (help from God) and modern medical techniques, their cancer will be eradicated. If the treatments are successful, they will claim God and not medicine healed them. This seems like an errant approach to me. If the treatments are not successful and the patient is declared terminal, then hope moves on to the acceptance stage and the afterlife—which is solely where all their hope should have been before any symptoms, diagnosis, or treatment.

But are we really to extend our hope in a God who is actively working for our good? Did biased hopes and desires lead us to claim God helped us when things went our way? Hope can accompany faith, and at other times, it can be responsible for leading us to false beliefs.

The following joke reminds me of where our true human hope lies when it comes to having any expectations that God is actively helping any of us.

A man falls over a mountains edge and grabs a tree branch that extends out from the cliff. He cries out for help, shouting, "Is anyone up there?" A voice comes from the sky, saying "Yes, it is me, Jesus! I will save you! Just let go of the branch and a big hand will materialize and catch you, lowering you gently to the ground." A moment of silence ensues. Then the man shouts, "Is there anybody else up there?"

I don't think God expects any of us to have the hope that he's going to supply a cosmic hand to deliver us from our problems like the guy in the joke. I also do not think that most people believe he really does act that way. However, it doesn't seem to inhibit intervention believers from looking at favorable outcomes, coincidences, or mysteries, and attributing them to the Creator who is supposedly working behind the scenes. We're all certain there's no big hand in the sky rescuing anyone. But why do so many continue to have hope in a God who removes cancer or provides protection to them during a bumpy flight? If we really don't believe in the "big hand", why would we extend our hope in a God who cures diseases? Aren't both scenarios equally improbable?

We need a rational hope-filled faith to believe that God exists and that Jesus died to remove the guilt and shame from our past. But we do not need to have any hope-filled faith that God is active. Again, there are no credible biblical requirements or suggestions for having hope that God is active today. I'm convinced we're falsely extending hope from the stories of godly activity from the biblical era and errantly trying to apply them to our lives today.

Belief[20]

Believe

noun

to have confidence in the truth, the existence, or the reliability of something although without absolute proof that one is right in doing so: Only if one believes in something can one act purposefully.

---

20.   "Believe," Random House Unabridged Dictionary (2021), dictionary.com.

verb

to have confidence or faith in the truth of (a positive assertion, story, etc.); give credence to.

to have confidence in the assertions of (a person).

Our beliefs are the foundation of our actions. Faith and / or solid circumstantial evidence are the operative words required to drive someone to the point of belief. In order to believe, one must have extreme confidence that what they are standing on is true.

When we process new information, we draw conclusions regarding its validity. But there are other factors influencing our abilities to process and validate or reject information. All of us bring our own subjective experiences, education, knowledge, and childhood religious biases when processing information. We approach new and conflicting information with our preconceived notions and burned-in beliefs from our past. All these factors play an enormous role in determining whether we will accept (believe) or reject new or conflicting information.

If you've been raised in one form of the Christian faith or another, you're likely to remain in that faith for life. If you're a Christian who believes in current supernatural activity, you have a built-in theological bias towards what you say you believe, and you will likely reject any conflicting information brought from outside of your Christian circle. If you believe in current divine intervention, you're more likely to accept any miraculous story from your friends or family.

And here lies one of the biggest issues with many forms of religious belief. We are all guilty of *confirmation bias*. Confirmation bias is also referred to as myside bias.[21] Brittanica.com explains it as the tendency to process information by looking for, or interpreting, information that is consistent

---

21.   "Confirmation Bias," Wikipedia, https://en.wikipedia.org/wiki/confirmation_bias.

with one's existing beliefs.[22] Confirmation bias actually conflicts with our deductive reasoning. Faced with evidence that disagrees with one's personal belief system, someone with confirmation bias is more likely to overlook it. This type of bias is even more evident for those who have a political, religious, or an emotional attachment to tightly held beliefs. Nearly all Christians have huge emotional attachments to their faith and beliefs. The depth of one's faith in specific religious matters will determine the time required to overcome any cognitive dissonance they may experience from conflicts with their tightly held positions.

We commonly see confirmation bias exercised in the political arena where one political party aligns itself with the president of that same party. If the president is accused of wrongdoing, people of that same party are likely to overlook or ignore evidence that points them in that direction.

When President Richard Nixon was under heavy suspicion for his involvement in wiretapping the democratic headquarters at the Watergate Hotel, his allies in the Republican party exercised their confirmation biases by defending him and overlooking any negative evidence. They continued to defend him even after Nixon's personal attorney testified Nixon was involved and willing to pay bribes to others to stay quiet. It wasn't until Nixon was required to release the damning audiotapes of his White House discussions regarding Watergate that his Republican allies considered impeaching him—before he resigned. Nixon's allies wanted him to be innocent and they didn't want to hear any evidence that would lead to his guilt.

We've all heard the phrase, "People only hear what they want to hear." This is exactly what intervention believing Christians are doing today regarding evidence that suggests God is not active today. Since they want and need a God who will help them in their greatest time of need, they have no interest in exposing their tightly held convictions regarding his current activities or engaging with anyone who opposes them. They will not consider statistics

---

22.   Bettina J. Casad, "Confirmation Bias," Brittanica, https://www.britannica.com/science/confirmation-bias.

clearly showing that prayed-for Christians are not favored over non-believers with the same terminal illnesses.

I would apply the following psychological terms to those who are hard-wired and unwilling to consider any other system of belief, worldview, or conflicting evidence:

Attitude polarization: when a disagreement becomes more extreme even though the different parties are exposed to the same evidence. Intervention-believing Christians will always refute the statistical evidence that clearly indicates prayed-for Christians die in car accidents at the same rate as non-believers per capita.

Belief perseverance: when beliefs persist after the evidence for them is shown to be false. In a later chapter we'll be discussing one of the most extensive prayer studies ever conducted. This study clearly shows that prayers do not affect the outcomes of people who are critically ill. Intervention-believing Christians with belief perseverance will likely discard the evidence-based results of this study. They simply refuse to believe that evidence because it would require them to accept that prayers of request are ineffective in causing God to act.

Illusory correlation: when people falsely perceive an association between two events or situations. This term perfectly describes attempts by intervention believing Christians who continue to errantly associate the outcomes of life events with supernatural godly activity. Coincidences become God-incidences.

The three terms listed above all influence our ability to rationally apply sound reasoning and to draw correct conclusions from life events we are exposed to.

Doubt[23]

1. To be undecided or skeptical about: *begin to doubt some accepted doctrines.*

2. To tend to disbelieve; distrust: *doubts politicians when they make sweeping statements.*

3. To regard as unlikely: *I doubt that we'll arrive on time.*

Everyone should have some level of skepticism in their lives in order to protect against deception. Without skepticism and doubt, most people would not have a real confidence for belief in anything. In the absence of skepticism and doubt, people's belief systems could at any time be subject to critical challenge—perhaps even destruction.

The apostle Peter even suggested in 1 Peter 3:15, "But in your hearts revere Christ as Lord. Always be prepared to give an answer to everyone who asks you to give the reason for the hope that you have. But do this with gentleness and respect."

"Prepared to give an answer" implies that one has thoroughly thought through the reasons why they've chosen to believe what they say they believe. If they've spent no time contemplating possible errors in their beliefs, then they become a person willing to follow anything. Therefore, we all should thoroughly investigate every aspect of our religious systems before we ever claim to say we believe they are 100% true. All people of any faith background will at some point be challenged to give an account for their reasoning regarding what they claim to believe. It may come by the challenges of another person or by circumstances they face during their lifetimes. Doubt challenges all of us to reasonably consider and even reconsider our systems of belief.

23.   "Doubt" (n.d.), *American Heritage Dictionary of the English Language*, Fifth Edition (2011), retrieved April 22, 2021 from www.thefreedictionary.com/doubt.

If you're just a Sunday-only pew-sitter who has never pondered the reasons behind your belief system, you may have a challenging time convincing someone else you have it right. If you're one who simply argues, "It's the religion I was taught as a child," it's not likely that reasoning alone will cause anyone to convert to your faith or accept your beliefs.

Many of us have doubts and disbelief when it comes to certain aspects of our faith; however, only a few of us publicly disclose them, for doing so would go contrary to accepted teachings. I know this firsthand because early in my journey when I desperately sought to speak about my faith-based doubts regarding godly inactivity, I didn't have the courage to do so with those in my Christian community who believed in an intervening God.

Is doubt equivalent to disbelief? It's not, and it's important to grasp the difference.

> *"Doubt" questions what one attempts to believe.*
> *"Disbelief" is an informed conscious REFUSAL to*
> *believe. Doubt is a struggle faced by the BELIEVER.*
> *Disbelief is a chosen position of the unbeliever.*

We all need to ask ourselves, which parts of our theology do we believe, doubt, or have disbelief? I doubt God is actively intervening here on this Earth today. And, from that deep inward doubt, I have freely (albeit kicking and screaming) chosen to move to a state of disbelief that he actively intervenes today. I forced myself to think critically and consider evidence that conflicted with my tightly held confirmation bias wanting to believe in a currently intervening God.

Not having tackled one's doubts, it's difficult to have a solid faith and believe in anything. That is, of course, if we're not the kind of people who, when faced with doubts, make the decision to sweep those doubts under the rug. To me, ignoring one's doubts is committing intellectual suicide. It refutes and circumvents the power of reasoning God instilled in his creation.

Here's Rick Warren's take on truth seekers[24] (those who are willing to face their doubts).

> There are two kinds of people in life when it comes to truth: speculators and seekers. Speculators make guesses about the truth. Speculators think they know what God is like.
>
> Speculators love to argue and discuss God, but they're just guessing—because they don't really want to know the truth. They only want to talk about him. On the other hand, God loves those who take the time to find the truth. Seekers do four things:
>
> 1. They ask questions.
>
> 2. They study.
>
> 3. *They observe what is happening around them.*
>
> 4. They do whatever it takes to find answers.
>
> They seek after Jesus with all they have. God loves seekers. The Bible tells us, "But if from there you seek the LORD your God, you will find him if you seek him with all your heart and with all your soul" (Deuteronomy 4:29 NIV).

And exactly where do Christians get their reassurances of the truth? It comes from their local churches, their small group Bible studies, and their local Christian radio stations. And even more prominently, today their truth comes from social media. And to further my point, Christians huddle up every Sunday to reaffirm portions of their faith they may have never really believed as truth. I know there are others like me, in larger numbers than most think, who do not believe that God is as active today as so many claim.

---

24. Warren, "Truth Seekers," PastorRick.com, emphasis mine. Retrieved October 2013. Removed from website, date unknown.

Yet, they continue as I did for so many years, attending church services and stuffing their doubts about that subject under the rug of faith.

When confronted with a miracle story from a fellow Christian that seems a bit farfetched, they say nothing in the way of expressing their doubts. They just silently think to themselves, "Wow! I find that a stretch, but if that's the way my friend wants to think about how God has come to his aid, then I won't challenge him on his conclusion. What's it going to hurt if my friend interprets an event as an action by the hands of God if it's really not true?"

But this is where most of us fall short. When we allow others to perpetuate these ways of thinking without challenging them, namely their miracle claims without knowledge in their validity, it reaffirms in others this is how God operates. Again, this perpetuation can lead other believers within earshot to have expectations for future godly assistance. They will comparatively expect God to act on their behalf in the future. If he doesn't act for them, it can rock their faith. These unchallenged claims also further alienate those who are certain current miracle claims are not true.

If we're honest with ourselves, everyone has wondered in times of crisis, "Is there a God?" or "Where are you, God?" We've all looked at difficult and even horrific life events and wondered just exactly where God was and why he offered no assistance. We've all felt emptiness in the same way David did when he wrote in Psalm 88:13–14, "But I cry to you for help, LORD | in the morning my prayer comes before you. | Why, LORD, do you reject me and hide your face from me?" In David's despair he went on to claim that darkness was his closest friend. It's in these desperate places that doubts find a way to creep in and carry with them the potential to diminish our faith even in God's existence.

No matter how much faith one can muster during their life, everyone will experience darkness and doubt. Many intervention-believing Christians may not know this yet, but they're only one tragic event away from being overwhelmed with doubt regarding God's current involvement in our world. The disciples of Jesus, unlike us, had more than just a confident faith as they followed him, because they were eyewitnesses to his miracles. Yet they all must have experienced a heavy load of uncertainty as they watched him hang on that cross. They must have doubted if, in fact, Jesus was who he said he was, even after witnessing so many of his previous miracles.

But doubt is neither a hindrance nor a destroyer of faith. Unless one is simply gullible enough to accept anything they are taught in the absence of critical thought, doubt challenges us to examine what we have grounded ourselves on and forces us to re-contemplate our positions. Doubt plays a crucial role in establishing our beliefs. It's not a sin to doubt. As Christopher Lane argued in *The Age of Doubt*,[25] "the explosion of questioning among Christian thinkers in the Victorian era transformed the idea of doubt from a sin or lapse, to necessary exploration."

Conversely, when we rely only on what we perceive as certainties or lock ourselves into a position in any matter, we become rigid and lose interest in exposing ourselves to or considering other positions that may conflict with our own. The philosopher Bertrand Russell wrote[26] "The whole problem with the world is that the stupid are cocksure, while the intelligent are full of doubt." No matter how certain we believe we are about any subject matter, we should always be open to exposing ourselves to and willing to consider conflicting evidence or views.

Cognitive Dissonance

Earlier, I touched on the psychological term, "cognitive dissonance," but I'd like to expound on it here. The theory of cognitive dissonance (CD) in social psychology proposes that people have a motivational drive to reduce dissonance (mental conflicts) by altering existing cognitions (understandings), adding new ones to create a consistent belief system, or alternatively by reducing the importance of any one of the dissonant (conflicting) elements.

---

25.   Christopher Lane, *The Age of Doubt* (New Haven, CT: Yale University Press, 2011).

26.   Bertrand Russell Quotes. (n.d.). BrainyQuote.com. Retrieved February 15, 2021, from www.brainyquote.com/quotes/bertrand_russell_101364.

It's the distressing mental state people feel when they find themselves doing or agreeing with things that don't fit with what they really believe or having opinions that do not fit with other opinions they hold.

A key assumption is that people want their expectations (that may or may not have been derived from critical thought) to meet their reality providing a sense of equilibrium. Likewise, another assumption is that a person who is unwilling to face their mental conflicts will avoid situations or information sources that would expose them to feelings of uneasiness (dissonance).

When applied to matters of faith, CD is a measure of one's uneasiness with conflicts that arise between one's belief system and their perception of their personal reality. When one begins to have doubts regarding certain matters of faith, some feel the need to sort them out so they can be at ease with knowing what they believe is true. Most people do not want to establish or ground themselves on falsehood—but there are others who are willing to ignore their conflicts to minimize their anguish.

The greater the uneasiness or CD value, the more likely one is to alter their belief system to fall in line with their reality. For example, during my early years, I desperately wanted to believe that God was actively involved in the day-to-day events of this Earth. I wanted to believe those who made miracle claims were being truthful and God was still in the prayer-answering business. I had a Bible that clearly stated God was active during the era in which it was written, albeit only 334 recorded times. I was surrounded by intervention-believing Christians who continually told me how God acted supernaturally for them. As I became older and witnessed so much earthly suffering and certainly countless unselfish prayers not answered, I became uneasy in my mind to the point where I could no longer believe current miracle claims. I also couldn't fathom a God who gave to some but ignored others. I could either pretend these claims were true and go along with everyone else or alter my way of thinking to a place where my thinking fit my reality. Pretending seemed hypocritical—living in constant confusion between what I was supposed to believe and what I had observed was no way to live.

Ignoring or dismissing miracle claims was too difficult when surrounding myself with so many intervention believing Christians. The needle on my cognitive dissonance meter maxed out.

The other method used to ease tension for those experiencing CD is to minimize their exposure to the realities that cause their uneasiness. I'm sure some readers never made it this far because of what they were exposed to in previous chapters. They may have aborted their read because they didn't want to expose themselves to further evidence that would cause greater mental anguish. It's the proverbial ostrich hiding its head in the sand.

For example, if one believes that Jesus loves all the little children of the world as the familiar Sunday school song suggests yet are simultaneously aware that 24,000 malnourished people will die today, they will probably not choose to vacation in foreign countries displaying such suffering. They are likely to quickly turn the TV channel to a different station when the World Aid commercials show up and display the real suffering occurring in those countries. If one lived amongst the starving with no way to ignore it, they may also have a challenging time singing "Jesus loves the little children."

PART 5:

WHAT ABOUT

SUFFERING?

[13] The Human Condition

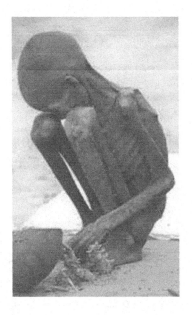

Haji

"Look at the birds of the air; they do not sow or reap or store away in barns, and yet your heavenly Father feeds them. Are you not much more valuable than they?"

Matthew 6:26

"Which of you, if your son asks for bread, will give him a stone? Or if he asks for a fish, will give him a snake? If you, then, though you are evil, know how to give good gifts to your children, how much more will your Father in heaven give good gifts to those who ask him!"

Matthew 7:9–11

He provides food for those who fear him; | he remembers his covenant forever.

Psalm 111:5

"I form the light and create darkness, | I bring prosperity and create disaster; | I, the LORD, do all these things."

Isaiah 45:7

And we know that in all things God works for the good of those who love him, who have been called according to his purpose.

Romans 8:28

AS PROMISED, ALLOW ME TO INTRODUCE YOU TO HAJI (pictured above), who sits on a dried dirt mound awaiting death. Haji's picture captures only a snippet of the horrific suffering in our world, and it disturbs me greatly. Before moving forward, we should ask ourselves if or how well we're able to reconcile the validity of the Bible verses listed above with Haji's circumstance?

As much as we may not want to believe it, there are 24,000 like Haji dying every day on our planet. I have shown this picture to many of my friends, asking them to compare their claims of godly favor to Haji's plight. Most people don't want to contemplate Haji's circumstance because it doesn't fit their understanding of a compassionate and loving God. It seems much easier to just live out their lives ignoring that many in our world live like

Haji in abject poverty and on the doorstep of death and continue to attach themselves to the notion of a favor-providing God.

My friends tell me that God has provided employment, saved their marriage, or cured them from disease. They tell me that during quiet times God has communicated with them audibly or even in their dreams. They tell me that God has supernaturally given them comfort during their most troubling times. They tell me they have "felt" God's presence. God seems to provide everything for them.

But what are we to make of claims like these? How can we look into the eyes of the Hajis of this world and ever consider clinging to the words of King David who said in Psalms 111:5 that God provides food for those who fear him? How are we to reconcile the differential between the "favor of God" claims with the circumstances of the Hajis of this world? Is a fair and just God doling out good parking spaces, strength to those who prayerfully request, selectively healing cancers—all while allowing (or perhaps even causing by his indifference) so many to suffer and die from a lack of sustenance or clean water? If God is not feeding the Hajis, should any of us have the courage or lack of empathy to think or claim God has supernaturally provided anything for our favor?

There is an immeasurable amount of suffering happening all over this Earth, and again, I'm convinced absolutely none of it has anything to do with Adam and Eve's original sin. As we've discussed, and contrary to many Christian pastors' claims, we don't have hurricanes, tsunamis, or famines that kill millions of people because of anything to do with the original sin. However, biblical authors of the Old Testament told us that God did use natural disasters to punish those who didn't follow his laws.

Are the Hajis of this world being punished? Is this cyclic form of generational suffering caused by the sins of Haji's forefathers? Or is it more likely some of the uninformed Bronze-age biblical authors just did their best to understand suffering and prosperity but incorrectly attributed the causation to God as the result of past or current unrepented sin?

God's Love in Light of Suffering

The Bible has a lot to say about God's love for us. According to Scripture, this God who is "righteous in all of his ways" is also "kind in all his works" (Ps. 145:17 ESV). Paul wrote that God promises he is still working all things together for our good in Christ (Romans 8:28). His heart is supposedly brimming over with compassion and affection for us. He calls us the "apple" of his eye (Deuteronomy 32:10; Psalm 17:8 ESV) and is so endeared to us that he lifts his voice to sing songs over us (Zephaniah 3:17). We are supposedly his "beloved" (Deuteronomy 33:12; Hosea 2:23), and his "banner" over us is "love" (Song of Solomon 2:4). "No good thing does he withhold | from those who walk uprightly" (Psalm 84:11 ESV).

And yet the horrific earthly suffering goes on and on—even to those who call upon his name and love him dearly. One may be able to pick up a Bible and randomly read one of the passages listed above which in turn may make the reader feel more loved by an active God. They may even tell us that God led them to that specific passage on that day because they really needed to hear it at that time.

But shouldn't we make some comparisons between that kind of biblically stated active love and what is really happening in our world? Do we need to reconsider the definition of the word "love"? Did God actively display his love to the people of the biblical era more than he does today?

I'm not saying God does not have a genuine deep heartfelt love for his creation. I'm convinced he does, and according to the NT he displayed it through Jesus on that cross. But I am saying that God's love as described in some Scriptures is most probably not the same kind of active love "good" earthly parents provide to their children. It seems the Hebrew authors desired and painted a picture of God's active love inaccurately. I'm convinced many of the biblical authors and the people of that era falsely believed the more obedience and praise they offered God, the greater their probability of being rewarded by God through his miraculous favor.

In the twenty-first century, we continue to have Christians perpetuating and believing what I have come to understand are misguided characterizations of God's active displays of intervening love. The sad result is disbelief by those whose obvious reality reflects that God has not acted favorably for them or even others less fortunate, contrary to what they have been told. So they inevitably begin to doubt God's existence.

If you're a compassionate person, Haji's photo should tear at your heart as it does mine. If you're like me, you ask, "Why is Haji the unlucky one?" or "Why am I the lucky one who has enough to eat while the Hajis of this world suffer?"

If God is active today, we should all be asking ourselves, "How can a God who we are told loves us all so much, allow this to be so?" Ironically, as some portion of the 24,000 malnourished people on this Earth prepare to die before midnight tonight, I will *ashamedly* search through my refrigerator and pantry, selectively disposing of items that have reached or exceeded their expiration dates.

More Valuable than Sparrows

Perhaps we should also be conflicted because of what the author of Matthew told us Jesus said doesn't align with everyone's experience. "'Look at the birds of the air; they do not sow or reap or store away in barns, and yet your heavenly Father feeds them. Are you not much more valuable than they?'" (6:26). If that is true, shouldn't we expect God would see that Haji and his brothers are fed?

If Matthew's quotation of Jesus in verse 26 is true for us today (we're more important than the birds of the air and God feeds them), how can there be 24,000 Hajis dying every day from lack of food? How can we possibly reconcile what Jesus said with what is happening in this world daily?

Every time I quote this verse, I receive pushback from other Christians. They tell me that I'm pulling this verse out of context and that Jesus was not promising to feed us. The group or surrounding verses from which Matthew

6:26 (25–34) is derived explicitly tells us not to *worry* about our sustenance. For many Christians, these verses are solely about worrying and not God promising to provide sustenance.

I agree with them somewhat. The main theme of these verses clearly tells us that we shouldn't worry about anything, but it seems to me that there's a lot more for us to glean from Jesus's statement which extends way past the subject of worry. And even if these verses are only telling us to not worry, does 24,000 malnourished people dying each day sit well with your understanding of an active God who loves and cares for us in the way the biblical authors have stated? Is the all-powerful, all-loving and caring God that you learned about in Sunday school the same God who is allowing this type of cyclical suffering every second of every day? Is he the same intervening and loving God who sits idle as a two-year-old drowns in his family's pool?

Let's look closely at the full passage from Matthew 6:

"Therefore I tell you, do not *worry* about your life, what you will eat or drink; or about your body, what you will wear. Is not life more than food, and the body more than clothes? Look at the birds of the air; they do not sow or reap or store away in barns, and yet your heavenly Father feeds them. Are you not much more valuable than they? Can any one of you by *worrying* add a single hour to your life?

"And why do you *worry* about clothes? See how the flowers of the field grow. They do not labor or spin. Yet I tell you that not even Solomon in all his splendor was dressed like one of these. If that is how God clothes the grass of the field, which is here today and tomorrow is thrown into the fire, will he not much more clothe you—you of little faith? So do not *worry*, saying, 'What shall we eat?' or 'What shall we drink?' or 'What shall we wear?' For the pagans run after all these things, and your heavenly Father knows that you need them. But seek first his kingdom and his righteousness, and all these things will be given to you as well. Therefore do not *worry* about tomorrow, for tomorrow will worry about itself. Each day has enough trouble of its own" (6:25–34, emphasis mine).

How can we reconcile verse 26 with those who assert that verses 25–34 are only instructing us to not worry? In this verse, Jesus seems to be clearly setting the hierarchy of where the animals stand in comparison to where humans stand in his eyes. He's clearly telling us we are more important to God than these creatures. And, if God is willing to take care of them by seeing that they are fed, shouldn't he be even more willing to see that we are fed? Are the 24,000 Hajis dying each day an oversight?

Since the beginning of time, countless weather phenomena have rendered billions of animals extinct from our planet. Fossil records show that 99% of all species that ever existed are extinct. Many have expired because of climactic (famine or drought) or meteoric catastrophes. One look at global news, and you'll observe famine, drought, hurricanes, and fires killing off millions of animals each year. Those same phenomena have contributed to the deaths of billions of humans (who are reportedly more important than all other earthly creatures) from the beginning of time. It appears God is not caring for us any more than he's been caring for the birds of the air. He might "care" for us from his heart, but I see no evidence that he's caring for us from an active, hands-on, provisional perspective. The world I live in displays an indifference to the suffering of all creatures by God.

There's another implication made by Jesus in verse 32 pertaining to what God knows we need. According to the end of verse 32, "God knows we need food, drink and clothing." I'm not doubting God knows his creatures require those provisions because he created us to need them. But isn't he aware, from where he sits, many are suffering and dying because they lack one or more of those three elements? If he is aware of those currently suffering without, why isn't he doing anything about it? I hope we can agree he's obviously not doing anything about it. If not, allow me to point you to our common reality from The World Counts website that lists the global malnutrition statistics[27]:

- 9 million: Total number who died from malnutrition

- 24,657: Total number of people who died daily

- 3.1 million: Total number of children who died of malnutrition

- 3.6 seconds: Time between all malnutrition deaths

- 10 seconds: Time between malnutrition deaths for children

- 822 million: Total number of people suffering globally from malnourishment (2018)

There are good people offering relief to the starving on behalf of God, but let's not confuse that with supernatural godly activity. As I will argue in the following chapters, there are "good" people who are sold out for God who act as God's hands and feet, but they are not God. These "hands and feet" are committed to the Jesus who died for them. With grateful hearts they sacrifice themselves in service to the starving and suffering because they are convinced God would want them to. There are also other caring people with compassionate hearts that have no religious affiliation helping those in need. And even with those "earthly hands and feet," millions continue to miserably suffer and die.

Action or Inaction by an All-Powerful God

I must credit the biblical authors who attested to a lot of suffering present amongst the people of their era. It's not as if those authors refused to address it. And Jesus also didn't promise us an easy life: "'I have told you these things, so that in me you may have peace. In this world you will have trouble. But take heart! I have overcome the world'" (John 16:33). But both the Hebrew

---

27.   People Who Died from Hunger, The World Counts, https://www.theworldcounts. com/challenges/people-and-poverty/hunger-and-obesity/how-many-people-die-from-hunger-each-year/story.

and the Christian Scriptures make many claims that God was the reliever of some of that suffering. I don't see any of that kind of relief happening in this era. For me, it's just another reason to conclude that 1) the biblical authors were probably not accurate with many of their claims regarding godly relief and 2) God is not participating in the events of today's world.

Let's go back to Matthew. It appears that Matthew 6:33 provides the answer to how we can obtain the three necessary elements to sustain ourselves: "'But seek first his kingdom and his righteousness, and all these things will be given to you as well.'"

Was the author of Matthew telling us that Jesus claimed if we seek God's kingdom and his righteousness, then God will see to it we receive food, water, and clothing? Maybe we can reasonably explain why there are so many starving today. Perhaps the reason for this horrific daily cycle of death by starvation has to do with Haji and his brethren worshiping either no god or the wrong god, or Haji and his brethren are just not seeking God's kingdom and his righteousness correctly. A few people have actually told me, "Those people in third world countries worship other gods or no gods, and therefore we can reasonably explain why the Christian God is not caring for them." But I can't accept that reasoning.

Is it possible that God doesn't want people to starve, but if he has chosen to not intervene on this Earth, he allows it to happen? We know it happens. If you believe in a God who actively cares for us as Matthew 6:26 states, then I think you might be conflicted as well.

It seems easy for many Christians to find alternative ways to interpret Scripture when it's contrary to what they want to believe about God. In their minds, God does love all his creation, yet billions of Hajis over the centuries have died miserable suffering deaths. This type of suffering has no moral explanation for causation. The root cause of this type of suffering is not the same as Adolph Hitler's killing of six million Jews, or Pol Pot's mass exterminations in Cambodia.

I've had other Christians tell me, "Well, so many corrupt governments are keeping the food and aid away from those who need it." But isn't our omnipotent (all-powerful) God capable of stopping corruption? Even if God was not miraculously the provider of the food and some corrupt governments are withholding aid, why won't he step in and ensure the aid gets to those who are in dire need? Most Christians believe he's capable.

An Example of Ancient Thinking

If we can agree that drought-causing famine is the prominent reason behind these deaths, then where is the God described in the book of Job who told us that God determined the location of rain that apparently was earmarked for the righteous? Allow me to run this biblical theory by the author of the book of Job by you.

Most of us wouldn't consider the biblical character Job an accredited meteorologist by today's standards, yet Job is quoted as saying that he knew (learned from God) exactly why it rained in one place and didn't in another. In the narrative, Job's friend Elihu claims to understand who directed the location of lightning strikes and who was actively causing and manipulating them.

> "He (God) draws up the drops of water,
> which distill as rain to the streams;
> the clouds pour down their moisture
> and abundant showers fall on mankind.
> Who can understand how he spreads out the clouds,
> how he thunders from his pavilion?
> See how he scatters his lightning about him,
> bathing the depths of the sea.
> *This is the way he governs the nations*
> *and provides food in abundance.*
> *He fills his hands with lightning*

and commands it to strike its mark.
His thunder announces the coming storm.
    even the cattle make known its approach." (Job 36:27–33)

"He loads the clouds with moisture;
    he scatters his lightning through them.
At his direction they swirl around
    over the face of the whole earth
    to do whatever *he commands them.*
He brings the clouds to punish people,
    or to water his earth and show his love." (Job 37:11–13, emphasis mine)

To the people of Job's time, God was more than just the Creator of the random atmospheric system he installed on Earth at the time of creation. God was always actively overseeing, generating, and locating each cloud and lightning bolt. God also supposedly governed the fate of nations by deciding who receives adequate rain and who will be left in drought. During the biblical era, these uneducated men believed that God sent rain for crops to those who were righteous, and horrific storms, droughts, or pestilence to those who were not obeying his laws.

If God is withholding the necessary rain to see that the Hajis of this world starve to death today, and there's anyone today who believes that Job's atmospheric theory is correct, then this could easily explain why they are starving. If Job's theory is correct, then God is purposefully withholding the necessary rain that would feed the starving. Again, I don't hold the author of the book of Job liable for his ignorance in meteorology. However, people today continue to errantly perpetuate this ignorance. The renowned physicist Neal deGrasse Tyson once said, "*Ignorance is a virus.* Once it starts spreading, it can only be *cured by reason*. For the sake of humanity, we must be that cure" (emphasis mine).

Examples of Applying the Bible Literally

The following is a more recent example of what I'm referring to regarding the perpetuation of biblical ignorance. The actor and Christian filmmaker, Kirk Cameron, referenced those verses in Job listed above when Hurricane Irma was approaching Florida in September of 2017. He posted a short selfie video on YouTube[28] from the airport as he was fleeing the coming storm. And he used Job's atmospheric theories to tell us that hurricane Irma was not a random or accidental event, nor was it a coincidence that Irma was arriving in Florida only two months after Hurricane Harvey decimated Houston, Texas. Mr. Cameron said in essence that God was reminding us of his power and Irma was "sent by God" to humble us and point us in his direction. Mr. Cameron even encouraged us to explain this to our children if they ask us why there are hurricanes and why people are killed by them. Apparently, Mr. Cameron chose not to be humbled and took the first plane out of Florida before the storm arrived.

Here's a few more modern-day errant extensions of biblical positions made by some prominent and influential clergy of our day:

- Pastor Luke Robinson of Quinn Chapel AME Church in Frederick, Maryland, told a crowd of same-sex marriage opponents that Hurricane Sandy hit New York City only after Mayor Michael Bloomberg made a sizable donation to a Maryland campaign defending the state's marriage equality law. Robinson continued, "'You better go back home and protect your stock because God is sending judgment. The [hurricane] came through the area. You

---

28.   Kirk Cameron, "Hurricanes Remind Us of God's Awesome Power," posted by Raymond7779 on YouTube, September 9, 2017, https://www.youtube.com/watch?v=IJs-J1LfAuI4.

have to understand the season and the time. It's almost the end of hurricane season, but God sent one of the biggest hurricanes ever.'"[29]

- In the wake of hurricane Katrina, Pastor John Hagee said, "'New Orleans had a level of sin that was offensive to God,'" because "'there was to be a homosexual parade there on the Monday that Katrina came.'" He concludes, "'I believe that hurricane Katrina was, in fact, the judgment of God against the city of New Orleans.'"[30]

- In an interview with Pat Robertson during his *700 Club* broadcast in reference to the 911 attacks, Reverend Jerry Falwell lists all the ways God has been thrown out of our country and said, "God will not be mocked." Then he laid blame for America's moral decay at the feet of the ACLU, abortionists, feminists, gays, and the People for the American Way with "you helped this happen." Pat Robertson responded in agreement.[31]

People are suffering from natural disasters all over this planet, but these events are not caused supernaturally and certainly not because of unrepented sin as the biblical authors believed. We need our atmosphere to have temperature differentials as God designed it—even extreme gradients that can lead to deadly tornadoes and hurricanes. Otherwise, there would be no means for water transport to different areas of our planet.

We're much more informed than we were 3,000 years ago. We understand the forces and intricacies of the atmosphere enough to know why there's something called the Tornado Alley. We understand what happens when

---

29.   Quoted by Tom McCarthy, "Pastor Blames Hurricane Sandy on Bloomberg's Support of Gay Rights," *The Guardian*, November 5, 2012, https://www.theguardian.com/world/us-news-blog/2012/nov/05/sandy-revenge-gay-michael-bloomberg.

30.   Quoted by Matthew Yglesias, "Hagee on Katrina," *The Atlantic*, March 5, 2008, https://www.theatlantic.com/politics/archive/2008/03/hagee-on-katrina/45516/.

31.   David Mickkelson quoting Jerry Falwell and Pat Robertson, "Falwell and Robertson Blame Liberal America," September 11th, Snopes, https://www.snopes.com/fact-check/falwell-and-above/.

warm, moist air from the equator travels through the Gulf coast and meets up with cooler air from the north. This explains why we don't see hurricanes and tornadoes in Los Angeles with the same frequency as the Southeast and Midwest. Hurricanes have a cyclic season, and they do not occur in the northern hemisphere in the dead of winter. Are the people of the midwestern or southeastern US Bible Belt living in the Tornado and Hurricane Alleys being picked on or punished by God more than those who live outside of those areas?

There are many examples where authors, mostly in the Hebrew Scriptures, interpret reality from a place of ignorance, and we need to make sure these misallocations are not perpetuated to future generations. If we continue to regard certain parts of the Bible and all its authors' theories as complete truth, it can lead us astray. Accepting these false biblical premises can also contribute to destroying our children's understanding of a supposed loving God as they contemplate why he would purposely want to harm people.

Moreover, as our children and their children become more informed than we are regarding how God designed our universe, they will increasingly be faced with the conflicts between some of these errant claims and their known reality. If we continue perpetuating the ignorance from the past, then we can expect a greater percentage of future generations to reject everything from the Bible. Haven't we already alienated enough humans from following Jesus because we have continued to perpetuate these false notions of how God works today?

[14] Isn't God All-Powerful?

MODERN CHRISTIANS TELL US THAT GOD HIMSELF understands our suffering because Jesus suffered miserably on the cross. "He knows what it's like to suffer, and he has compassion for all of us as we suffer." I'm not saying Jesus didn't suffer miserably or God does not have compassion for those suffering, but I take no solace in using it to explain why God doesn't intervene and provide for the starving and the suffering. Unless of course, he's chosen to intervene for no one as I will continue to argue as we move forward.

God's refusal to intervene for anyone would be fair and just, and it should motivate us to help those in need. It would confirm that the current miracle claims made by so many today are as false as the biblical authors' attempts to explain the causation of suffering, and why the Hajis in our world are not being fed. Haji is not dying because God is punishing him by withholding rain.

I'm no longer a rocket scientist, but based on the statistics listed above and contrary to what the author of Matthew wrote in verse 6:26, I think 24,000 humans on a planet without an active God need to be worried about where their next meal is coming from every day. On average, every 3.6 seconds, someone on this planet will take their last breath because they did not have enough food to eat.

For me, this is not God's problem, albeit Jesus seemed to have claimed we are more important than the birds and see that we are fed. This is our (your and my) collective problem. There is enough food on this Earth to feed those who are perishing at such an alarming rate. What are you and I really doing to eliminate starvation deaths on this planet?

Doing God's Work

Perhaps if we'd all stop making prayerful requests for God to actively solve the world's problems, we'd all be more apt to get off our bottoms or present our credit cards and do something to help the less fortunate and those who are suffering. If it's not feasible for us to go to the world regions affected by famine, perhaps those who can afford to give should consider making donations to World Aid organizations who are there. When my children were younger, we began financially sponsoring less fortunate children from other poverty-stricken countries. That aid organization sent us pictures of a few of those children and my wife and I placed those pictures on our refrigerator. We wanted to ensure our children understood what was really happening in the world.

Perhaps we should all acknowledge that "letting go and letting God" or offering "thoughts and prayers" are all false premises that accomplish nothing. If we could just accept that manna is not going to fall from the heavens or cancers will not be miraculously cured, we would engage more with others less fortunate. I think it's much more likely that God wonders why most of us are not in the game helping the needy than he's relying on us to pray for change before miraculously providing aid.

Assume for the moment that my interpretation of Matthew 6:26 is completely incorrect: we are not valued more than the animals and Jesus never promised to feed us like the birds. If Jesus created this metaphor only to tell us not to worry, does it not create conflict deep within your heart? This conflict should make you ask yourself: How can God supposedly "actively" love the whole of humankind as the Bible and Christians claim, yet allow 24,000 people to starve on this planet daily?

Such a conflict that would create cognitive dissonance only occurs if you are a believer that God is an active participant in our world. If you could accept the fact that God is not active in our era, you will be able to use reason and logic to explain the causation of this horror. You could resolve any of your internal conflicts (cognitive dissonance) because you won't need to continue to ask yourself why God is not intervening. But there's a price to pay for accepting that fact. Accepting the fact that God is not active should force you to feel some sense of responsibility to do what you can to help those in need. It's solely on us to be the helpers.

Sunday-School Song Errancy

If you are a believer in God's current intervention, could you look into the eyes of Haji and sing the previously mentioned song that so many of us were taught in Sunday school? You know, the song we all understood to mean that Jesus actively cares for the less fortunate children of color just as he does for us here in the US.

> Jesus loves the little children
> All the children of the world.
> Red and yellow, black and white
> They are precious in his sight.
> Jesus loves the little children of the world.

The only way that song can carry any truth is if it solely refers to the love that Jesus holds in his heart for the little children. Reality has clearly shown us over the past two millennia that he is not physically taking care of us. Perhaps we should stop teaching our younger children this song or at least explain to them that the term "love" referenced within it is not a verb in this case but simply a feeling held by Jesus and his Father. Perhaps we should wait until our children are at a more appropriate age and show them pictures of Haji. In that way, we could clearly explain to them that Jesus has called all of us to be his hands and feet and that we are responsible for helping people in need. If we continue to have them sing "the song" in their youth, only to be faced later in life with the horrific suffering realities of this world, I contend it will surely force them to reconsider the validity of that song, our biblical misapplications, or even perhaps Jesus and his sacrificial love when they are older.

According to the CDC[32], in 2018, malaria was responsible for an estimated 228 million medical episodes and 405,000 deaths. An estimated 91% of deaths in 2010 were in the African region. Mosquito bites are causing 405,000 deaths per year, or 33,750 deaths per month. That's 1,125 deaths per day! As I write today, the coronavirus (Covid –19) pandemic has killed over 670,000 Americans and over 4.5 million globally. Mercifully, the vaccine developed solely by scientific methods is just beginning to be distributed.

Are we willing to acknowledge once and for all that God is not taking care of us in any physical way? Are these malnutrition, malaria, and virus statistics not evidence enough to stop us from believing God has shown us specific favor? Shouldn't they force us to question the validity of current miracle claims, or the God-incidences that are so rampantly purported within Christian circles? If God is not caring for the starving or protecting people from deadly mosquito bites, why would any of us believe the bazillions of miraculous claims from others today? If any of the miracle claims made by so many today have any merit, it can only mean God favors his select while purposely ignoring the majority suffering amongst us.

Theodicy: Reasoning Out God's Love, Power, and Suffering

Let's discuss the conundrum with the philosophical term, theodicy. Most believers do not recognize this term, but many have struggled with the simultaneous realities of its assertions during their lives. The term theodicy asserts the following:

1. God is omnipotent (all powerful and without limits)

---

32. "World Malaria Day 2020: CDC and Partners Continue the Fight against a Global Killer," Malaria, Centers for Disease Control and Prevention, https://www.cdc.gov/malaria/features/wmd_feature_2020.html.

2. God is omnibenevolent (all loving)

3. There is suffering

Most of us find it difficult to simultaneously reconcile those three terms. Think about it. If God is all powerful and he actively loves (intervenes) as the Bible tells us he did and others suggest he does today—even enough to die on a cross for us—then why is there so much suffering taking place on this Earth?

I'm convinced "love" should be fully expressed as a verb demonstrated by action. It's not enough to think our spouses love us or even tell us they love us. We show our love to our spouses and children with our actions. God demonstrated his love by actively hanging on a cross, but where are God's loving actions today?

I am also convinced God cares about us, but not actively. Today, he doesn't love us (by action) in the same way that we love our children. We love our children in an active way. We are there with "skin on" nurturing and caring for them when they are sick. "Good" parents see their children are adequately fed and sheltered to the best of their ability. Who can say with any certainty God provides for our needs in that way?

Rejecting False Claims

Moreover, I think it's wrong for Christians to teach and agree with some of the biblical authors' claims that stated God was always looking out for the best interests of humankind. Believers in this falsehood experience a dismaying dichotomy when God doesn't come through for them during difficult times. If we stopped claiming God was actively taking care of us—refuting what I contend are false claims of many Christians today—no one would be left on the roadside contemplating why God did not intervene to help them.

Let me give you a vivid example / analogy to demonstrate God is not actively feeding us like a good parent would feed their child. It will also show how false expectations based on false premises derived from specific

Scriptures can lead to disgruntled followers when their realities do not meet their expectations.

Let's say my family and I are about to sit down at the dinner table. My kids are grown now so let's imagine it was about 25 years ago when they were young children. However, before we have dinner, I approach my wife privately and announce that we will only feed our daughter and withhold food from our son until he expires. Let's say for the sake of argument that my wife decides to go along with my plan. I certainly had the financial means to feed my family at that time. My wife and I were all powerful (theodicy assertion #1 from above) with respect to providing food. Adding to that, there cannot be another parent on this Earth who could ever say they loved their children more than my wife and I (theodicy assertion #2 from above).

So, in an analogous way to God's supposed "theodistic" attributes, my wife and I were omnipotent with respect to food and we loved our children at least as much as God is said to love all of us. After the first day of refusing to feed my son, he starts to become weak while my daughter is witnessing her brother not being fed. Day two: more of the same, and now my son does not have the strength to get out of bed. As much as it hurts my wife and me, as well as my daughter who is being fed, we continue to withhold sustenance from our son. After an extended period, we all watch as my son takes his last breath.

What would my daughter think about the actions of her parents? Would she look at us with disdain? Should she be thankful to us for feeding her in the same way we seemingly overlook the starving on this planet yet prayerfully thank God from whom we claim to have been blessed with our food? Would she have the courage to ask us why we allowed that to happen in the same way we ask God why he allows the same for the Hajis of this world?

We claimed we loved her brother, and our daughter knew we had the ability to feed him, just as we believe in God's sustenance-providing capabilities. Wouldn't you expect her to be questioning the authenticity of our sincere love for her brother or concerned about being the next to starve?

At some point, I would expect my daughter to become angry with us. Yet, no one seems to be angry with God or at those who teach about his overwhelming active love for us despite the suffering occurring today. Manna does not fall from heaven for the starving in this world.

What would this fictitious scenario have looked like from my son's perspective? He would have been playing the role of our present-day Haji. As food was being withheld from him, he would have questioned our sincere love for him. How devastated would he have been if his sister praised my wife and me for the food we provided her? He certainly would have considered his sister more favored.

If our daughter would have shown sympathy for her brother during that time, I doubt she would have been thanking and praising us for her good fortune. I would have expected nothing less from her. And this analogy is exactly the reason I'm writing this book. I'm asking Christians to reconsider the notion that God is showing them special favor and to be sympathetic towards others less fortunate by ceasing to make public favor claims.

It is this unfortunate reality which forces me to conclude God does not love us in the same way that we love our children. He loved us enough to die for us, and I can't think of any greater demonstration of love. Almost every Christian agrees with this premise, yet they continue to have hope and expectations God will act on their behalf—notwithstanding the horrific suffering occurring on this planet to others less fortunate.

For the Least of These

Lastly, I think Jesus may have been telling us in Matthew chapter 25 that we will be the responsible parties for taking care of the needy, because he wouldn't be here after his death to do it himself. Perhaps it's another indicator Jesus knew the days of miracles would cease at the end of his era. He also told us that when we do care for those who suffer, it's as if we were doing it on his behalf.

If you recall the parable of the sheep and the goats found in Matthew 25:34–40, Jesus teaches about his selection process during the end times and how he will separate the "good" (sheep) people from the "bad" (goats). Jesus says,

> "Then the King (Jesus) will say to those on his right, 'Come, you who are blessed by my Father; take your inheritance, the kingdom prepared for you since the creation of the world. For I was hungry and you gave me something to eat, I was thirsty and you gave me something to drink, I was a stranger and you invited me in, I needed clothes and you clothed me, I was sick and you looked after me, I was in prison and you came to visit me.'"
>
> But the righteous were confused by what he said, and they told the King they didn't remember a time that he needed anything. Jesus then tells them, "'The King will reply, "Truly I tell you, whatever you did for one of the least of these brothers and sisters of mine, you did for me."'"

It seems that Jesus could have been teaching on at least two different levels here.

- First, when we help those in need, we are doing it on behalf of Jesus. In other words, we would be acting as his hands and feet in providing physical intervention and care.

- Secondly, Jesus may also have been suggesting to us that it would be our duty to carry out these merciful tasks because he was about to leave this planet.

Perhaps he was preparing his disciples for his departure and how he would not be here to continue physically caring for anyone. Multitudes of people were not going to be miraculously fed with five loaves of bread and two fish after he ascended. There would be no more leper healings or restoring sight to the blind. Doesn't this theory appear to fit with our observations and common realities today? Isn't it possible Jesus was reluctant to heal or feed people when he was on Earth, only performing miracles when he was here to draw larger crowds to hear his message and to validate who he said he was?

One may certainly argue when we help the poor and the destitute, we simply act as a substitute for God, and God could or would have helped without our intervention. But there's clearly no current earthly evidence to support that position. Even with all the current world aid organizations, nine million people will starve to death this year.

I am convinced God is not supernaturally changing anyone's circumstances for the better. When we care for those suffering on this planet, we are their only hope for physical relief. When we accept that God is not changing the circumstances for those suffering and he has commissioned us for that task, no one will feel disappointed. There is no need to be confused or feel hurt by God for his inactivity. Again, the liability for relieving suffering rests solely on all of us.

Despite what David wrote in Psalm 46:1, "God is our refuge and strength, | an ever-present help in trouble," I have demonstrated that there is no truth in it as it relates to physical caregiving, protection, or providing sustenance to the starving. That verse was written to the people of Israel by David and not to us in the twenty-first century. And I question whether that statement was true for the people of Israel at that time and not just a simple embellishment. But it doesn't stop people from trying to apply it to their lives today.

It may have seemed that way to someone writing centuries ago, but it's not the way of the world today. I'll refer you to the picture of Haji at the beginning of this chapter if you're in disagreement with my premise. If you think I'm delusional, maybe we should ask all the world aid organizations to take a few months off from their benevolent endeavors and see just how much God provides to the needy. The death rate from starvation would explode immeasurably during that time. In some ways, that's a hard pill for most of us to swallow. But the sooner we accept this, the sooner we can move forward responsibly.

It has always bothered me when Christians say, "God is doing great things." We might hear that when church members are serving in their community or certainly in cases where missionaries are risking their own lives to care for those less fortunate around our globe. I've heard that when a Christian organization like Habitat for Humanity recruits compassionate volunteers to build homes for the homeless. But I would argue God is not doing those great things, people are.

Compassionate gratitude-filled people sold out for God are doing great things. If they stopped their benevolent actions, the evidence clearly shows us God would not serve the less fortunate in any physical way. Wasn't it God's inactivity towards those suffering that stimulated others to step in and provide help in the first place?

The Miracle Question

I find it much easier to reconcile my reality of the world's events (both good and bad) by accepting that God is not miraculously intervening. In that way, I never need to consider anyone more favored for their good life outcomes. If God really does love all of us equally, then we all should be on a level playing field. Either no one should be receiving divine intervention or all of us should. I think we can all agree *everyone* has not or is not receiving supernatural godly favor.

Although the Bible records only 334 miracles over about the 3,000-year period it covers, Christians make daily claims about the millions of interventions that supposedly continue to occur. I don't live in a world that demonstrates the miracles that are listed in the Bible or even a world that displays with any known certainty the miracle claims of today. This does not mean all the miracles recorded in the Bible are false. It might make them seem unlikely when we compare them to the observable known events of today.

But, since I am convinced God created the universe and the first inhabitants, I must be open to the possibility of miracles occurring today or which occurred during biblical times. And as crazy as this sounds, we cannot concern ourselves with investigating the miracle claims from the Bible since we have no way to know if they were true. Even when archeological discoveries confirm the existence of societies listed in the Bible, in no way does that confirm any miracle story from ancient times.

Hoping or wondering if they are true is a much different matter than saying I know they are true because these claims are in the Bible. It's extremely hard for me to stretch my reason by applying faith and just blindly accepting all the biblical miracle stories as true. We have a lot of other miraculous mythical stories from ancient times we know were not real. We even have other religious texts outside of Christianity that Christians wholeheartedly reject—even though people of these other religions believe their ancient miraculous stories and apply faith to do so.

[15] Reasoning from the Bible

THE BIBLICAL AUTHORS EXPLAIN THE SOURCE OF SUF-
fering using multiple approaches. I find one of these explanations completely
at odds with the others. The biblical book of Job states that suffering can
be brought by God to test the faithfulness of his followers. The stories of
both Joseph and Jesus suggest that God-ordained suffering can be used for
redemptive purposes. The prophetic authors tell us in many places that suffering was a punishment brought directly from God because of sin.

The account that contrasts with all the rest comes from the book of
Ecclesiastes (the author purported to be Solomon, although most scholars
believe the book was written at least 400 years after his death). This wisdom
book tells us there's no God-attributed rhyme or reason as to why people
suffer. The writer tells us that bad things happen to good people and good
things happen to bad people. Solomon was supposedly the wisest man on
Earth, and if he indeed was the author, he deduced that suffering occurs
randomly in everyone's life without godly causation. According to the Book
of Ecclesiastes, since suffering is not orchestrated by the Almighty, we should
seek as much moral pleasure as we can while we're here.

Suffering as a Test (The Story of Job)

Most Christians are familiar with the story of Job, so I will simply paraphrase
it here for those who are not. Job was the wealthiest, most blessed man on
the planet. He was a righteous man, loved God very much, and honored him
by following his commands. At some point, Satan (many scholars believe

this Satan-like figure was not the chief fallen angel as described in the New Testament) approaches God and asks God to put Job to the test.

After God boasts to Satan about how faithful Job was to him, Satan states that the only reason Job was faithful to God was because God had given him everything he could ever want: family, wealth, land, etc. So, God grants Satan permission to take all those things away from Job in order to see if Job would still be faithful to God. In essence, God made a cosmic wager with Satan. Is that how God operated then, or even today?

So, Satan (not God) causes Job to lose everything including his ten children. He even becomes infected with leprosy. He is in terrible agony both physically and emotionally. Even Job's wife tells him to curse God and just die, but despite all this Job remains faithful to God.

Most of the remainder of Job's story involves discussions with three of his friends. One of his friends suggests that the reason Job is suffering is because he must have some unrepented sin. The people of the ancient world including many of the prophets, believed suffering was clearly a punishment by God for personal sin. To people of this time, the origin of this type of punishment was not by random earthly consequence or reasoned cause and effect but rather by divine targeting. And I believe faulty extensions from that era of these types of beliefs cause many Christians to believe God operates this way today. Christian karma?

Job finally gives in and becomes increasingly angry with God for ever allowing him, a "righteous man," to suffer like he is. Job even curses the day he was born. Then, God bombards Job with a plethora of questions that Job is not capable of answering. God asks Job if he was there when he set the foundations and dimensions of the universe and if he knows how the Earth's oceans know their boundaries. He asks him if he knows how the stars were hung in the sky, how lighting emanates from the clouds, and who is responsible for providing rain to the desert regions. Finally, he asks Job if he knows who endowed wisdom to the human heart and provided understanding to the mind.

God overwhelmed Job with his authority, and Job sat and humbly took all of it. Ironically, God doesn't give Job an answer as to why he's been suffering. Based on what God has told him, the answer to Job's miserable suffering is, "There is no answer." Similar to what parents are known for saying, "Because I said so."

Job finally repents and decides to trust God even while he is suffering. Because of his trust, God rewards Job with more than he was blessed with before his suffering. God replaces Job's wealth, bestows ten new children, and ensures he lives a long and prosperous life.

If these atrocities and blessings happened to a man named Job, certainly they were not caused by the hands of God or some figure of evil. There is no supernatural reason why an innocent person decided at an unfortunate time to travel down a specific road and be killed by a drunk driver. There is not a God who ordained, caused, or controls those kinds of outcomes to test others. Yet, I can understand men living during the biblical era who thought that the Lord pulled the strings for each good and horrific event. They too looked for explanations to describe earthly events. They just didn't have present day knowledge, experience, and practical understanding that have come to us over thousands of years since.

So, what is the real reason why Job suffered in this story? If you believe that the story occurred the way it's described, I think you'll find it difficult to believe anything other than God causes righteous people to suffer while testing their faithfulness in order to win a bet. Let's not forget the story of Noah, where apparently wiping out the entire human race was a viable option available to God. If you are on the same page with me, then Job's story is meant as an extreme literary example of how we should remain faithful to God during rough times in our lives, even when we don't feel we deserve the misery we might be going through. I can accept Job's story on that basis. It's a reminder that when bad things happen in my life, they shouldn't cause me to abandon my allegiance to God.

Suffering as Punishment for Sin

"God is a mean kid with a magnifying glass sitting on an anthill, and I'm the ant. He could fix my life in five minutes, but he'd rather burn my feelers off and watch me squirm." (Jim Carrey, *Bruce Almighty*).

I found the movie *Bruce Almighty* very humorous. In places it reflected the hidden attitudes many people have regarding if or how God operates. In the middle of all of Bruce's struggles, he pictured God as a tyrant who cared less about remedying his circumstances and more about pleasurably watching him suffer. And because this fictional character believed God had the power to stop his suffering and didn't, he considered God the liable party with bad intentions. I think many people look at the causation of their circumstances that way today. Let's look at the biblical reasoning for causation as it relates to the "feeler burning" process that Bruce assumed he was experiencing at the hands of the Almighty.

The Old Testament is filled with references to sin as the cause for most suffering. When a person was suffering, people of that time believed God was punishing them—as we discussed in Job's story. To the Jewish people of the Old Testament era, this was a different type of cause and effect than many of us understand it today. Many Christians today have latched onto the Eastern religious view of karma and apply it as a God-orchestrated form of punishment. The faulty reasoning found throughout the OT causes them to make a correlation between suffering and God. People believe you don't just get what you deserve from natural cause and effect. God also sees to it that you pay for your sin one way or another on this side of eternity. Let's examine just how pervasive this way of thinking was for the Jews in the OT times.

The major prophets (longer writings) were Isaiah, Jeremiah, and Ezekiel. There are also twelve minor prophets (shorter books) listed in the OT, namely, Hosea, Malachi, Haggai, Habakkuk, Joel, Obadiah, Jonah, Micah, Nahum, Haggai, Amos, and Zechariah. For the record, there won't be a quiz at the end of this chapter asking you to recall or correctly pronounce any of those names.

Prophets were viewed as mouthpieces for God. We are told God provided the prophets with instructions regarding how the Jews of Israel were to conduct themselves. The prophets then relayed the messages to the people of Israel. In many instances, it's purported that God through the prophets warned the people of Israel of what would happen to them if they failed to obey his instructions.

Prophets were certain that if the people of Israel did not adhere to God's instructions, they would be punished directly by God. They believed God would send drought, famine, pestilence, economic hardship, and military defeat. It's interesting to note that most of the prophets initiated their work around the time of the two huge disasters which befell Israel: the destruction of the northern kingdom by Assyria in the eighth century BCE and the destruction of Southern Israel by the Babylonians in the sixth century BCE. It was during these times of immense suffering under the rule of other nations that the prophets continually urged the Jewish people to repent of their wicked ways and return to their God if they wanted any chance to live in prosperity again.

The Bible clearly states that sin requires punishment. Again, the book of Genesis claims God destroyed the entire human race except Noah and his family because sin had spread everywhere. The two cities of Sodom and Gomorrah were destroyed. Everywhere in the Old Testament God rewards the good and punishes the sinners. Since there was no belief in an afterlife for most of that period,[33] people were seen to be rewarded and punished on this side of eternity. Rewards / blessings for good behavior included health, long life, and prosperity, while illness, defeat in battle, or any other calamity were believed to be an expression of God's judgment and anger.

The OT clearly paints the picture that God was deeply offended by sin. His wrath was aroused, and he punished the sinner. The New Testament

---

33. T. Desmond Alexander, "The Old Testament View of Life After Death," *Themelios* 11:2, https://www.thegospelcoalition.org/themelios/article/the-old-testament-view-of-life-after-death/.

continues this picture. We see a picture of God's anger in the treatment given to the servant who showed no mercy (Matthew 18:23–35), to the unfaithful servant (Matthew 24:45–51), to those who murdered his messengers inviting them to the wedding feast (Matthew 22:2–7), and to the man without a wedding garment (Matthew 22:8–13).

Jesus made it even more clear when referring to the unbelieving towns: "'But I tell you that it will be more bearable for Sodom on the day of judgment than for you'" (Matthew 11:24). In his description of the final judgment, Jesus warns, "'Then he will say to those on his left, "Depart from me, you who are cursed, into the eternal fire prepared for the devil and his angels"'" (Matthew 25:41).

The Almighty described in the Old Testament was a pretty nasty God. But tell me what you'd expect God's characterizations to be like coming from superstitious, desert-dwelling nomads in the Middle East during that era? How else were they to explain their suffering? Even if those stories of God's causal punishments were true at that time, is there any credible evidence he operates that way today? Is this what God is doing to Haji?

It's beyond me to understand this way of thinking, but as I've mentioned, Christians continue to believe God is still in the business of punishing sinners and rewarding those who love him. Shouldn't we consider the causation of earthly suffering today for what it really is without supernatural explanations? If our societies continue to lose their moral standards, then we can safely say we will suffer more earthly consequences that are directly related to our sin. But those consequences will not be orchestrated by God here on Earth. We cannot continue to perpetuate this false way of thinking anymore. I'm convinced the authors of the Hebrew Scriptures and the people living at that time misattributed the causes of at least some if not all of their suffering to God.

We know today that smoking increases one's chances of getting cancer over those who don't smoke. We don't consider their disease as something brought to the victim directly from God. If someone in the ancient times viewed smoking as a sin—violating the godly principle that our bodies are temples for God and we should take care of them, they would have considered a cancer victim as being punished directly by the Almighty. They neither knew nor understood what we know today about the damage caused by carcinogens to lung tissues. Being drunk was considered a sin because it also violated the godly principle of keeping our bodies as a holy temple. If someone during that era fell off their camel while intoxicated and died, people of those times would have attributed the event as direct God-orchestrated punishment for sin. You and I would simply recognize the effects of alcohol as the cause behind that event.

Most of us are cognizant of the moral compass God genetically instilled within the fabric of his first human creation. As their descendants, assuming one is not mentally impaired, we possess those same attributes. Of course, today we understand when we violate God's laws, or principles derived by his laws, we can suffer direct consequences. These consequences do not occur because of karma or a God who actively manipulates our circumstances to see us suffer. They are natural, logical consequences having reasonable explanations because God has provided us free will, and that is exactly how God designed the universe.

Redemptive Suffering

Some people believe God causes certain types of suffering for redemptive purposes. God causes suffering to some to help or save others from suffering. Two biblical examples can be found in the OT story of Joseph and the NT gospel accounts of Jesus's death and resurrection.

If you recall, Jacob's sons grew jealous of their youngest brother, Joseph, who was their father's favorite son. When Joseph comes to them in his beautiful, multi-colored coat, the eleven elder jealous brothers consider killing him, but then sell Joseph into slavery. They tell their father that Joseph is dead.

Joseph was sold to Potiphar, a high-ranking official in Egypt who favors Joseph. But Potiphar's flirtatious wife accuses Joseph of trying to sleep with her, and Potiphar sends him to prison. Later, because of his faith, Joseph earns favor with the head of the prison.

After proving himself as an interpreter of dreams, he waits several more years for his release. When Egypt's Pharaoh is in turmoil over two dreams, Joseph's former fellow inmate tells Pharaoh of Joseph and his ability to interpret dreams. Pharaoh summons Joseph, and his interpretations indicate a great famine will decimate Egypt after seven years. Pharaoh, impressed by Joseph's abilities, elevates Joseph to be his highest official and assigns him to organize Egypt's plan to set aside food in preparation for the famine.

When Joseph's brothers are also facing starvation, they learn of the Egyptian supply of grain, and go there to purchase food. When the men present themselves to Joseph, he recognizes them immediately but stops short of revealing his identity. Joseph tests his brothers next.

He first tosses them in jail and then sends them back to Canaan to retrieve their youngest brother, Benjamin. They delay, but finally in desperation return with their father's new favorite son, and Joseph continues his game. His officials plant a silver cup in his youngest brother's satchel, and then Joseph threatens to kill him when the cup is discovered. Upon Judah offering his own life in exchange for Benjamin's, Joseph finally reveals his identity. Joseph convinces his brothers to return to Egypt for their father Jacob, who, overjoyed, moves to Egypt with his family of seventy and escapes the famine.

In Joseph's story, he was first with his father and last with his brothers. He was betrayed by his brothers and suffered greatly during the time he was sold and then enslaved. He was later redeemed as he became Pharaoh's right-hand man and was able to save (redeem) his entire family. According to this story in Genesis, all these events in Joseph's life were orchestrated by God. God permitted Joseph's suffering so that later God could use the situation to redeem Joseph and his family.

Likewise, the New Testament places the eternal destiny of all mankind in the redeeming story of Jesus. As we know, Jesus's story involved a great deal of suffering, and for us to be redeemed, Jesus needed to die. According to some biblical texts, the reason some people suffer is to bring about the best for others. The Bible tells us that Jesus suffered to redeem the whole of mankind.

Ecclesiastes' Explanation for Suffering

Many Christians are unaware the Bible gives us another explanation as to why mankind suffers which conflicts with the biblical reasonings mentioned above. The book of Ecclesiastes presents us a naturalistic vision of life—one that sees life through human eyes. This is certainly a biblical book I can relate to, because it takes the liability for suffering away from God. This more humanistic quality has made the book especially popular among younger audiences today as well as others who have experienced more than their fair share of pain and suffering.

The Book of Ecclesiastes takes an interesting perspective to answer the question, "Is life worth living?" It's surprising to discover that the author concludes it is not. He analyzes the many things people strive for and deduces that life brings only vanity and frustration.

He does not believe in progress but rather that history simply repeats itself: Ecclesiastes 1:9 "What has been will be again, | what has been done will be done again; | there is nothing new under the sun." He thinks every generation believes it has created something new, but any advancements from his generation or from those before, will all be forgotten. Moreover, the writer sees no point in trying to make the world better: "'What is crooked cannot be straightened; | what is lacking cannot be counted'" (1:15).

He goes on to show the vanity of life itself, "Yet when I surveyed all that my hands had done | and what I had toiled to achieve, | everything was meaningless, a chasing after the wind; | nothing was gained under the sun" (Ecclesiastes 2:11). The author refers to himself as a man who has already tried all the ways by which people pursue a meaningful life. Ironically, he concludes that life is self-defeating. He finds no satisfaction in riches, wisdom, or fame, and his pursuit of those goals only left him emotionally bankrupt.

The author appears to be familiar with some people's belief that rewards and punishments will be dealt to individuals in a future life beyond the grave, but he doesn't believe that. He tells us that the death of a human is comparable to that of an animal, and he observes, "All have the same breath; humans have no advantage over animals. Everything is meaningless. . . . Who knows if the human spirit rises upward and if the spirit of the animal goes down into the earth?" (Ecclesiastes 3:19, 21).

People's desires cannot be satisfied, for the more people see, the more they want to see; the more things people acquire, the less satisfied they become with what they have obtained. The Ecclesiastes writer is skeptical but not angry with the world. He is just trying to make the best of what he can. Unlike Job, who was emotionally troubled that innocent people suffer, this author accepts bad life circumstances as they are and refuses to become upset about them. Throughout the book, repeatedly he says, "A person can do nothing better than to eat and drink and find satisfaction in their own toil." (2:24).

The author knows that many people of his era believed they would be rewarded here on earth for their good deeds, but he is convinced that there are no cosmic reasons for earthly rewards. His observations tell him that a good person fares no better than a wicked person, and, at times, the righteous person doesn't even fare as well. Regardless of how an individual lives, we will all be forgotten after we die, for death comes to the righteous and the wicked alike. Earthly rewards come to the wicked as much as they come to the righteous.

The book of Ecclesiastes is filled with advice on how a person should live in order to extract the greatest enjoyment from life. He instructs his readers: "Do not be over righteous, | neither be over wise— | why destroy yourself?" (7:16). A person should find a happy medium. He argues that no one should waste their time saving up money in anticipation for old age and they should enjoy their lives when they're younger. Old age will only bring weakness and sickness right before "the dust returns to the ground it came from..." (12:7).

The Book of Ecclesiastes is skeptical, unorthodox, and different in tone than other biblical teachings in many ways. It amazes me it was incorporated into the Hebrew Scriptures and later the entire biblical canon. It appeals to many individuals because of its straightforward and honest approach. It's clear the author is aware his arguments are not the generally accepted ideas of his era, but he has the courage to say what he believes to be true. And, since the name of King Solomon had long been associated with this book, it added even more merit to its validity. But this book probably would have been excluded from the Bible had it not been for an addition that appears to have been made to the last chapter.

Almost every biblical scholar believes the last words in the book of Ecclesiastes were a late addition by someone other than the author. And they think this because it completely conflicts with the premises the author makes throughout his entire book. The author of Ecclesiastes, as most of the people of that era, does not believe there is an afterlife throughout the body of his book, and yet the last words of the book, Ecclesiastes 12:13–14, suggest there is an afterlife. The book ends with, "Fear God and keep his commandments, | for this is the duty of all mankind. | For God will bring every deed into judgment, | including every hidden thing, | whether it is good or evil."

In summary, the Bible has multiple explanations as to why we suffer. For me, it's hard to see the validity in a direct causation by the active hand of God *today* to bring suffering to his creatures as a test, as a redeeming quality, or as a punishment. There's a significant differential in perspective between natural consequences and thinking there's a whip-carrying "big judge" in the sky actively doling out earthly punishments or actively creating life-altering circumstances of hardship for some reasoned purpose. But this is how the Jewish people understood suffering. They are also the same people who believed that thunder and lightning were, at times, God's anger and wrath. They saw earthquakes and famine along those same lines.

We are not that unenlightened today, and we should not allow ourselves to interpret present-day life events in such a way. It's time to break away from some of the misguided ink and parchment way of thinking, accept only the portions of the Bible that meet with our common realities, and continue building on the observable knowledge we have attained.

PART 6:

PRAYER

EXAMINED

[16] Requests, Benedictions, and Giving Thanks

A man who makes prayers of request is one who thinks that God has arranged matters all wrong, but who also thinks he can instruct God how to put them right.

—Christopher Hitchens[34]

Once a man was asked, "What did you gain from asking God through prayer to change your circumstances?" The man answered, *"Nothing.... but let me tell you what I lost: anger, ego, greed, depression, insecurity, and fear of death."*

—Author Unknown

I used to believe prayer changes things, but now I know that prayer changes us, and we change things.

—Mother Teresa of Calcutta

AS WE BEGIN THIS DISCUSSION ON PRAYER, I WANT TO make it clear I am one hundred percent pro prayer. I am convinced prayer, if aligned in non-supernatural reality, is a great method for changing this

---

34.   Christopher Hitchens, *Mortality* (New York: Grand Central Publishing, 2012).

world for the better. Prayer should be about changing us, and not an attempt to carry with it any hope to entice God to act in a supernatural way.

Prayer can be a meditative time for giving thanks to God for what he has already provided through his creation and his forgiving grace, focusing and realigning ourselves to the standards of Jesus, acknowledging our shortcomings, and committing ourselves to do better going forward. But prayer does not entice God to supernaturally change anyone's circumstances. Meditatively aligning ourselves through prayer with the principles of Jesus can change us—which in turn can change our attitudes, positions, decisions, and actions.

I'm convinced God does not answer prayer by circumventing the laws of nature or by supernaturally altering human intentions or circumstances. He does not save praying people in specific seats in plane crashes, nor does he heal praying people from diseases. He does not instill disease-curing solutions into the minds of scientific researchers at the time of his choosing. He does not provide selected favored praying people with cars, jobs, or preferential parking spaces.

God will not feed the 24,000 people who will die every day from malnutrition no matter how many people pray for him to do so. He will not save any of the 405,000 praying people who will die from a malaria-carrying mosquito which bites them this year. He will not quiet the Earth such that earthquake causing tsunamis will not claim the lives of thousands.

He did not stop Adolf Hitler and his band of Nazi thugs from exterminating six million Jews (God's purported chosen people) at the prayerful requests by so many, nor is it likely he will interfere with other evil people in the future. He does not steer or deflect hurricanes and tornadoes from any portion of the Earth irrespective of claims made by prayerful local survivors.

None of these calamities occur because God is incapable of stopping them but rather because God has chosen not to intervene. For most Christians, it's inconceivable for a loving God to be characterized in this way. But how can Christians reconcile the horrific events we all observe daily? It seems God

willingly suspended his right to intervene when he gave mankind its libertarian free will. He also set this universe up in such a way that randomness
in the natural world and the intentions and actions of free-willed people are
the causation behind the events on this planet. His choice to provide us our
free will allows us seemingly unlimited opportunities yet also subjects us to
the consequences stemming from satisfying the desires of our fleshly bodies
(sin) and the random chaotic risks of this natural world.

Some have devalued God's forgiving gracious act of love and substi-
tuted it with a miracle dispensing deity who, through prayer, is purportedly
actively involved in all the events of their lives. We have accepted and misapplied some of the Bronze Age biblical authors' claims that through prayer,
God currently oversees and continually controls the outcomes of earthly
events. We've aligned ourselves with and extrapolated those same authors'
superstitious beliefs that suggested there was a God who punished people
for sin, rewarded others for virtuous deeds, and continues to do so today. We
have accepted the notion that every word and concept in the Bible is truth
because they are all of God's words and values. We continue to believe that
all the biblical prayer promises made during that era also apply to us today.
We've clearly been mistaken.

Prayer is an important component to Christianity, and, for most, prayer
is synonymous with making requests to God. In fact, most Christians only
know how to pray that way. But I will argue within this chapter that those
making prayerful requests to God to alter anyone's circumstances or to ask
God to supernaturally to give us anything tangible or even spiritual while
harboring expectations he will provide, employ prayer ineffectively.

Others use prayer as a form of one-way communication to God—
sharing their heart and their life, an important component of prayer that
I encourage. Through prayer, we can bolster our strength and come away
with more peace because during our prayer time we should be focusing
and aligning ourselves with God and his precepts. I don't believe we receive
strength, wisdom, or invisible cosmic peace wave packets from God during

prayer. Prayer can also be used to make comparative assessments of our daily lives and how well we've been living up to godly standards, the way in which Jesus asked us to live. It can be a time to convey our thoughts and concerns toward God as we assess our life's struggles.

Prayer is also a venue in which we can confess our shortcomings and make commitments to God that we will try to honor him by being more obedient. However, prayer should not involve requests for items in a never-ending shopping list, or for aid to solve our life problems. God has already acted supernaturally for all eternity, and he has provided us with everything we need. He's already solved our greatest problem.

From 2 Peter 1:3 "His divine power has given us *everything we need* for a godly life *through our knowledge of him* who called us by his own glory and goodness" (emphasis mine). If Peter claimed the people of his era had *everything* they needed to live a godly life through knowledge of him, why would we continue to make prayerful requests with expectations for intervention? Yet some continue to seek answers through prayer and claim to have received revelations directly from God. During prayer, some even claim to have heard God's answers in audible form.

Many people see prayer as a method to change God's mind or attempt to get God's permission and agreement to do what they want to do. Should they buy a certain house or sell their car or take a new position for employment? They pray fervently that God would reveal his desires and direction for them in such matters.

But don't we already know what God's general desires are for us from the biblical teachings of Jesus? Don't we already know the principles and standards that are revealed in portions of the Bible—especially how Jesus asked us to live? Assuming the Bible (in part or in whole) is really the revealed words of God, hasn't Jesus already equipped us with the capacity for, and challenge to, apply his principles and standards to the details of our lives? Does our God really care whether we should buy a certain house or not, unless doing so would be out of line with principles Jesus taught? Didn't Jesus provide sufficient guidance for discerning what decisions we should make during trying times of our lives?

God shouldn't need to actively provide selective wisdom-filled answers to the problems in our lives, nor do I believe that he does. The answers we seek to receive from God through prayer stare directly at us if we read the words of Jesus. These godly principles should be ingrained in us. They are not supernaturally flowing from the heavens into our minds upon prayerful request. Moreover, how would we learn valuable life lessons if God were bailing us out by providing answers to our life's problems through prayerful requests? *The challenge and beauty of this life is applying the standards of Jesus to the difficult circumstances in our lives.*

If it's true that Jesus suffered on that cross for our benefit, then how much more could God have done to show his love for us? Honestly, what other godly intervention through prayer today could be required to meet our deepest needs? During challenging times in our lives, we all desire a helper, healer, or protector; we can't imagine living life without one. But reality is not in the business of lying nor is reality a function of hope.

There are no miracle gift cards in anyone's wallet with value. The moment we accept this important fact, we will set ourselves free from the pitfalls of potential disappointments when our unselfish requesting prayers are not answered in the way we'd hoped for. We will be able to rationally explain the outcomes of life events without needing to consider mysterious godly intervention. We will also avoid the need to scramble and defend God by declaring a higher godly purpose for not intervening. No longer will we need to consider a God who plays favorites. I know this sounds extremely frightening to many Christians. But I can tell you from my personal experience, life is so much more fulfilling when one only looks to God with thanksgiving and gratitude for his overall creation and his promise to forgive our sins rather than expecting God to alter our circumstances through prayerful requests.

I use prayer as nothing more than a form of meditation—measuring myself against what I perceive to be God's standards and my past actions. I take time during prayer to think about my circumstances, the circumstances of my friends and family, and consider ways in which I may be able to help them. For me, viewing prayer as a means of getting what I want—be it gaining godly acceptance, receiving material or financial gain, healing cancer, etc.—is to fail to genuinely pray. Of course, my thoughts run completely counter to how Christians generally interpret and apply what the Bible seems to teach regarding requesting and receiving through prayer. I believe that occurs because they have errantly taken the prayer promises of Jesus or other examples of prayer listed in the Bible and have believed those promises and examples of intervention apply to us.

You might be saying: Hold up, Jeff. Doesn't the Bible tell us we should ask God for help? Paul wrote in Philippians 4:6–7: "Do not be anxious about anything, but in every situation, by prayer and petition, with thanksgiving, *present your requests to God*. And the peace of God, which transcends all understanding, will guard your hearts and your minds in Christ Jesus" (emphasis mine). I think it can be a healthy practice to present our needs to God, as long as we're not carrying an expectation or hope he will provide supernatural relief. Notice verse 7 doesn't say God *will* provide help by providing answers or relief to our requests. It says we will receive *peace*. I believe that's only true because we have shared our concerns with God as we might with a close friend, not because God will change our circumstance.

What Is Prayer?

In my view, authentic prayer falls into four categories:

- Reviewing and assessing our most recent attempts to emulate the life of Jesus and how he taught us to live.
- Giving thanks for God's creation, for the gift of Jesus's life instruction, and our salvation through his death and resurrection.

- Meditatively committing ourselves to changing the areas of our lives where we continually do things against what we believe God would desire of us.

- Expressing exactly what we are feeling to God.

On that last point, most Christians believe God already knows our circumstances and even our thoughts. But God can be an outlet for dumping our truck during prayer time, like we would with a close friend, a psychologically healthy practice.

I differ with the way many Christians interpret Scripture regarding how God answered prayer during the biblical era. I don't believe prayer alone will directly affect the outcome of events via God's manipulation in our current age. It may have worked that way when Jesus walked this Earth because he was physically present or even through some of his apostles after his death, but not today. And, if you'd like a good biblical example that suggests the miracle days ended when Jesus and his disciples departed this Earth, you only need to look at the apostle Paul's situational prayer he made three times to have his thorn (which caused some sort of suffering) removed from his flesh. Paul tells us that Jesus said, "'My grace (forgiveness) is sufficient for you, for my power is made perfect in weakness'" (2 Corinthians 12:9).

Living solely in gratitude for what Jesus did on that cross should lead us to peace. As much as we want an active God who will bail us out of our troubles (addictions, health issues, unemployment, finances, thorns in our flesh, etc.), his grace and not his intervention should be enough for all of us. We've been given life from God as randomly created descendants of his first creation, and Jesus told us he died to set us free from guilt and shame. Please tell me what else we really need to live a life filled with freedom, gratitude, and love, even when, at times, our circumstances are difficult. Paul seemed to understand and accept it. Why isn't it enough for so many today?

I do, however, think prayer can affect the attitude of the person praying, assuming they are not expecting God to show them favor. If one aligns themselves with God's goodness, principles, and his love while contemplating certain dilemmas they're currently facing, then that could certainly affect their future choices, hopefully for the better. As we know, those decisions could also alter the course of events for others who are within the sphere of influence of the person who prayed.

But this scenario does not happen because God directly intervened to change an event because someone prayed. Prayers of the non-requesting type can change the thoughts and mindset of the person praying because they have contemplated life's issues in light of what they believe to be God's standards and desires. Petitionary prayers to the Almighty do not cause God to supernaturally alter any of our thoughts or circumstances because that would violate the free will God has extended to us.

Any prayer that includes expectations for godly relief can also lead us to abandon our responsibility to help someone else. It will also set us up for the disappointments that will surely follow when our requesting prayers are not answered the way we hoped. We shouldn't just prayerfully petition God to help someone and think, "God will take care of it." We should accept the responsibility of acting in ways within our control (not with the old thoughts-and-prayers cliché), and we should be contemplating what we should do to help the situation when we pray.

> *During prayer, we should align our lives with, and commit*
> *ourselves to God's principles, rather than ask God to realign*
> *our circumstances. We are responsible for changing and*
> *aligning ourselves with the moral principles of Jesus.*

During prayer, I remind myself of the life lessons Jesus taught when he was here. Prayer for me is a way of assessing how well I've been doing with answering the age-old question "What would Jesus do?" Have I really been emulating how he lived and loved others? Have I been too judgmental? Have

I looked at others as if they were below me? Have I humbly considered others greater than myself as Jesus asked us to do?

During my prayer time, I ask myself, "Has my mouth been honoring God and others, or has the overflow of my mouth been horrific and reflective of my rotten selfish heart?" Who do I need to make amends with?

My personal prayers are an interrogation and assessment of how I've been doing both inside and out. I remind and recommit myself to acting in the future as best I can, to be more like Jesus. I do tell God during prayer that I'm sorry for my shortcomings and commit to him to try to do better.

When praying, I formulate viable solutions and weigh them against what I think God would want me to do. I ask myself, "Are the solutions only about me?" and, "How will they affect others?" "What will God think about my solutions, and will they honor him?" This isn't about seeking God's answers to my problems, spoken or felt. If our lives are truly aligned with God's standards, then we are less likely to choose a solution to our life's problems that exist outside of those standards.

Prayer is a method to align ourselves with God, not for God to provide information or actively direct us towards a specific path which could cancel our free will. But if you think God does act supernaturally, or you've claimed that he has acted on your behalf, again I challenge you: look around and see just how effective he's been at bequeathing the desired results. Our world is a mess, and I'm really hoping it has not been caused by godly intervention through anyone's prayerful request to make it so. God certainly has the right and the power to alter anything, but the evidence of life's events suggests that he does not act that way. At least I hope he hasn't been.

As I previously mentioned, many Christians say they receive special feelings during prayer, and from those feelings they make decisions in their life. They operate as if the feelings they received came directly from God. As fallible humans, can we really count on our feelings alone to make critical decisions in our lives? Most of us know that feelings are fickle and not to be trusted. Feelings certainly don't always tell the truth. God produced the human brain to be logical and capable of functioning with keen reasoning capabilities. We should use that same reasoning to make critical decisions in our lives and not believe our feelings are the result of divinely sent messages from God. There are no supernatural divine directives. There are only mindful, reasonable choices that either sit well with us or do not—because they are either synchronous with or against what we perceive to be God's desires for us.

I also use prayer to give thanks to God but not necessarily in the same way as most traditional Christians. I am thankful for God's creation, the life instructions of Jesus, and for him offering himself as our sacrifice. But I would never prayerfully thank God for a promotion I received at my job, nor would I prayerfully thank God for seeing I was not harmed after avoiding a close call. I do not thank God for my finances. I can't have a God who is providing these things to me while countless others go without. I'm not that deserving. I have what I have because of calculated decisions and a whole lot of luck.

I once heard a story of a little boy who was asked if he prayed every night. He answered, "No not every night, because there's some nights I don't need nothing." When things are going well in a Christian's life, they may not remember to make prayerful requests. But when life's problems are greater than their ability to solve, even the non-believer may call out to God for relief. It's been said many times, "When the devil is sick, the devil a saint would be."

Let's think about this more deeply. Have you ever considered just how chaotic life might be if everyone's prayers were granted by God? What would happen when the people of two different virtuous Christian nations at war were both praying for victory? What if you believed God answered your prayers by miraculously remediating your terminal cancer, and three years later you accidentally run a red light, killing three people in a car wreck? What would happen when a bride prayed for a beautiful sunny day for her wedding while local farmers were praying for rain the night before to save their crops? Since any changes made by God through prayerful request will create a cascading ripple effect on other fellow humans, wouldn't that require

God to constantly consider the endless ramifications his decisions to act may cause? How many more interventions would be required and how many more people would be affected? Is that how God really operates, or is it more likely he's allowed us to steer the course of events on this planet and to corporately deal with the outcomes of our choices?

In the New Testament portion of the Bible, Jesus seemed to make multiple promises to his followers that they could ask him for anything, and he would *unconditionally* provide for them. Those promises are notably referred to as the "name-it and claim-it" prayer promises that we'll examine in the next section. Were these biblical promises to his followers also applicable to everyone who has lived after his death and ascension? Most Christians believe they apply today, and that explains why they continue to make prayerful requests to him. I've been hinting at this along the way, but throughout the remainder of this book I will unequivocally postulate the following:

> *We have unreasonably and errantly hijacked the prayer promises of Jesus from 2,000 years ago and delivered them to a future realm in which he did not intend for them to apply. If he performed miracles during his time on earth, their usage was solely to prove his divinity and draw people to hear his message. His miraculous interventions were never intended to extend past his or his disciples' time on earth.*

Are there other interpretations or contexts that mitigate Jesus's promises to intervene today? Many Christians apologetically argue these promises are not absolute and none of them come to fruition without the condition that God's will be in place. "You'll only receive what you ask for today if and only if it is God's will." But, as you will discover, those verses clearly do not state that condition. Nowhere in those verses or in any verses surrounding them does the Bible mention a condition requiring God's will to line up with our request as a condition of fulfillment. One may argue that it's simply assumed that God's will must be in place to receive what we ask for because God is always the arbiter and final decision maker. But most Christians who read the Bible don't rely on an apologetic answer or excuse to explain why promises don't always come to fruition. Most are only relying on the exact words and phrases (as they do for every other biblical verse they scrutinize and dissect) of those prayer promises, which at face value, clearly tell us God will give us *anything* we ask for in prayer.

Grace Supersedes Miracles

There's a small sect of Christianity who call themselves The Berean Bible Society (BBS). Their name originates from the city of Berea, where the apostle Paul visited during his ministry. Their understanding regarding prayer lines up with my beliefs, and they offer a very credible explanation as to why God is not honoring his prayer promises in our era. For clarification, not every church with a name that includes "Berean" shares the same understanding regarding what you're about to read.

For the BBS, the application of Jesus's prayer promises went away after Jesus and his apostles left this Earth. They believe the miraculous sign gifts were part of the formation of the early Church, the body of Christ, at the beginning of this age. They believe miracles passed off the scene by the latter part of Paul's ministry after Acts 28, because in Paul's prison epistles (Ephesians, Philippians, Colossians, and Philemon) written after Acts 28, we don't find the miraculous gifts any longer. They assert the sign gifts of speaking in tongues, interpretation of tongues, healings, etc., were used by Jesus and his apostles to carry out their ministry and show God's authority. The Bereans believe there is no need for miracles today because we now have the canonized Bible and can know God through his written word, and by the grace he has extended to everyone after Jesus's death and ascension.

According to the BBS, the fundamental fallacy in today's prayer arena comes from a failure to apply 2 Timothy 2:15: "Do your best to present yourself to God as one approved, a worker who does not need to be ashamed and *who correctly handles the word of truth.*" The BBS argue that the prayer promises of Jesus have nothing to do with the dispensation in which we live today, but rather belonged to a program which God himself has interrupted and is temporarily holding in abeyance. To be clear, the term "dispensation" can be a reference to what is being dispensed or "doled" out (favors), in this case by God. It's also considered a division in time between what occurred at a particular time but does not occur after that time.

The BBS claim God dispensed miracles during the time of Jesus and his apostles but stopped dispensing them after God fully revealed his message of grace to Paul for this dispensation by the latter part of his ministry. They assert, after Jesus and Paul's ministry times, we have been dispensed grace and no longer will we experience miracles through the prayer promises Jesus made until right before his second coming.

For those who fail to recognize the distinctive ministry and message committed to the Apostle Paul, the topic of prayer creates a difficult and perplexing problem. Consider some of the notable name-it-and-claim-it prayer promises made during Jesus's earthly ministry:

"Again, truly I tell you that if two of you on earth agree about any-thing they ask for, it will be done for them by my Father in heaven." (Matthew 18:19)

"If you believe, you will receive whatever you ask for in prayer." (Matthew 21:22)

"Therefore I tell you, whatever you ask for in prayer, believe that you have received it, and it will be yours." (Mark 11:24)

"And I will do whatever you ask in my name, so that the Father may be glorified in the Son. You may ask me for anything in my name, and I will do it." (John 14:13–14)

TRADING MIRACLES FOR GRACE

These are wonderful promises. But we all know the disappointment, confusion, and heartache when claiming one of these promises and not receiving the answer we hoped for. It's certainly the main reason that made me begin to question the authenticity of certain canonized promises of Jesus, and because I knew they were not guaranteed in today's world. Since we know these promises are not guaranteed today, we have no other choice but to accept that they were only valid during the era of Jesus—unless the words of Jesus were never true.

This conundrum forced me to consider the reason and context in which Jesus made his promises and exactly for whom they were intended. I also couldn't accept the Christian apologetic that the prayer promises made by Jesus all carry with them the caveat that everything we ask for needs to be "in accordance with God's will" for these verses to be true for us today. Again, those verses do not state God's will as a condition. Our prayers are not rejected today because they fail to be in sync with what God desires. Our requesting prayers are never supernaturally answered because those promises were not meant for us. If a favorable event occurs and is what we asked for in prayer, it was a coincidence—it wasn't God—and the event we prayed for would have come to fruition through the flow of natural earthly processes whether we prayed or not.

Christians develop and employ excuses (what they call apologetics) to explain away some of the seeming failures of biblical Scriptures and their general interpretations when their expectations do not meet with their realities. There are Christian apologetic books numbering in the tens of thousands that attempt to explain away why, at times, God doesn't always intervene to help us. According to the BBS, these promises do not work for us because they do not apply to our dispensation. God doesn't dispense miracles in our current world. We should be living by grace through faith today, not miracles through faith. Although I must say, one could easily argue the BBS's position could be just another apologetic argument to explain why the prayer promises of Jesus fail today, but I find validity in their arguments. Their arguments completely agree with what I see as reality, that God is not active today. This inactivity also substantiates that Jesus only performed miracles to prove his divinity.

If Jesus performed miracles while standing on this planet, he would have successfully used them to convince others that he was God in the flesh and to draw thousands to hear his message–just as the NT tells us he did. Since the NT authors clearly tell us that Jesus completely delivered his message when he declared, "It is finished," what purpose would miracles serve today? Consider this: before Jesus came to Earth, he obviously was not performing miracles. The NT books do not mention Jesus performing miracles before he was born in the flesh. According to the NT, he did perform miracles while on Earth. After his death and departure from Earth, why would we continue to think or believe he continues to perform miracles today? God has obviously kept himself hidden from all mankind since the era of Jesus, and that's why we're required to extend faith in him. Again, we're supposed to be living by faith, not sight. If miraculous interventions were occurring today, who would need to extend faith in his existence?

The name-it-and-claim-it verses above need to be faced honestly so they have their full impact: namely that the prayer promises made by Jesus during his earthly ministry have nothing to do with the grace that God has dispensed for us today through Jesus's death and resurrection. Bereans argue that we simply can't go back to the so-called four Gospels or the early Acts period to find instructions for living in this current time, when we are only being dispensed biblical instructions and grace (God's forgiveness). They argue this is the reason why these prayer promises are not for today.

In biblical times, these promises functioned perfectly, and each had purpose. We can't just remove them from their era and expect them to be true today. But this is exactly what today's Christians continue to do. It seems to me that the BBS have formulated a perspective that meets with most of our realities, whether Christians are willing to accept it or not. Jesus's past prayer promises to the people of Israel do not function in our era.

As I mentioned previously, we have no way of knowing if any of the biblical miracles are factual. We can't know that Noah built an ark and filled it with pairs of every creature on Earth. Nor can we know with any certainty that Jesus healed anyone or was even resurrected. In reality, we are hoping and operating as if some of those biblical intervention claims are true—especially Jesus's resurrection and promise to forgive us.

I'm convinced godly interventions do not occur today. I make that claim by observation, cognition, and because I don't associate individual favoritism with God. I also reject current godly intervention because good solid evidence is nonexistent. It appears to me that misguided, biased, fallible humans make illusory correlations between good outcomes and godly activity to make themselves feel better.

Prayers for Peace and Strength

As I've mentioned, I do not believe God supernaturally provides a calming peace or strength to us through prayerful request. Neither does God offer these favors for someone else through any intercessory prayer on our part. There's no effectiveness to me saying to God "Please give Barry more strength to get through his situation" no matter how badly I want Barry's strength to increase. It would better serve Barry if I called or met with him and listened to his concerns, offered encouragement, and explained to him that I would be there for him in any way possible.

Social media sites are constantly loaded with people requesting prayers for their loved one whose life is in jeopardy. I see updates every day that include people telling the original poster they are praying for their loved one's healing. They may or may not include some of the prayer promises of Jesus. They may also include the phrase, "Sending thoughts and prayers," of course, often including the praying hands emoji. And I often wonder what percentage of those commentors actually set any time aside to ask for God's healing after claiming they will.

When the prayer requester's loved one dies and everyone realizes their prayers were ineffective in having God heal, the commenters redirect their prayers for God to provide peace and strength to the family members left behind. They seem to have forgotten their initial prayers for healing were not answered the way in which they asked. What would make them believe that God will now be actively providing peace and comfort to the family members when he didn't provide physical healing to their loved one? Did God choose to not intervene to heal their loved one, so later he could infuse the family with peace and strength at the request of those praying?

I always find it confusing when people tell me they've asked God (though prayer) for strength or peace during trying times and then report he did provide it. I've heard people say, "I never would have made it through that situation without the peace and strength God provided me during that horrible time." It's as if they are telling me, they may have committed suicide in their horrible circumstance had it not been for God providing the strength or the capacities to endure it.

The truth is, they most likely would have made it through that situation with or without that prayer request or the claimed provision from God. How do non-believers get through exceedingly difficult times in their lives? Do they face less pain and suffering in their lives than Christians?

I believe we are interpreting things backwards when it comes to these types of godly provisions. Rather than claiming, "God provided peace and strength," we should be claiming, "We have peace and strength because we are confident God has our back in the end." In doing so, we can feel a sense of comfort and peace because we're aligned with God.

Rather than claiming, "God is working things out for me behind the scenes which provides peace," we should be claiming, "We're doing our best during a trying time to use godly principles in our decisions and actions." In that way, it helps us sort through our difficult circumstances in a moral and godly manner. In the aftermath of our circumstance, we will have exercised our faith muscles by clinging to God as we persevered through a trying time—irrespective of the outcome.

By applying this method in our lives, we can feel a sense of peace and comfort because, irrespective of our circumstances, we will remain loyal and committed to God. This is what the author of Job was saying and how the fictional character Job eventually found peace when facing his trials. Even when an undeserving Job believed God was destroying his life, he remained faithful to God. Let's be the Jobs of our era and abandon the notion that God is selectively providing these spiritual favors to the select few. If God loves all of his creation, it's unlikely he's providing spiritual wave packets of peace and strength to some but not others.

[17] When Two or More . . .

WHEN I USED TO ATTEND A COUPLES' SMALL GROUP, WE would participate in a Bible study or watch a video of a popular Christian speaker of the leader's choice. We always saved the last thirty minutes of our study for prayer requests—sharing our struggles and concerns for ourselves and our families. Upon the conclusion of our sharing time, our leader would re-recite our requests and concerns in a formal prayer for relief directly to God.

Perhaps group members felt better upon hearing another member ask for God's favor on their behalf and it seemed more powerful when we all bowed our heads in unison. But should we believe the outcome of a specific prayer would be any different if we simply expressed our concerns for each person's needs and told each other that we will be carrying some of their burdens? When we have big problems that are not within our control like a terminal illness or a drug-addicted child, that's when we feel we should gather in group prayer to ask God for help. Again, I think it's great when people make their requests known to God, albeit doing it a group setting is no more effective than making those requests to God alone or not making any requests. But many people who pray in a group falsely carry greater expectations and believe God is more likely to act on these prayers than what one offers in solitude.

Although Pastor Rick Warren admits he's unable to understand how it works, he argues group prayers are much more powerful and effective than praying alone. Again, he cites biblical reasoning because he, along with most

Christians, believes all reasoning offered in the New Testament applies to us today. This false reasoning regarding group prayer drives intervention-believing Christians to recruit as many people as possible into their prayer rally when there are earthly problems with no simple or practical solutions.

From his Daily Hope email broadcast[35], Pastor Warren says,

> To get through what you're going through, you need to recruit other people to pray for you.
>
> This is very easy when you're in a small group. When you're going through a tough time and you're not in a small group, *you are unprotected*. You don't have the strength that people in a small group do because you don't have people praying for you.
>
> Paul says in 2 Corinthians 1:11 (NLT), "You are helping us by praying for us. Then many people will give thanks because God has graciously answered so many prayers for our safety." (Emphasis mine.)

Did Paul have this correct, or was he simply wanting to have more followers or supporters who were emotionally supporting his efforts? The disciples who suffered torturous deaths apparently did not receive any help from God when others prayed for them. Warren continues,

> I'll be honest with you: I don't know how this works. But there is additional power in group prayer that is not there when you just pray for yourself. There is more power in group prayer than in the single power of you praying for yourself.
>
> The Bible says, "If any two agree as touching anything it shall be done" and "Where two or more are gathered in my name, there am I in the midst of them" (Matthew 18:19–20 KJV).

35.　Rick Warren, Daily Hope email broadcast, "The Power in Group Prayer." Moved to https://www.danielplan.com/the-power-in-group-prayer/.

Christians plaster social media sites daily requesting prayer for their friends or loved ones because they sincerely believe there's a better chance to receive what they ask for when a request is made by a group, as Pastor Warren suggests. For many, the intensity and power level to entice God to act through prayer is directly proportional to the number of petitionary participants.

Christians solicit as many prayers as possible—as if they're circulating a political petition that requires x number of signatures. Does God have a prayer count threshold before choosing to intervene? Or does God have some method unknown to us that calculates the total measure of faith for each supplicant, and after averaging that number, decide whether to intervene? I don't think it works this way.

I found another meme on social media that showed a surgeon in his scrubs standing in the lobby facing a man whose wife had just passed away. The surgeon says to the man, "I'm sorry Mr. Henderson, we were just two Facebook prayers short of saving your wife." This is not an attempt to make light of a situation like this, yet this is how many Christians seem to view this subject when recruiting people to pray for healing.

What Christians truly accomplish when making these public requests is attracting sympathizers—which I think is a healthy practice. It's a way to let a large audience of their friends and family know about their difficult circumstance. There is something therapeutic when we reveal our burdens to others and receive sympathy that comforts and connects us to them. But coupling that sympathy with hope for potential godly intervention leads to false expectations and potential future disappointments for others.

I sent a text to one of my cancer-stricken loved ones last week. This relative knows my positions on godly inactivity. She was having an MRI of her brain that morning to determine if her cancer had spread. I texted, "Good morning. I know you're having your MRI today, and I just want you to know I'll be thinking about you and carrying some of your fears and concerns deep within me. You know I won't be making a formal request to God to heal or provide good test results, but please don't mistake that for how much I love you and want your test results to be good."

What's the difference between my message listed above and prayers requesting godly intervention with or without the little praying hands emoji? My heartfelt message shows my love for my family member and is centered in the realities of this world. Invoking God into the equation in some ways accomplishes the very same thing, but it contradicts reality and has the potential to create false hope. If I would have told my loved one I was praying and asking God for good test results, and the results indicated her cancer spread, she would only be able to conclude that God rejected everyone's prayers for her. The message I sent her could never cause that.

So, let's get back to our couple's small group. When the leader prays, he usually starts each subject of concern with, "We pray for Johnny to find employment, Cindy's uncle's cancer to be cured, Billy's medical test to be negative and that he will feel peace while waiting on the test results, Sandy's son to overcome his meth addiction, safety during Steve's family's vacation and that you (God) will watch over them."

I've been involved in enough group prayer sessions to know these group prayers are no more effective than individual prayers, or not praying at all. If we really believed there was any merit in group prayer, why is it our nation never makes any positive progress when millions of Christians unite on the National Day of Prayer? If there was any truth in this notion, we could get a group together and pray for everyone's diseases to be cured.

I recall one of our group members texting the entire group, asking us all to pray for her boyfriend to get a lucrative business deal. She texted the following: "Hi everyone. My boyfriend has the potential to land a huge national advertising client. He has his proposal in and is waiting to hear from them. Please pray that he gets it!!!!"

Her text was followed with a flood of texts by the other group members with things like "Praying for him," "I'm on it," "That's so exciting, I'm praying now," etc. etc. I replied with, "I'm rooting for him to get that deal."

I didn't invoke God into the equation because I personally don't think God manipulates the outcomes of business transactions. I'm sure the other group members saw my "rooting" text as being negative because I wasn't calling on God to get the deal finalized.

I speculate there have been many times when a group member has not included me in their group text prayer requests. They probably feel like they would be wasting their time since they know I wouldn't ask God to help them. Ironically, I do want to know when friends have life problems because I would like to offer my concern and comfort, and maybe even a potential solution when possible. But that doesn't seem good enough for their life problems. They need someone who's going to pray and get God moving for their benefit. Concern and comfort from me probably won't fix anything.

I understand her and her boyfriend really wanted this deal. All of us in the group wanted him to get that deal. But I couldn't help asking myself, "Is this the way God operates?" Does God really care or favor some people through seeing that someone gains a lucrative business deal over the needs of so many others on this Earth?

Perhaps you're thinking, "Maybe God has a reason to see he gets or doesn't get the deal. God's reasons to act or not act may have a bigger purpose that we just don't understand." Maybe God knew if he helped our group member get the deal, he would give away some portion of his earnings to the needy. Or maybe God wouldn't allow him to get the deal because he suspects the group member will do something immoral with his earnings. Sure, these two speculations are possibilities, but how are we to ascertain the truth in either scenario? The answer is we cannot, unless we believe that God is constantly manipulating the outcomes of earthly events. If that's the case, again our free will would be compromised, making us puppets acting out God's scripted desires.

It turned out the boyfriend did land that lucrative deal. When the announcement came by another group text, it was returned with texts from some of the members with, "God is good!" "Praise God," "God is faithful,"

"God still answers prayer," etc. Without evidence connecting God to the favorable outcome and never considering their prayers simply were synchronous with what would have played out even without prayer, they gave God the glory.

Of course, I'll never be able to know if he received that job because of God's handiwork or if it really was solely because of his skills and abilities. My logic and reasoning tell me it was the latter. If no one would have prayed, would his skills and abilities have been minimized and therefore his proposal rejected by his client? After all, her boyfriend had already submitted his proposal before our group prayed, so our prayers could not have affected the contents of his proposal unless God later "doctored" them up. Or perhaps our group's prayers caused God to coerce the big client to select her boyfriend's proposal.

I'm not saying the concerns of so many are not legitimate or important, because I know they are—especially to the requestor. We all struggle during our lifetime with so many different needs, but we shouldn't expect God to fix our problems through prayer. The best that I can do is offer whatever love, support, and encouragement I can to the members of my group for the things I can reasonably help with. For the struggles I cannot remedy, cancer for example, I can only offer my love and a servant's heart. I cannot do anything about their cancer, but I can do things to offer comfort. I can take time to listen to their concerns, bring them meals, or mow their lawn as they go through their treatment.

Let's look again at Matthew 18:19–20: "If two of you agree on earth about anything that they may ask, it shall be done for them by My Father who is in heaven. For where two or three have gathered together in My name, I am there in their midst" (NASB).

You'll note, again, there are no conditions on this biblical passage. One cannot explain it away by saying the Christian God is or was not viewed as a name-it-and-claim-it kind of God. Jesus seemed to be that kind of God when he lived on this Earth. Many argue we should take it in context with the entire Bible and not as an excerpt from the individual book of Matthew. Others say God doesn't operate that way as a whole and direct us to gather teachings on prayer from the other books of the Bible. Maybe the proponents of "context" theories don't realize that the author of Matthew didn't write what Jesus said within the context of other NT biblical books apart from the Hebrew Scriptures. There was only one other NT gospel book, Mark, in circulation at the time of Matthew's writing. The gospel books of Luke and John came later. There was no other context for the author Matthew to be concerned with.

Can you imagine what it would have been like if Jesus told the people during his era that he would provide them what they asked for in group prayer, as he reportedly did, but then rejected those requests? We know we don't always get what we ask for 2,000 years later, so doesn't that lend itself more towards Jesus's prayer promises (individual and group) applying only to people when he was here on Earth? And, if true, doesn't that give merit to the notion that prayers that God seems to answer happen simply by coincidence? The author, Matthew, supposedly quoted Jesus for that time and place, and the author reported that Jesus did heal people who asked him. Why would we think he continues to perform miracles? I suggest it's only because we want it to be so.

I believe the author of Matthew intended to write exactly what he wrote because he witnessed Jesus provide favor to those who asked him. Most Christians today think this continues to work in our era because they want or even need to believe it. Perhaps they never selfishly request to receive a Mercedes or a mansion, but they want to believe in a compassionate God who will come to their aid in life and death situations. In my mind, Matthew 18:19–20 tells us it only takes a minimum of two people to get God moving, and this condition should guarantee that we will have our prayers answered affirmatively. I also believe if this were ever true, it could only have been true during the earthly life of Jesus.

As I've gone through great pain to establish, we do not always get what we ask for through prayerful request, and we never get what we ask for because our God actively manipulated a circumstance with his supernatural powers. Again, Jesus claimed he produced miracles for those in his presence to bring glory to the Father and to show that he was God in the flesh. The Gospels say that he healed the sick, walked on water, and even raised the dead. These miracles helped to support his claim that he was the true God who came to Earth to save mankind.

Jesus also said, "'Believe me when I say that I am in the Father and the Father is in me; or *at least believe on the evidence of the works themselves*'" (John 14:11, emphasis mine). Apparently, Jesus needed the skeptics of his time to see his miraculous power to convince them of his divinity. But Jesus's miracles did more than just support his divine claims. Jesus's miracles provided an audience for his message. Some came to see Jesus drawn by the prospect of seeing or receiving a miracle. When they came, Jesus capitalized on the opportunity and taught them how they should live and the good news of salvation.

Here's another possible clue to help us understand that miracles would be ending after his earthly era. Jesus told Thomas, "'Because you have seen me [alive after my resurrection], you have believed; blessed are those who have not seen and yet have believed'" (John 20:29).

I think Jesus may have been also speaking to us while speaking to Thomas. "Thomas, you are fortunate and have believed and feel satisfied because you have witnessed my miracles and resurrection with your own eyes. You didn't need faith to believe who I claimed to be because you were an observer to everything. You've seen the scars in my hands, and now see that I am alive again. But those who have not witnessed my resurrection (during this time and all future generations after I leave this Earth), they will be blessed as well—even without witnessing my resurrection or seeing any miracles during their lifetime."

Is it possible Jesus was telling Thomas and all future generations that the miracle days were coming to an end and the real blessing to future generations would be only his gracious sacrifice? My observations in life tell me this is exactly what Jesus was proclaiming.

What did Jesus tell the Pharisees (Jewish religious leaders) when they asked him to perform a miracle? "He answered, 'A wicked and adulterous generation asks for a sign!'" (Matthew 12:39). But Christians continue to prayerfully ask for signs and miracles today—most with pure motives.

What did Jesus tell the royal official in Galilee when the official asked Jesus to heal his son in Capernaum? "'Unless you people see signs and wonders,' Jesus told him, 'you will never believe'" (John 4:48). When the royal official heard of the healing upon arriving at home, only then did he and his family genuinely believe.

What did Paul tell us in 2 Corinthians 5:7? "For we live by faith, not by sight." Again, if miracles were happening today and we could clearly observe them, we wouldn't need faith in the existence or divinity of Jesus.

What do these passages indicate to us? We should seek to experience God by exercising our faith in the risen Jesus and not by observing physical signs and miraculous healings. If you agree, then there is no logical reason to expect God to act on our behalf through prayer. We should exercise faith and hope in God's existence and the death and resurrection of Jesus that saves us from our sin, not the potential for present-day relief.

Wouldn't it have been great if, after his resurrection, Jesus explicitly came out and said, "Listen up, my brethren. I'm leaving this Earth, and there will be no more miracles until the day I return to establish my kingdom." If Jesus made that claim, Christians would not be recruiting us for prayer or bombarding all comers with active godly claims of favor today. Many non-believers would never feel a desire to avoid God because they would never have to reconcile any current miracle claims. I certainly wouldn't be typing right now—at least not about this subject.

If Jesus would have been explicit in that way, Christian prayers today would not include requests. Their prayers would be centered on expressing their grateful hearts to God for his creation and sacrifice. For me, that's the way it should be.

I have thought about these supposed name-it-and-claim-it prayer promises for many years. Both "baby" Christians and those with deep faith should know these verses cannot be true for us today. These verses are also not dependent upon God deciding to act or not act based on his desires or the number of people making requests. In the early years of my Christian faith, I prayed with a lot more than just two people for cancers to be remediated and for marriages to survive, and yet the heavens were silent.

I concluded that my theology was wrong, and it needed to be corrected to match reality. No longer could I try to convince myself or others that God was acting in order to make some of us happy, or not acting to teach us a lesson—all to fall in line with his supposed desires or plans.

[18] Christian Apologetic Theory for Answered Prayer

CHRISTIANS HAVE A THEORY REGARDING HOW GOD answers our prayers and attempts to explain why our prayers don't always get answered on time or affirmatively. They claim he does so with one of the following three answers:

1. **Yes!** We ask for something and God supernaturally provides in a timely manner.

2. **Slow.** His answer is coming, but not immediately. We'll need to wait for God's timing because of his unknown greater plan for us or others. Our request could negatively affect someone else's life circumstance. So, we don't receive the answer on our timeline.

3. **No!** The door has obviously been shut, and we will not receive what we have requested. And because God loves us, he must have good reason for denial. Our request was never in line with his plans.

Keep in mind that one may need to go through answer #2 (slow) for some undetermined span of time before he provides them with either answer #1 (yes) or answer #3 (no) above. If #2 (slow) never comes to fruition during one's lifetime, then #2 (slow) defaults to #3 (no). So, given a person's lifespan and assuming the prayer is personally for themselves, there are only two possible outcomes to prayer. At some point, it's either you do get what you ask for, or you don't. At first glance, and notwithstanding circumstantial probability differentials, it's effectively a 50–50 proposition. I'll provide reasoning later indicating the actual average odds of someone perceiving to receive what they ask for in prayer are much lower than 50% because most Christians only make requests to God for the improbable circumstances they cannot control.

But I would like to show you that "Yes, No, Slow" is an errant theory for attempting to explain how God operates. The three answered prayer outcomes above are the only possible outcomes even if God doesn't exist. With or without prayer, or God for that matter, or even if you're only a believer in the tooth fairy, one of those three answers will come to fruition in any life circumstance we desire.

The bigger question is, who believes that God through prayer alters what might have happened had one not prayed? Would God's present concern or love for us have been diminished had we or our loved ones not prayed for an intervention? If God is active, and his will is going to be done no matter what we pray—as many Christians believe—then why would we believe our prayers could entice God to act in the way we asked for?

Perhaps our only prayer in any circumstance should be, "Your will be done, Lord," as we accept the fact that God's will is to allow this Earth to run its course through our freewilled choices absent intervention. If we take that position, then we're effectively saying, "We're willing to accept any circumstance this physical world offers us because the outcome of any event will only be controlled by those world forces." What we hope for in any life circumstance, without prayer requests, the natural world will offer us one of the same three answers that Christians claim God provides. And those answers will come non-supernaturally, by the intentions and actions for those involved in creating those outcomes.

The STEP Prayer Study

Many scientific studies have been conducted on the efficacy of prayer dating back to the late 1800s. I'd like to focus on the most recent extensive study conducted in 2006. It was called the *Study of the Therapeutic Effects of Intercessory Prayer*, referred to as (STEP)[36]. The longitudinal study took ten years and $2.4 million to complete, underwritten primarily by the John Templeton Foundation, a supporter of studies that explore the intersection between religion and science. To date, this has been the largest and most comprehensive study ever conducted on the efficacy of prayer.

A group of 1,802 patients, all admitted for coronary artery bypass graft surgery, were divided into three randomized groups. Two of the groups received prayer from committed Christians with experience praying for the sick. But only one group's members knew they were being prayed for. The result: The group whose members knew they were being prayed for did slightly worse in terms of post-operative complications (59%) than those whose members were unsure if they were receiving prayer. The knowledge that they were being prayed for by an exclusive group of intercessors, or the prayers they received on their behalf seemed to have a slight though unremarkable negative effect on their health.

The two groups that were unaware if they were receiving prayer were also compared. One group received prayer (the same group mentioned above), while the other did not. This time, the group that received prayer experienced slightly more major complications (52 %) than the group without additional prayer (51%). In other words, the study seemed to show that prayer—at least prayer from a large group of strangers—had no beneficial effects. The results were disappointing to those who had hoped to see the positive effects of additional intercessory prayer.

As a side note, there are some mainstream Christians who discredit the qualifications of the people who performed the prayer for this study. Many of the prayer participants in the study were all from a Unitarian sect of Christianity. Because some of their doctrines do not conform to standard tenets, some mainstream Christians do not believe the study to be

---

36.   Herbert Benson, et. al., "Study of the Therapeutic Effects of Intercessory Prayer (STEP) in Cardiac Bypass Patients," *American Heart Journal* 151, no. 4, April 2006: 934–42, doi.org/10.1016/j.ahj.2005.05.028. Retrieved March 2014.

credible. I find this arrogant, to say the least. How can any of these main-stream Christians know the integrity or the true desires of the people who prayed or just how much they wanted their prayers to be effective? If God is active, would he care or decide to act or not act based on the supplicant's religious foundation? If God answers prayer, and if the people praying were Mormon, would God not take to heart the passion with which they prayed and their desire to help the patient?

The study's actual conclusion is that there is no effect on those who were prayed for since the statistical variances were so small. Can you imagine what we would have heard from those who believe that prayer affects the outcomes of healing if the study would have concluded that 95% of those who were blindly prayed for had completely recovered from their illnesses with no complications? Many miracle believers aware of the studies like STEP will quote Matthew 4:7, "'Do not put the Lord your God to the test'" as justification for the study's conclusion that prayer showed no positive effect. But I believe if the study would have showed a favorable outcome confirming their belief that God through prayer can bring healing, then they would say it was ok for them to test God in that way.

The famed British author and former atheist convert to Christianity, C.S. Lewis, predicted in the 1950s that there would be more extensive prayer studies in the future, but he did not think they would show any positive, measurable "results." He argued such an approach to prayer acts "as if it were magic, or a machinated—something that functions automatically." Lewis argued such attempts always end up trying to measure something more like magic than a real movement of God. But for me, facts are facts, and I surmise Lewis did not want to face the fact that a future study like STEP would have an outcome that did not favor an active prayer-answering God.

I wonder if Lewis would have been willing to tell the families of those who died during the study that God was withholding his divine healing from their loved one because it was all part of a prayer study. With all due respect to Mr. Lewis, and I have great respect for that man and what he stood for, most

Christians would rather look for an apologetic reason to explain away why some biblical interpretations fail rather than accept the statistical outcomes of a study like this. They will rely on scientific evidence in so many other areas of their lives, but not for scientific evidence like STEP. They'll defend positions like these to the bitter end rather than being ok with accepting that that most Christians are misapplying portions of Scripture and that miracles have not occurred since the era of Jesus. I find freedom in accepting that, in places, the Bible isn't always correct, or that God is not intervening today. Yet others will continue to hold on to the notion of biblical inerrancy and hope for godly intervention at all costs—even when science refutes biblical positions or the interpretations that have been derived from those positions.

Praying According to His Will

The Bible tells us God's ways are higher than our ways and his thoughts are not our thoughts. If God is active, how are we to pray for things that are according to God's will if understanding his will is something above our intellectual paygrade? Are we unable to know his will because only he can see the big picture, as so many claim, and we as mere mortals are incapable of determining what's best for humanity as a whole?

I read a Christian apologetic book that used the following analogy to differentiate between our perspective and God's perspective. Imagine you are a sergeant in the marine corps, and you and your platoon of fifty men are engaged in battle with the enemy. Before you know it, artillery is raining down on you, and you realize the bombs are coming from your own army ten miles behind you. Your men are being killed and wounded, so you immediately radio the artillery brigade and tell them you are being destroyed by friendly fire and demand they cease bombing. Your commander informs you that they cannot stop sending the artillery because there's a cache of enemy weapons located exactly where you are, and the enemy, less than a mile away, is attempting to retrieve it. He tells you there are so many weapons buried in your location, your country could lose the entire war if the enemy retrieves them. The commander tells you to do your best to fall back and navigate what's left of your men to a safer location.

The analogy here is that you as a soldier do not have the same information or perspective as the commander (God). It's unfortunate that you and your men may need to be sacrificed, but the commander needs to ensure the enemy does not retrieve that huge stockpile of weapons. Your commander (God) is concerned about the big picture (winning the war) and less about your well-being. He hates to be responsible for the death of your men, but the mission / plan or, "his will," is to win the war at all costs. And "his will" be done.

As I've been arguing, everything that happens on this Earth is "God's will": free-willed human intention and the random outcomes of our chaotic world. Those intentions and outcomes may not be "his desires," but they must be his will, because he is allowing this world to run its course. Since most of us believe that he has the power to force his desires, most Christians expect his intervention to carry out his plans to see his desires come to fruition. But as I mentioned earlier, this is how I see it:

> *God's will is simply the outcomes of free-willed human choices and the results of the natural laws and randomness of our physical world.*

If you're an interventionist, and you say that God's will is being carried out through some form of intervention on our planet, then you must be saying God is responsible for the earthly chaos we experience. If, as I suggest, God's will is only to allow for our free-willed choices and this Earth to run its course, then we are responsible for most of the mess that's being made here on Earth. I'm asking you again to look around this globe. Does it look like the God described in Scriptures is supernaturally intervening today? If the events of this world are caused by his interventive will, shouldn't we expect better outcomes?

Is it possible that it's God's will that a man rapes a woman? Rapes occur in our world by the thousands daily. Is an earthquake that causes a tsunami which kills 230,000 people God's will? It happened in December of 2004, and they've occurred since the beginning of time. How about the Holocaust? Was it God's will for six million Jews to be exterminated during the early to mid-1940s? We all want to believe that these events were not God's desires, but didn't all the above listed tragedies have to be his will? If not, wouldn't he have stepped in and altered the course or outcomes of those events? With this line of reasoning, it must be God's will that 24,000 people die every day from malnutrition. If it wasn't his will, God would feed them. I'm fairly sure it's not God's desire that so many starve, but it must be his will to allow it because this is the suffering occurring on this planet.

Since I'm convinced God's will is our will, praying according to God's will is effectively our willingness to accept the natural event outcomes (not caused by God) occurring on this Earth.

[19] Prayers for Healing

WE BRIEFLY TOUCHED ON THE HEALING REMEDY VERSES
from the biblical book of James, but I'd like to provide more detail. Some
people argue the following verses only apply to spiritual healing, but I do
not think that is the correct interpretation, and it's obvious most Christians
don't interpret it that way either. Many churches today practice this method,
prayer along with "anointing with oil" to bring about physical healings. But it
should be our common reality that refutes these verses because prayer studies
like STEP mentioned previously clearly show this methodology is no better
than not praying at all.

> Is anyone among you in trouble? Let them pray. Is anyone happy? Let
> them sing songs of praise. Is anyone among you sick? Let them call
> the elders of the church to pray over them and anoint them with oil
> in the name of the Lord. And the prayer offered in faith will make the
> sick person well; the Lord will raise them up. If they have sinned, they
> will be forgiven. Therefore confess your sins to each other and pray
> for each other so that you may be healed. The prayer of a righteous
> person is powerful and effective. (James 5:13–16)

I have witnessed the aftermaths of many ailing people anointed with
oil and prayed over by elders within the churches I have attended, and the
statistical outcomes have not been as favorable as James 5:13–16 suggests.
Either the author of these verses was not correct when he suggested there
will be a favorable outcome, or perhaps the elders praying were deficient

in righteousness and therefore not powerful and effective. Or these favors were only applicable in the era of Jesus. You should also note that nowhere in those verses does James say a prayer of this type requires God's will to make it come to fruition. To me, this is yet another claim by superstitious men from thousands of years ago who believed this methodology would be effective for healing the afflicted.

Let's not forget that men from the biblical era also casted lots (like rolling dice or flipping a coin) to find godly answers to specific questions. It was believed God would line up the lot in a certain way to help one make the right decision that would be in line with God's will or desires. We don't use this superstitious way of making decisions today because we know they are not effective and certainly not a method employed by God to deliver messages. They most likely never were.

The fact is, today, most of us rely on medical science to remedy our illnesses. Yes, many pray for God to help them, but they place higher confidence in medicine than in believing God will heal them. There are a few people who refuse medical treatment and rely only on God to save them from disease, but that's an exceedingly small camp. That camp shrinks every time someone like that gets seriously ill.

Jehovah's Witnesses will allow medical attention for their loved ones if blood transfusions are not required. They will allow their family member to die if a blood transfusion is needed because they interpret the same Christian Bible differently than most other Christian sects. They consider blood to be sacred, neither to be ingested or transfused.

As I briefly discussed, before the advent of the polio vaccine, there were millions of expectant mothers on their knees praying to God that their newborn children would not contract polio. Not long after 1953 when the vaccine was introduced, the numbers of new polio cases dropped off immensely, and today the disease within the United States has effectively been eradicated. Did God invent the new vaccine, or did he lead the inventor Jonas Salk to it? If God had anything to do with the timing or the discovery itself, what are we to think about the millions before that time who became paralyzed or died from that horrific disease? Why did God wait if he was behind the scientist's discovery in the early 1950s?

If a Christian or their loved one was diagnosed with cancer, and they were forced to choose between medicine and prayer, there's no question most, if not nearly all, would choose medicine. Faced with a medical emergency, most people call 911, and an ambulance takes them directly to the emergency room of a hospital. I've never heard of anyone experiencing a medical emergency asking the ambulance driver to take them or their loved one to a church to be placed in front of a praying clergyman. Why do you suppose that is? Isn't it simply that we have more confidence and realistic hope in medical science than we do in God solving our medical emergencies or illnesses? Christians have more faith in medicine than in God, and we should know that because every Christian who can afford health insurance pays for it.

But, when the chips are down and we have no control (waiting on a medical test, standing over a loved one in a coma, a rebellious child has committed a heinous crime), we want to believe God can offer help in our helplessness. It's many people's last straw. Or, as my mother-in-law so eloquently said to me after I asked her if she believed God heals people from disease through prayer, "Probably not, but it's worth a shot to ask him."

My mother-in-law's comment reminded me of a Jim Carrey line from the movie *Dumb and Dumber*, "So, you're saying there's a chance." People seem to make prayers of request to God like it's a potential insurance policy of some sort. If the doctors can't help someone, then maybe calling on God will offer some backup coverage, and we'll have both bases covered.

However, most Christians continue to add prayer to their healing regimen and claim that both medical science and prayer can be equally effective. For some, God even manipulates the hands of certain specialty surgeons to ensure that the medical procedure is carried out to perfection. I've also heard many ask God to provide wisdom to the doctor during the treatment of their loved one. Forget the surgeon's experience and medical training, as if that's not the main reason they selected a specific doctor. If God is involved in manipulating surgeons, why don't we just hire an auto mechanic and pray over him so that God will make sure their loved one's surgery is successful? Don't we choose the surgeon with the best qualifications and experience in dealing with the disease we are trying to remediate? We do our homework and ask others for referrals to make sure the surgeon we hire has the knowledge and the expertise to maximize our chance of a good outcome. This is logical, and for those who are able to be selective, I think this is how it plays out. There's a logical reason we don't hire and pray over kindergarten teachers to perform open heart surgeries.

Here in Las Vegas, it's common knowledge that we lack "good" local specialty research and treatment hospitals. Many of my friends facing life-threatening diseases have always looked for better hospitals and treatment options in places like California or Arizona. I don't blame them for doing so, but if God is actively healing people, why couldn't they just seek "decent" treatment here, and have God cover the potential insufficiencies through prayer?

Care over Prayer

Personally, I would rather have someone tell me they are thinking and concerned about me when they are aware that I am in the middle of a health crisis—rather than prayerfully invoke God to heal me. I'd prefer they just tell me they care about me or ask me if there's something practical they can do to help me when I am in need. I've had people tell me they are carrying some of my burdens with them as I go through medical testing, and I've appreciated that. I'm thankful when they check in on me during trying times like that.

I do want to mention what I believe to be a potential benefit that "prayer" can offer, but only if those prayers are not petitioning God to act. I know that sounds foreign to Christians because again, for most Christians, prayer is synonymous with making requests to God. But I contend that even non-requesting prayers with or for others unlocks our empathy towards those who are suffering. Telling someone we are caring for them from our heart is an expression of love that binds us to that person and their suffering. It can be viewed as a sacred act of kindness even if we're simply telling the person we're thinking about them and carrying their burdens. It's what I was trying to convey to my loved one who was having her MRI that I previously mentioned. In Galatians 6:2, Paul wrote, "Carry each other's burdens, and in this way you will fulfill the law of Christ." If God is love, and caring (physically or in thought) for others is an act of love, then in some way our caring for others connects us all to God and each other in a personal way.

Admittedly, it's humbling when someone thinks enough of me to go to the creator of the universe and is willing to ask for help on my behalf. I know their intentions are good, and I don't want to argue with them that there's no solution there. I have come to the place that when a friend is struggling with a serious health crisis, I don't try to prayerfully fix them anymore. I don't try to help them see a bright side past what medical science can offer or try to make them feel more hope for survival. I have their back while they're here, and God will have their back when they leave here. I just want to make sure they know I'm present with them.

When I pray for someone who is ill, it is not with the intent to have God alter his obvious stance to allow life's events to run their course. I might pray something like:

God, we are committed to accepting any possible outcome for Justin. We are relying on medical advancements to either cure or manage this disease and are completely relying on you for our eternity. No matter how this turns out, along this journey we will continue to align ourselves in accordance with your precepts and values and the love you displayed on that cross. We know you are not involved in life and death matters on this Earth, and we willingly submit ourselves to that understanding and always to you. We love Justin, and as much as we want him to be fully restored physically, all our hope is in eternity with you. We have a confident assurance (faith) you didn't create humankind to eventually discard it.

It's difficult for me to admit this, but I only pray like that when I'm alone. As much as I'd like to say an honest prayer like that with others who are sick, I won't do it. I know my ill family member or friend doesn't want to hear an honest prayer like that. They and their family want a prayer that gives them hope for survival. The type of prayer mentioned above doesn't offer any extra earthly hope to the sick, but I contend it also has zero potential to hurt either the patient or their loved ones if things start to go downhill. And at some point, in everyone's life, things will go downhill. Whether the family is relying on the misapplied prayer promises of Jesus or simply hoping that God will perform a miracle, people will certainly wonder why God didn't offer help if their loved one dies.

Let's take the onus away from God for physical healing—which in turn will take away the potential for our own frustration when we just can't make sense of why it didn't prayerfully go our way. If we take the position that God is not involved in these matters, then we can make complete logical sense of all outcomes. Losing a loved one is hard enough without adding greater disappointment when people feel God has abandoned them.

And exactly what is the purpose of asking God to heal someone, and what or who might we be trying to save them from? If you think about this a little deeper, and either you or your ailing loved one has any hope or faith in eternity with God, as every Christian will tell you they do, doesn't it appear as if we are trying to save our loved one from God? Are our prayers not an attempt to keep our loved one away from a paradise that we all claim to desire? I know our interest in offering healing prayers to others has the following three components:

1. We don't want to be separated from our loved ones, and we don't know how we'll be able to carry on in life without them.

2. We need to give them hope because it will be even more difficult for all of us when there is no hope for survival.

3. We know our loved one carries some measure of uncertainty about what the future will be in a place they have no familiarity with.

We all can say that we hope for some heavenly realm in eternity with God, but none of us knows with certainty if that place exists or what it will be like if or when we get there. Some Christians are also concerned whether they are qualified to get there. The unknown after death creates some measure of anxiety for all of us.

If one believes that prayer can heal people from disease, why do they or their loved ones only pray for the single person who is sick? If we sincerely believe God really heals, why don't we ask God to heal everyone in the world who is stricken with disease? Doesn't it seem a bit selfish to only be praying for the person we care about?

There are many purported medical miracle stories out there for us to ponder, but to me, they are just stories. And I am certain that many readers here will have a plethora of medical miracle stories to attempt to refute my positions. I've heard the holy water—or miracle oil—in conjunction with prayer stories many times. I have heard the stories of medically confirmed tumors mysteriously disappearing. But show me the evidence that validates these "miracles" are from the active hands of God who answers prayers, and I'll readily provide the statistical evidence that clearly shows prayed-for Christians fare no better than non-believers with the same disease. In 2020, prayed for Christians and non-Christians were being infected and dying at the same rate from the coronavirus. This data reflects not just my reality but our common realities—even if some refuse to believe it.

Why Won't God Heal Amputees?

Many years ago, I stumbled on an intriguing website titled, Why Won't God Heal Amputees?[37] It was authored by a prominent non-believer named Marshall Brain, who also is the founder of the TV show, *How Stuff Works*. Although I completely agree with his example of amputees never regenerating their limbs by prayerful request nor anyone being cured from a disease by prayer, I reject his overall conclusion that God is imaginary.

Why Won't God Heal Amputees contains some very juicy claims I believe are founded in truth. The website poses an important question, "How is it that so many people are supposedly healed by God from so many different diseases, and yet, there's never been one recorded case of an amputee miraculously regenerating their missing limb by prayerful request?" It certainly makes one think deeply about reported medical miracle claims by Christians and why God would seemingly ignore the needs of the amputee.

Do Christian amputees or their families pray for God to regenerate limbs? Perhaps they don't. But why not? Shouldn't amputees and their families pray to God for a restored limb just as those with cancer pray to be healed? Christians always pray for God's involvement and oversight when their loved ones are only having a simple procedure like a gall bladder removal or a knee replacement. And we know Christians consistently give thanks to God when simple surgeries like those go well. They'll tell everyone that God's hands were actively involved.

Does God not care for the amputee as he has supposedly cared for and cured so many others with different forms of cancer? Every Christian will tell you they believe God can do anything, so restoring a limb shouldn't be any more difficult for God than removing cancer. Amputees must wonder why they are excluded. Is God more compassionate towards select cancer patients than he is with amputees? Have you ever heard of a child born with a cleft

37.   Marshall Brain, "Chapter 5 – Why Won't God Heal Amputees?" Why Won't God Heal Amputees, https://whywontgodhealamputees.com/god5.htm. Used by permission. Retrieved February 2014.

pallet miraculously healed through prayer? Has prayer ever caused God to reorient the genetic codes of a child born with Down syndrome?

Unlike a cancer patient receiving chemo, radiation, surgery, and prayer, there's no unknown mystery for the amputee. We would all be able to observe the results of a miraculously regenerated limb. Multitudes of people can pray their hearts out to God for an amputee to regenerate a limb, but we know it will never occur. As I previously mentioned, so many people make their miracle claims after receiving medical treatment and prayer, but no one can know with absolute certainty if it was really God or medicine. Christians must love to say it was God, and this claim cannot be disproven because the miracle cannot be substantiated nor refuted by observation.

But again, we do have statistics that clearly show no favor to prayed-for Christians over non-believers. We also have statistics from the past that clearly show decreasing morbidity rates for many diseases over the past thirty years, and not coincidentally, we've had incredible medical advancements during that period.

With the amputee, there's nothing to debate and certainly no mystery. They will remain limbless for the remainder of their lives. Prayer won't reverse birth defects, and yet people continue to attach themselves to the false notion that prayer is effective in remediating diseases. It seems to me that Christians who claim divine healing tend to pray for results that are observably indeterminate but have little or no interest in praying for anything where outcomes would be plainly obvious to everyone.

The author of the website Why Won't God Heal Amputees quotes many Scriptures, and most quotations are the name-it-and-claim-it type that we have previously discussed[38]. He uses these Christian Scriptures to solidify that God does not honor Jesus's supposed promises, thus the Bible is not inerrant, leading to his conclusion that God is imaginary. He quotes the following Scriptures in the NKJV translation, and I'm purposely including

---

38.   Such as Matthew 18:19; 21:22; Mark 11:24.

them again as well as a few additional verses for readers who are not that familiar with them:

> "Ask and it will be given you; seek and you will find; knock and it will be opened to you. For everyone who asks receives, and he who seeks finds, and to him who knocks it will be opened. Or what man is there among you, if his son asks him for bread, will give him a stone? Or if he asks for a fish, will give him a serpent? If you then, being evil, know how to give good gifts to your children, how much more will your Father who is in heaven give good things to those who ask Him!" (Matthew 7:7–11 NKJV)

Jesus reiterates that same message later: "'If you have faith the size of a mustard seed, you will say to this mountain, "Move from here to there," and it will move; and nothing will be impossible to you'" (Matthew 17:20 NASB). Since a mustard seed is a tiny inanimate object about the size of a grain of salt, what Jesus is saying is that if you have the tiniest bit of faith, you can move a mountain.

Jesus then says something similar in Matthew 21:21: "'If you have faith and do not doubt, not only can you do what was done to the fig tree, but also you can say to this mountain, "Go, throw yourself into the sea," and it will be done. If you believe, you will receive whatever you ask for in prayer.'" The Gospel of Mark reiterates this message, "'Therefore I tell you, whatever you ask for in prayer, believe that you have received it, and it will be yours'" (11:24).

Jesus tells all of us just how easy prayer can be: "'Again I say to you that if two of you agree on earth concerning anything that they ask, it will be done for them by My Father in heaven. For where two or three are gathered in My name, I am there in the midst of them'" (Matthew 18:19 NKJV). John also recorded a similar statement, "'Most assuredly, I say to you, he who believes in Me, the works that I do he will do also; and greater works than these he will do, because I go to My Father. And whatever you ask in My name, that

I will do, that the Father may be glorified in the Son. If you ask anything in My name, I will do it.'" (John 14:12–14 NKJV).

So, when the author of this website applies Jesus's words to the amputee or anyone who has prayerfully asked for anything and does not receive it, he argues that Jesus was not telling the truth and therefore he could not have been God. Like me, he asserts that all current miracle claims by anyone are false. I clearly understand the dilemma the author Marshall Brain faces, because we know with certainty that the above listed Scriptures are not true for us today.

Brain adds, "No matter how many people pray, no matter how often they pray, no matter how sincere they are, no matter how much they believe, no matter how deserving the amputee, what we know is that prayers do not inspire God to regenerate amputated legs."

But rather than considering those Scriptures only applicable to the people living during Jesus's time on Earth or extended temporarily to certain disciples after his ascension, the author concludes that God is imaginary.

This is exactly my point. When Christians suggest miracle claims from the Bible and claim current intervention today, they do not engender faith in those who doubt. Instead, they drive away skeptics like Marshall Brain from Christianity who will never consider God. This is how Christians turn skeptics into atheists.

I'm sure Brain has many other arguments that refute the existence of God, but I must say the Scriptures he listed turn many people away from even considering God. We are all being bombarded with one prayer request and miracle claim after the other by fellow Christians who stand on verses like those listed above. When someone like this author hears what he believes to be delusional babble, he runs to the nearest exit: God is imaginary.

He cannot reconcile a God who shows favoritism to people of certain religious sects any more than I can. He cannot reconcile an active God, with the mass suffering and injustices occurring every second on this planet. The author sees nothing miraculous happening in our world, as I do. So, if we want to introduce the wisdom of Jesus to nonbelievers, we should discontinue making claims that God is actively favoring select people through prayer, which clearly flies in the face of our common realties.

[20] God-Incidence or Coincidence

THERE'S A GREAT QUOTE FROM THE MOVIE *FLIGHT* THAT speaks volumes regarding how Christians perceive what seems to be mysterious events in their lives. In this movie, Denzel Washington says, "Once you believe that all the coincidences in your life are God, you'll live a much happier life."

There seems to be a strong motivation on the part of many Christians to associate an active God with the events in their lives, but I am convinced there are no supernatural connections. It's simply an illusory correlation (when people falsely perceive an association between two events or situations) that we discussed in an earlier chapter. Christians are always concocting scenarios which attempt to include God's involvement in specific life events because they want or need to believe God always actively looks out for them. For them, the supernatural is always in play to explain all of life's favorable circumstances.

My son and I had a very weird experience / coincidence happen when he was eighteen and living at home. He was working as a waiter in a nice restaurant here in Las Vegas. He came home one afternoon and said to me, "Dad, you're never going to believe who came into my restaurant today."

I thought for just a brief moment and said, "Dr. J" (also known as Julius Erving—the famous basketball player who had retired twenty-five years earlier). I wish you could have seen the look on my son's face when I answered him.

After helping my son pick his jaw up off the floor, he looked at me and asked, "How could you have possibly guessed that?" Then he continued, "You must have heard that Dr. J was in town on the news or something." I told him truthfully, I had not.

Before I give you the reason behind my unlikely guess, I want to calculate the probability that I would have guessed Dr. J. It's only a rough calculation, but it will show just how crazy it was to successfully make a guess like that, and to show that God did not, and would not, have any possible motivation to have provided the correct answer to me.

Since I had to know that my son was referring to someone "special," the person he was referring to must have been some sort of celebrity. What are the number of possible celebrities (actors, athletes, politicians, musicians etc.), over the last fifty years, I could choose from? I'm going to be conservative by saying 20,000 possibilities, but I will show you the actual odds are much lower. So that presents a 1 in 20,000 chance I would select the right answer, and as crazy as it sounds, I did.

So, what caused me to guess Dr. J? I was watching ESPN that Saturday morning, and they were showing tennis shoe commercials from the past. Some of these commercials were at least twenty years removed from airing on TV. I saw at least four of the old commercials that had Michael Jordan, Magic Johnson, or Larry Bird in them. Then they showed one of my favorite commercials that Dr. J was in. It had such a catchy tune. It went like this, "Hey Dr. J, where did you get those moves?" and Dr. J's songful reply rhymed with, "from my Converse tennis shoes." I just watched that old commercial about an hour before my son came home from his restaurant, and I was singing it in my mind even up to the time my son arrived. When he asked me that question, I responded with Dr. J only because that tune was stuck in my head.

If you really want to calculate the true probability of guessing correctly, then we would need to also incorporate the probability of ESPN placing that commercial on the same day that I was home to watch it, on the same day that Dr. J was in Las Vegas at my son's restaurant, and at the same time when my son was working. What if my son was working on another side of the restaurant and had never noticed Dr. J that morning? We would also need to include in our calculation all the other TV channels available to me at that time. Let's also not forget the probability that something else could have distracted me away from having that tune stuck in my head before my son came home and asked me that question.

In other words, the probability that I would have guessed Dr. J was astronomically low. This is clearly a coincidence and not a God-incidence. There can be no divine purpose for God having anything to do with my selecting Dr. J, and yet I did. The same thing goes for people who randomly select six numbers in a lottery and hit all six. The true probability that one would select all five white numbered balls and the extra red Powerball is 1 chance in 292,201,338. That's 1 chance in 292 million! We all know people hit this jackpot all the time, and there's nothing mysterious or honestly attributed to God's hands when people win. It follows the laws of probability. It's a coincidence, not a God-incidence or miracle.

Dreams from God—or Not?

My friend Mike told me an interesting story regarding one of his recent dreams. He first told me about his close childhood friend he hadn't seen in twelve years. They were great friends, and could always be found together during their youth. Mike thought many times about calling his friend over those twelve years but never did.

When sleeping one night, he had a dream about his friend, which had never happened before. He said his dream consisted of things they had done during their childhood and the fun they had had together. When he woke up that next morning, he told his wife about his dream, and she encouraged him to call the friend. Mike also mentioned his dream to some of his siblings who knew his friend, and they also encouraged him to call. But Mike never called. Three days after his dream, Mike's sister called and informed Mike that his friend's father died. So, Mike concluded the following:

1. God caused him to dream about his friend.

2. God wanted him to contact his friend because God knew his friend's father was going to die three days later.

3. This was not a coincidence, but rather it was a God-incidence. According to Mike, God placed that dream in his mind that night

I love Mike, but his reasoning is not sound to me. I'm compelled to ask myself where the fairness is in our God planting a dream in Mike's mind for who knows what purpose, while there are so many other horrific things happening here on Earth and God does nothing about them. For me, Mike's dream is a coincidence of the highest order. If Mike dreamt about someone he never knew, then I might be able to buy a portion of his story. Mike had a dream about someone he knew very well at one time in his life, which is totally plausible.

Chance or Higher Purpose

We want to believe there's a godly reason behind why our forty-year-old mother suffered and died from breast cancer. We want to believe there's a higher purpose behind our brother being killed by a drunk driver. So, what do we do? We try to convince ourselves and others it's all part of a divine plan orchestrated by our Creator. Or we errantly believe there was a higher purpose for his allowance of it. We try to make sense of life's bad outcomes by connecting irrational supernatural dots that do not exist.

Why do Christians do that? I believe it's because during our greatest times of loss, it's better to have some divine explanation than to accept that "bad" outcomes occur out of randomness or beyond our control. We'll rationalize our circumstance by saying things like "God allowed something bad to happen so something good will come of it."

When a soldier returns from war as an amputee and begins helping other vets cope with their limb loss, some claim God allowed (or even caused) his wounds for the greater purpose of helping others later. An amputee soldier could have accomplished this charitable feat even if God didn't exist. One may claim being laid off from a particular job was orchestrated by God, so the next job will be more financially rewarding. A more favorable job could be obtained even if God did not exist. Isn't this simply Christians trying to make the best out of difficult circumstances through erroneous reasoning?

Randomness is unpredictable. It's uncomfortable for us to live in a random, and chaotic world with the constant possibility for tragic events to occur. And so many would rather convince themselves there's a preplanned reason, and therefore a "Reason-er," who trumps randomness.

Rather than accept the bad random events that happen to us, we'll concoct a story that God allowed it because he had some higher purpose to fulfill. We'll either say that God orchestrated the adverse event, or the extremely misguided might tell us Satan was the culprit. Again, I wonder what God thinks when we do this. It seems so unfair to God when Christians consider him the responsible party for their perceptions of his action or inaction, yet they continue explaining random events in this manner.

Miracles and Probability

As I've gone to great lengths to establish, requesting prayers have no effect on the outcomes of life events. Life events happen independent of any action by God. Likewise, when someone prays for God to act, and the outcome of the future event falls in line with that person's prayer, the same outcome would have occurred even if that person had not prayed. It's merely a coincidence that the outcome matched the petitioner's request.

Earlier, I mentioned that the Christian apologetic reasoning for prayer always results in either a yes or no, which equates to a 50/50 chance of getting what they want. But a one in two chance is hardly anyone's definition of a miracle, is it? Of course, that assumes we ensure there are enough sampling points. But to be statistically and circumstantially correct, each specific circumstance has its own weighted probability of going the way we might want it to go.

The probability of receiving an affirmative answer for one who prays or hopes to gain employment with a college degree is much higher than a person who is praying for a loved one to be cured from a terminal illness. Prayers for safety prior to a flight have a much greater probability of appearing to be answered in the affirmative than an amputee who might pray for limb regeneration. But since most people only go to God with more difficult life circumstances, we can expect their perceived prayer affirmation rate to be well below 50%. Perhaps the "easy" stuff, like hoping a mechanic doesn't overcharge someone during a car repair, isn't big enough to warrant going to God.

My point is this: Christians who believe that God always answers our prayers with either a yes or a no will always claim that God is the overseer and is involved in every circumstance in their lives. He's always in charge because at some point in their life, they always get a yes or no answer. When a frequent flyer prays for a safe flight prior to each departure and has survived each flight, they're likely to believe God has answered their prayers affirmatively. But we know that the chances of dying in a plane crash are 1 in 11 million. Prayer seems remarkably effective when you're calling on God's favor with statistical probabilities like that.

The probability that God will act is the same for those who seek medical attention and pray as for those who forgo medical attention and only pray. They are both zero. Some have claimed they have been diagnosed with a terminal disease, refused treatment, and yet somehow became healed.

We know that our immune systems are extraordinarily strong defenses in fighting diseases, but sometimes they become weakened. In fact, immunotherapy treatments (infusions that boost one's immune system) are being used to successfully manage and treat certain cancers and have recently been a giant leap in medical science. When someone is healed from what appeared to be a terminal disease without the aid of medicine, isn't it possible their immune system reawakened and killed that same disease at a later point in time?

Many have experienced false positive test results and were incorrectly diagnosed by their physicians, then claim God healed them when the second doctor disagrees with the first doctor's diagnosis. That's why most of us seek a second opinion when given unwelcome news, to make sure that the first doctor got it right. Doctors are not infallible.

Misdiagnosis

I have a personal example regarding medical second opinions and how the illusion of prayer and godly intervention appeared to be behind a miraculous healing. In 1987, when my son was about six months old, he appeared to have a serious reaction to the pertussis vaccine. Pertussis is used to vaccinate against whooping cough. Those who contract whooping cough normally have horrible coughing episodes, but they can also become very disabled both physically and mentally. In rare and extreme cases, when the vaccination serum is tainted and not pure, it can cause horrific brain damage.

The day my son received that injection, my wife noticed later that he was having some type of spasmodic seizures. His eyes would blink rapidly, and his head would violently jerk backwards. At first, our son was experiencing a seizure every ten minutes or so, but later that night we noticed the frequency of the seizures increasing. We took him to our pediatrician the next day and he suggested we see a neurologist as soon as possible.

We checked with our insurance carrier to ensure that we found someone within our coverage network. Luckily, we were able to get him to a neurologist the next day. I can't remember if either my wife or I had begun our praying regimen for our son's situation at that time, because I'm not sure if we knew just how potentially serious the situation could become.

First Looks Can be Deceiving

I clearly remember walking into the neurologist's office and being horrified by what I witnessed. There must have been ten to fifteen patients in that lobby who all seemed to be either in a vegetative state, or at minimum, disfigured, paralyzed, and confined to wheelchairs. Many of these patients were younger children, and I remember how frightened I was. I wondered as we waited in the lobby if this was to be my son's eventual fate. When we walked into the doctor's private office, I recall noticing how young he was. The bookshelf behind his desk gave the appearance as though he had received his medical degree from the Time-Life collection of magazines. The doctor examined our son and asked us to confirm with him that the seizure episodes began right after the vaccination. This doctor did not measure the electrical activity of our son's brain using an EEG testing procedure.

Then the doctor dropped what felt like a nuclear bomb on both of us. He told us that he was sure our son's seizures were caused by the vaccination. He went on to explain that each time our son spasmodically seized; it was causing brain damage. These internal neurological "sparks" were killing brain cells, and our son had a 90% chance of being mentally retarded. He told us that it was rare, but some children react differently to vaccines that are tainted and not pure.

We were told the only hope to *minimally* reduce the severity of this reaction was to immediately start him on a heavy regimen of steroids and antibiotics. He told us he believed that our son was going to suffer debilitating side effects, both physical and neurological, from this reaction and was also highly likely to suffer other serious side effects from the highly concentrated steroid treatments. The pressure was on to hurry and start this steroid treatment to minimize brain damage.

Decision Time

My wife and I began crying as we held our son in that office. We didn't know what to say or do. The doctor told us he would make the arrangements for the hospital and the treatment, and he would call us the next day to provide us the information we needed to get started. We went home that night scared and worried. I held my son that night and cried as he continued to spasm—fearing and wondering how much damage the seizures were causing.

My tears rolled down my cheeks and landed on my son's cheeks as I called out, and even begged God to remove this disorder from him. My wife started calling our family and friends from church, reporting the shocking news and asking for prayer. I remember one of my wife's aunts in another state calling a local Christian radio station asking the DJ to ask others to pray for our son over the air.

Rather than simply accept the unwelcome news from one doctor, I decided to review our health care provider list to find another neurologist for a second opinion. God did not lead me to choose the next doctor. How do I know that? Because our directory only had two neurologists listed in the area where we lived, and it wasn't apparent to me until later that I chose the wrong doctor first. I used common sense and recommendations from other friends and family who agreed that we should seek a second opinion.

The Second Opinion

It's been over thirty-five years, but I can still remember the second doctor's name—Dr. Rice. We scheduled an appointment with him within the same week, while putting off the first doctor's recommendation to get our son into the hospital for treatment as soon as possible. As we later discovered, Dr. Rice had completed all his postdoctoral research in a foreign country specializing in vaccination disorders. If someone was going to know about this sort of disorder, it would be Dr. Rice.

Dr. Rice performed his examination and tested our son's brain activity with an EEG, unlike the first doctor. He told us that he wanted our son to be tested on a biweekly basis for the next six months, but he didn't think that our son's seizures were of the type to cause brain damage. According to Dr. Rice, our son would have displayed completely different seizure-like symptoms if there was a concern that the brain was being affected. He was certain we were dealing with a reaction to the vaccine, but it was not going to cause long-term brain damage. His diagnosis was "myoclonic seizures," resulting from the vaccination.

Our son continued seizing as we brought him in for testing every other week. Over that next year, the seizures began to subside until they vanished completely. Our family and friends were giving glory to God for intervening and removing the horrific disorder we first thought we were dealing with.

Flip of the Coin

Was I happy my son had shown remarkable improvement? Absolutely! The problem was that the rest of our friends and family were giving God the glory for removing something that Dr. Rice had said was never there. Our son was showing the same outward signs for Dr. Rice as he had for the first inexperienced doctor who diagnosed him with brain-debilitating seizures the day before. It's not as if God had miraculously intervened between the two doctor visits and after we prayed so that his symptoms disappeared or were different in the presence of the second doctor.

The seizures took about a year to subside, so it's unlikely God performed a miracle that would have caused the seizures to stop immediately. Yet, all glory was given to God the great physician by our family for intervening on our behalf. When I look back on it, I always think, if we would have selected Dr. Rice first, all this would have been much ado about nothing. My wife and I would never have traveled the path of fear and anguish that we did. No one would have needed to pray about something that ended up being nothing.

At the time, however, I wanted to believe that God miraculously helped us. I wanted to think since we were a "Christian" family, God would always look out for us. He was our protector and a shield about us. We were the apple of his eye, and he wanted to give us good gifts. I wanted to believe we were special because we not only humbly worshiped him, but we also took a leap of faith and asked him to help us.

Looking Back

Some time later, I recalled thinking about all those children sitting in those two doctors' lobbies who were not healed. I saw them every two weeks as we had our son tested. The damage from their vaccinations or other debilitating conditions had run their course, and there would be no return to any "normalcy." Certainly, there were other Christian families in the lobbies of both doctors who had prayed over their children for God to remove their child's disorders, and yet he obviously did not.

I was in a place in my life where, out of a sense of fairness, I found myself contemplating the humble truth regarding our "special favor" over the families who received nothing. To me, a fair God is one who either gives freely to all who ask with good intentions, or he gives nothing to anyone. I just could not bring myself to believe that he heals some for his own reasoning and ignores the needs and requests of other humble souls. I simply stuffed those feelings of reality deep down inside and continued leaving room for God to show up in an active way somewhere in my future. But that never happened.

The Peril of Contingencies

It freed my soul when I chose to believe God is not intervening in our world today. You don't feel obligated to give him credit for the specific good things that come your way, and you never need to ponder if he either caused or allowed something bad to occur because he had some greater purpose.

Would it be bad in God's eyes for someone to not give credit to him if he did act on their behalf and not recognize or praise him? Maybe so. On the flip side, what would God think about someone publicly giving him credit and praise for something favorable that he did not provide—especially when God knows that favor claim will hurt others who have received nothing? Those who appear favored seem to have no consideration for those who are less fortunate. Could you imagine me sitting in that second doctor's lobby during our last visit and sharing with the parents of the other disabled children about how God had miraculously healed my son?

Of course, those who believe God continues to be in the miracle business will probably say that my son really had a brain debilitating disorder caused by that vaccination. They will probably say God started to remove it between the time we saw the first doctor and the second doctor—even though the seizures were presented to both doctors in the same exact manner. I'm sure there are some who will suggest God led us to the second doctor so that we would be even more blessed.

Here's an example of intervention believers dismissing the observable and seemingly getting away with claiming that God performed a miracle with not a shred of evidence. We received a diagnosis, prayed between doctor visits, and after a year, our son was not having seizures. Looks like a miracle.

But one young, inexperienced doctor said he was suffering brain damage, and the other more experienced specialized physician said he was not. As I've already mentioned, no one can know with certainty if my son was becoming brain damaged, but I challenge them to go to the amputee with their claims. No one will ever be able to dispute a leg regeneration at the request of God, but who's willing to pray and wait that long for one to occur?

Let's look at it from another angle. What if the second doctor gave us the same diagnosis as the first doctor, as most families waiting in those doctor's lobbies received? I don't think I would have sought a third opinion—even if there were more than two neurologists available in my insurance plan.

More than likely, my wife and I would have started our son on his steroid regimen with the second doctor, and who knows what would have happened to him? As I mentioned, the steroid regimen was expected to cause a lot of other damage, but according to the first doctor, it was worth the risks to marginally minimize the ongoing brain damage. We were just one decision away from our son experiencing horrific drug-induced consequences of highly concentrated steroidal treatments, all because the first doctor misdiagnosed our son's symptoms. There are many instances in which doctors make an incorrect diagnosis.

What happens when a doctor makes the diagnosis that someone is terminal, but later needs to reverse their opinion when the patient is later deemed in remission with or without medical treatment? Christians will claim that God was behind the patient's remission even with medical treatment. If they are willing to make that claim, what claim should they make when a doctor declares a patient to be in remission, but the patient later dies from the same disease they were originally diagnosed with? This happens all the time, but I've never heard a Christian claim that God was involved or responsible for that scenario.

[21] The False Hope Elevator

WITH THIS NEXT EXAMPLE, I HOPE TO DRIVE HOME TWO points: how risky it is when petitioners allow themselves to hope for any supernatural intervention and how doing so can lead to greater disappointment in God. As I previously argued, the magnitude of one's disappointments will always be directly proportional to the amount of hope one places in miraculous favor. Taking the God-spun "false hope elevator" to the top floor and having the godly supporting cables fail can be devastating to anyone's faith. When one has zero expectations for godly intervention on this Earth, they remain on the ground floor with no risks to be let down by God.

> *When our hope for aid in a health crisis centers only on medical science and we fixate our spiritual hope solely on the premise of eternity with God, we keep ourselves emotionally gratified and grounded on the solid foundation of his amazing grace.*

What causes people to rely on God for supernatural physical healing and not solely on medical science? I believe it's because the Bible tells us repeatedly just how much God loves us, because we believe he has the power to heal us, and because there are examples of Jesus healing people in Scripture. We are also emotionally connected to God—a connection we can never have with medical science.

Have you ever heard anyone gravely ill ever say they were disappointed in what medical science provided when their treatments were not successful? Probably not. And that's because no one has ever written a book declaring medical science loves us. Nor has medicine ever promised to give us what we ask of it—whether we asked alone or with a group of petitioners. Medical science has never claimed to die and provide salvation for us.

But with God, most Christians believe that he cares about them so much that he would be willing to provide help in their greatest time of need. Jesus also made promises to the people of his era that they could ask for anything and he would provide for them. He told those same people that group requests would assure them they would receive whatever they asked for. These types of claims emotionally connect us to God, and in times of crises, we errantly rely on God for miraculous help. But I am convinced we need to keep hope for our physicality and spirituality separated. We should extend our hope for earthly survival to medical science alone, and only to the reasonable extent it can physically remedy our illness. Any extension of hope past the actual probability for healing can also lead us to greater disappointment. We should never extend any hope for God to remedy our illnesses but only to his promise to forgive and to provide an eternity with him.

Riding the Yo-Yo

Many years ago, my Christian friend Robert was diagnosed with terminal stage four colon cancer. He was a candidate for a radical surgery which attempted to remove portions of his colon and the cancer that metastasized within some of his other organs. Most people with this type and stage of cancer do not live long. Hope for long-term survival is miniscule. Following his surgery, Robert was treated with chemotherapy and radiation, and the last time I saw him he had lost a lot of weight. He was a great guy who always made me laugh, and I loved spending time with him.

Since advanced staged colon cancer is difficult to manage and spreads quickly, Robert was required to have blood tests and PET scans on a regular basis to determine if the cancer continued to spread or metastasize to other areas of his body. His wife, Susan, continually posted updates on her social media page during Robert's treatment and testing along with requests for prayer. Obviously, Susan knew the diagnosis was terminal, but she wasn't about to let go of hope that her husband would be healed by God. She was clearly riding the false hope elevator, and that was noticeably reflected in each of her posts during their journey.

Each time Robert was tested, Susan requested prayer for good results. When the results were either the same or better than expected, Susan put the God spin on it and claimed that God was still in the miracle business. Those unchanged or better results were falsely being interpreted by Susan as godly favor. She wrote, "I just want the people around us and the people we are in contact with to realize how powerful our God is and how much he wants and loves to show us. We thank God for these good test results through all of your faithful prayers."

And every time people received "good" news from Susan's posts, they responded with prayer and praise to God for his intervention and oversight of Robert's treatments. I've listed a few of their replies below.

- "They that wait upon The Lord shall renew their strength and mount up with wings as eagles. . . . Praise be to God our loving miracle providing Father."

- "Amen, Amen, and Amen! Just goes to show you, the Christians praying, believing with great faith, miracles are beating the Dr.'s theories all the time. Doctors need to learn; you don't play with God and his work!! YAY God!"

- "Your word says we have not because we ask not. We are asking Father God that you completely heal Robert. Let your mercy and grace be seen by all as you completely restore and renew his body and spirit. Father, your word says where two or more are gathered in your name that you are there in the midst. There are many joined together praying for Robert, and we are trusting that you will move in a mighty and miraculous way for Robert and his family. Guide the doctors as they provide care."

Susan was interpreting these "better" test results as godly favor and, most likely unbeknownst to her, was riding the false hope elevator to the upper floors. Then her friends decided it was best to get on the same elevator as reflected by their replies to her posts. They seemed to have confidence God was favorably involved.

Waiting on medical test results can be as horrible as receiving bad results. Trust me. I know. I'm sure Susan was so excited at times when Robert's test results were not devastating; and after receiving godly encouraging prayer comments from her friends and family, she never considered nor would allow herself to consider those results could have solely been from some of the treatments Robert was receiving.

Reactions to a Downward Trend

Later, when the results weren't what they'd hoped and prayed for, Susan would again request prayer and remind us that God could do the impossible—never giving up her hope that God could completely heal Robert. Medical science hadn't given up on trying to manage the cancer and extend Robert's life, but their terminal diagnosis confirmed they had resigned themselves to the fact that Robert's cancer would take his life. When Robert's health started to go downhill, Susan and Robert's family and friends posted the following comments:

- "It doesn't matter what your doctors say, it doesn't matter what your specialists say, it doesn't matter what the people around you say. IT IS WELL!!! God will heal Robert!"

- "Father God, we thank you that you are still in the miracle-working business; we give you all the praise and glory for the miracle you're about to provide, in Jesus's name Amen."

- "Father, we take authority over the cancer spreading and command it to cease being a problem. The devil has no authority over your children. We command your spirit to completely cleanse Robert right now, in Jesus's name! Thank you for showing your glory, Father, and that signs and wonders do follow all who believe! Hallelujah!"

Robert died about eleven months after he was initially diagnosed. Have Susan or any of her friends and family gone back to review what they said during that process? Have they considered the false hope laid on all of us—and more importantly on Robert? Have they ever asked themselves retrospectively if they were correct when claiming God was initially involved in keeping Robert's health from crashing? They probably all have selective memories now. You must wonder though, when the next medical crisis comes along, are they going to continue with the same line of reasoning and the claims they applied to Robert's situation?

Unable to Help

You may be thinking it's calloused for me to suggest we shouldn't have hope for godly intervention when one is facing a serious health crisis. I've had many people tell me they would never adopt my theology regarding God's inactivity because they claim my theology would take away their hope. If or when they are faced with a difficult crisis in their life, they tell me they need to have hope that God would intervene for them. I carefully and in a loving way, try to remind them that prayed-for Christians and atheists die at the same rate from the same diseases. I also try to convince them that hope for a health crisis needs to be solely fixed on medical science, not on God. But I also remind them of what Paul wrote in Colossians 3:1–2: our hope should only be centered on eternity with God, not earthly matters (interventions).

I know it can be exceedingly difficult when a friend or a loved one is enduring a life-threatening disease or injury. Obviously, it's hard for the person who is dealing with it, but it's also hard for the ones on the outside who have no way of changing the outcome. Everyone is desperate to find help, and the fear of losing someone is unimaginable. I've experienced this many times in my life—even when I was open to God as an active, intervening healer.

When another close friend was diagnosed with terminal cancer, the doctors had no medical solutions to offer. Each time we met, there was this feeling that I couldn't just leave him without offering some measure of hope for survival. I couldn't just say, "See you later," or "Talk to you next week." It seemed at the time there was no other place to turn but to the biblical God who we are told healed people during his time on Earth.

So, back when I was open to believing in an active God, I would hold my friend's hands and ask God for a miraculous healing. I prayed for healing more out of a desire to give my friend hope than to witness God provide healing. I didn't know how much time my friend had, but I didn't want him to spend his remaining time without any hope for recovery. And I believe this is where we get into trouble.

False Hope?

When doctors are out of solutions and we know we can do nothing physically to remedy the situation, we'll go to the Almighty and his intervening promises that I contend were not meant for us. We make these prayers in the solitude of our bedrooms, but we also feel compelled to tell the patient and their family we are praying for them. We'll hold the patient's hands, just as I did, and pray for their healing. It's all about giving a person hope—even when God's reputation and the emotional stability of the patient could be on the line.

Do we think about what effect our requesting prayers for healing will have on the person being prayed for and their family when they come to the realization that they are dying? They'll have no choice but to conclude God didn't help them, and it will force them to reconsider just how much God loves them. Accepting that God is not physically healing people today, we are set free from the potential of godly rejection, and no one will consider the prayer promises of Jesus (applicable only when Jesus was here) to have ever been false. I trust medical science for my physicality, knowing its limits, and I trust God with my eternity.

Psychologically Speaking

Consider the following question: Is it better and more psychologically healthy for the patient or the intercessory praying family and friends to make potentially false claims regarding God's supernatural involvement during a health crisis? Or is it better to say nothing miraculously is happening during that time—relying on what medical science can offer and centering one's hope only on eternity with God?

I ask this because, in Robert's case, obviously God did not provide miraculous healing. But Robert and many friends and family members were being misled by Susan and her friends to believe God was helping. Initially the PET scans after surgery and treatment looked better than before, but the family members made it seem like God was actively involved. Did this approach make Robert and all his family members feel better at the time when they received the good medical news, as they believed (I contend falsely) that it was God who provided? I'm sure it did. Putting the God spin on it certainly brought temporary happiness and hope to all of them. Everybody was riding the false hope elevator to the top floor.

But what about later when everyone came to the realization that the cancer was never remediated despite the best efforts of medical science and their prayers? What are we to think in hindsight? If God was involved in any way with Robert's temporary "better" test results, now it appears God was unwilling to completely heal him. We were all left standing on the side of the road, wondering if any of what Susan ever said about God's involvement had any merit. I guess I hope they were wrong. Everyone will be forced to conclude that God was never involved in providing healing in any physical way to Robert.

Nothing but the Truth

Let's ask ourselves a different question. What if the doctors saw the spread of cancer in the PET scan after Robert was initially treated, but they lied to him by telling him that every scan was clean? What if they assured Robert, without evidence to the contrary, that the cancer appeared to be remediated? Obviously, doctors falsifying evidence and not being truthful would be deplorable by most of our standards, but it certainly would have created temporary hope and happiness for Robert and his family.

Now compare such heinous (and fantasized) behavior by doctors to what Susan and so many others did, claiming with no evidence that God intervenes in this world. Happiness was gained, not through intentional deception, but through otherwise similar false hope.

Most Christians find the first scenario with deceptive doctors to be reprehensible, and yet the second scenario, Susan making claims of intermediate godly intervention, to be completely acceptable. I consider both practices unconscionable, because neither one of those scenarios would have been grounded in truth. You must wonder what Robert's thoughts were regarding the effectiveness of prayer or God's love for him as he began to die.

The Bottom Line

Either we're not interpreting Scriptures correctly regarding God's current intervention policies or the biblical authors have unintentionally misled us into believing God would act in the future after Jesus left the Earth. The evidence is noticeably clear. We've errantly hijacked the biblical miracle stories and promises from that era, attempting to apply them to our era.

I need to make sure the reader understands what I'm saying is not from a cold, factual heart. I hurt for anyone struggling with difficult circumstances, and my sympathy overflows towards them. I wanted Robert to live because I cared about him, and I was crushed when he died. I want to urge others to stop allowing our human weaknesses to get in the way of reality and truth. We must stop making claims about the unknown with respect to God's activities. When we make these claims, we set others up for future unmet expectations. We also smear God's reputation, and at times, give false hope to the hopeless.

> *No temporary hope for supernatural healing is better than false hope.*

As difficult as it can be, I believe it's better to speak the truth about these matters that may hurt but cannot mislead than to speak potential falsehoods providing temporary comfort, but which may leave others emotionally train wrecked in disappointment.

Over the years I have found it very difficult to engage in discussions with intervention-believing Christians who claim God continues to be in the miracle business. I've concluded it would be much easier to simply refer them to my book, thus eliminating the likelihood for emotional conflict. I'm not opposed to that type of conflict, but I have discovered through trial and error that direct arguments and emotional conflict rarely change minds.

When having those discussions, I always tell the intervention believer, "If you've got the courage to make a miracle claim, you should have overwhelming, remarkable, and non-disputable evidence to back it up." I also tell them, "I hope you've got this right, because you're putting God's reputation on the line, and it may mislead others if the supposed miracle is proven to have another cause or is completely false. It also may not sit well with God because you have him appear to show favor to you yet not to the countless others less fortunate."

Eventually, the interventionist claimer will always tell me, "You can't know or prove it wasn't a miracle, so you don't have the right to say God wasn't involved." But why should I have to prove something that cannot be known with certainty or disprove a claim I never made? I'm not the one making the miracle claim, so the burden of proof should be on the person making the miracle claim, and they should have sound factual evidence to easily convince us all.

[22] Hedging Bets

I HEARD A HORRIFIC STORY ABOUT A PASTOR AND HIS family during one of their annual family vacations. The pastor shared that every time they left on a long road trip, he would lead his wife and four children in prayer, calling on God to protect them during their journey. On the highway during the first day of a vacation, a piece of metal dislodged from a semi-truck ahead of them and landed under their van, rupturing their fuel tank. Before they knew it, the rear section of their van was engulfed in flames.

After quickly pulling over, the pastor and his wife were able to get out of their front doors, but they were initially unable to get to their four children. They could hear the children screaming and struggling as they burned, but there was nothing they could do to help them. Eventually, the pastor was able to break out one of the windows, but he was only able to pull one of his children to safety. The other three were already deceased. The lone surviving son was horrifically burned and near death.

As faithful Christians who believed that God could heal, he and his wife held a bedside prayer vigil in their surviving son's hospital room that night. Along with some of their parishioners, they collectively called on God to save their child. The heavens appeared silent as their son died the following morning.

Was it simply that God just said "no" to this pastor's prayerful request for safety prior to their trip and then "no" to healing their last living child? I can't speak for the pastor or his wife and children by telling you I know with certainty that they felt more secure when he prayed for their safety before they embarked, but I would bet they did. I know from my own experiences when I used to say humble prayers like that with my family before our long road trips, I felt like God had our back.

I've come to realize those types of prayers are really just providing false hope and security. Again, when we stand on false hope and things go wrong, we fall from a much higher position than we would have if our hope was not falsely elevated.

Deadly Prayer or Unfortunate Timing?

If the pastor hadn't prayed and the same event would have happened, then his angst may have been marginally reduced because God hadn't been called upon for safety. He would be able to illogically conclude his family wasn't covered by prayer to explain their horror. However, without prayer, no family member would have had false hope for security as they backed out of their driveway. If the pastor had not prayed, I'm sure they would have told us the reason they went through that horrific day was because they didn't call on God for safety.

If we really want to look at this in a realistic way, think about this: if the pastor had not spent two minutes in their driveway prayerfully asking God for safety prior to their departure, their family van would not have been in that exact place when the metal fragment was dislodged from that truck. Most likely, no one would have been hurt. This is clearly a random event that occurred only because their van was in that unfortunate position. This pastor's horrific experience was not from a God who said "no."

I saw another post on FB that reminds me of this situation. It said, "Sometimes a delay in your plans is God's protection," to which I would respond, "Sometimes a delay in your plans can be devastatingly lethal." The horrific event mentioned above was not caused by God nor was there any intent on anyone's part to cause this tragedy. The "delay" caused by the pastor's prayers randomly placed them behind that truck at the exact time when the metal was dislodged. That is the logical reason they lost their four children that day.

This pastor has a deep-spirited faith, but I'm not sure about the reasoning he provided in the aftermath of this tragedy. The pastor claimed he still has faith in a God who actively loves and intervenes on behalf of his creation. He also admitted he cannot understand why God provided no protection for his family on the day of their tragedy.

Unfortunately, he concluded that God must have a higher purpose for not intervening. It's obviously a coping mechanism. He never seemed to consider the possibility that we're all on our own on this planet from a physical perspective, and God has chosen to allow for the random events caused the by free-willed choices of humans.

Combination Prayer

Another social-media friend posted the following just hours before a massive hurricane was about to hit Mexico: "I am going to pray for my brothers and sisters in Jalisco as they prepare for Hurricane Patricia. May God watch over you, and may you protect yourselves as much as you can."

My friend's workable solutions for the people who may be affected in the Mexican city of Jalisco were interesting to me. He used a sort of combination of theology and reasoning. Pray for God's protection and simultaneously use your reasoning minds to find the safest place during the storm.

I'm picturing a cartoon with a word bubble over God's head saying to the people in the path of the hurricane, "Stop wasting your limited time praying for me to protect you and make a decision where you should take shelter!" If my friend and the people facing the hurricane really believed God would protect them, there would be no need to seek shelter. My friend's FB prayer shows what most of us honestly believe about the likelihood of God solving our problems through prayer. In real-life situations, we all really believe in the nonbiblical statement, "God helps those who help themselves."

Subliminal Scoreboards

This may seem difficult to believe, but many Christians also apply a running point system to their lives to earn God's future favor. It's a subliminal scoreboard that keeps a running average of their good and bad deeds. I believe some people operate this way because I committed this error earlier in my life and heard others make the same claim.

It's sort of a Christian karma, and its roots seem to stem from the OT authors who suggested they were rewarded for their honorable deeds and punished for their sins. Since Christians today believe God operated in that way during the biblical era, they extend this erroneous theory into our era. For some Christians, each of their deeds are assigned different positive or negative values.

For example, Christians feel they receive some positive good merit points when they attend church weekly. They feel better about their relationship with God because of their commitment to him. If they help an elderly woman with her groceries, it's another plus for their scorecard. If they take too many office supplies from work, they've reduced their overall merit-based score with God. We all think murder or rape probably have much greater negative point values than swearing. When Christians do what they believe God sees as good, they believe they are more likely to be protected, cared for, or more apt to receive godly blessings through prayer. If their overall score with God is diminished, they are at greater risk for God to reject their prayer requests or see their lives are riddled with problems.

This way of thinking even runs counterintuitive to what most Christians are taught from the pulpit. Most of us are taught God doesn't keep score for those who sincerely love him. It only takes accepting his sacrifice to clean one's negative scorecard values and be worthy of eternity with him. Even though the Bible records events suggesting godly favoritism, we know and experience that no one—righteous or unrighteous in the sight of God—is shown any selective favor based on merit. We are, however, protected and "blessed" more by honoring God's laws, precepts, and principles only because we are not exposing ourselves to the earthly perils that might come our way by disregarding them. But even minimizing consequences by following godly principles doesn't exempt any of us from contracting cancer at an early age nor guarantee a distracted motorist will not kill us.

These false-merit premises are mostly found in the OT Scriptures, but they are also present in the NT. Consider the popular verse Paul wrote, "And we know that in all things God works for the good of those who love him, who have been called according to his purpose" (Romans 8:28). To paraphrase this verse, God is intervening to work good things out for those who obediently love him and have been called by him for his purposes. If there is any truth to this, how would we be able to reconcile that verse with the many tragedies that Christians have experienced?

The nineteen-year-old son of one of our church staff members was killed on a motorcycle a few years back. This young man served God by teaching in our youth ministry. If godly scorecards have merit, I'd like to think this young man's card was largely positive. Rich Mullins, a famous Christian songwriter and musician, was killed in an accidental rollover years ago. The example above of the pastor who prayed for safety lost all his children.

The talented Christian musician Steven Curtis Chapman lost his five-year-old daughter when his eldest son accidentally ran over her with his car in their driveway. I want to think Mr. Chapman and his wife were worthy of God's favor, having God work for their good, based on the way they have lived their lives, and yet they were exposed to the horrific realities of our random, chaotic world.

Pastor Rick Warren's son committed suicide despite all the prayerful requests made by his church and family for his son to become more mentally stable. From these examples, it would appear that God is not offering protection, specific blessings, or working things for the better for anyone based on merit or the intensity of their love for God. Romans 8:28 is simply a feel-good verse and based on a false premise that does not meet with our common realities.

Perhaps God was working things out behind the scenes for the select few during the biblical era, but there's no evidence of that today. Again, whether you accept my interpretation of that verse or not, I can tell you that nearly every Christian interprets this verse in the way I've represented it. It's yet another apologetic way for Christians to believe in an active God, notwithstanding their horrific circumstances. God is always at work behind the scenes for their betterment.

What kind of life will we experience if it's based on falsehoods that make us feel happy in the short term but end up untrue? We may be happy during our short belief in something that might be false (i.e., God is actively healing or protecting us or working behind the scenes for our benefit), but if it later turns out false, we're bound to experience greater pain. Grieving is also different for the intervention believer because they are forced to contemplate why a beseeched God didn't provide help.

We should all actively seek the truth, even if it's not what we desire. When I was diagnosed with a form of blood cancer, I hoped the doctor would tell me there was a cure and that I might live another forty years, but that was only what I hoped to hear. Again, reality is not a function of hope.

What I truly desired, no matter what the doctor was about to tell me, was the absolute truth. I wanted to know what the real statistical probabilities were for my life expectancy. I certainly didn't want him to sugarcoat how much time I might have remaining, and I told him that from the very start. "Give it to me straight."

I don't want false hope from my doctors, and I'd rather not receive it from fellow Christians invoking God through prayer to heal me—even knowing their motives are sincere. I certainly won't set myself up to believe false biblical premises that lead me to consider God is working behind the scenes through prayer for my benefit. I'm just not that special.

Lastly, I had a close friend of mine tell me something very funny regarding prayer after he finished reading this manuscript. He said, "Jeff, if you make it inside those pearly gates, and you think you'll just be chilling out for eternity, I hope they hand you a phone headset and lead you into a giant call center for requesting prayers." Wouldn't that be ironic?

PART 7:
PERSONAL
APPLICATION

[23] "Blessed"

I MUST ADMIT, I'VE BEEN FAIRLY LUCKY THROUGHOUT my life. I was born in a country that can grow its own food, and my vocation and hard work have provided ample monetary gain. I cannot believe or suggest God has orchestrated either of those two favorable outcomes because these circumstances would suggest he plays favorites. Although my sins have been forgiven, I deserve no more earthly blessings by God's active hand than Charles Manson, Adolf Hitler, or certainly Haji starving in an African mudhole.

Have you ever considered what it would be like to live somewhere that wouldn't allow you to feed or educate your children? Do you consider yourself lucky because of the circumstance of where you were born? Or, rather, would you say that God has shown his blessing [favoritism] to you but not to others on this globe who are unable to provide those "blessings" to their children?

The apostle Luke wrote in Acts 17:26, "From one man he made all the nations, that they should inhabit the whole earth; and he marked out their appointed times in history and the boundaries of their lands." There may be many ways to interpret that verse, but many Christians take it to mean that God has always determined where people live. At first glance, I can understand why they believe that, but it does not align with our common realities regarding free will.

I hope the author Luke was only trying to convey that out of one created man, God allowed the disbursement of his creation into different parts of the world. Perhaps he references the establishment of different nations (non-Jewish or non-Christian nations away from Israel) living on other continents, not necessarily nations as we know them today. In my view, it's certainly not a reference to God intervening in which country or city our forefathers lived. But such reasoning would be consistent with people of that era who believed God controlled everything and even everyone.

Many Western Christians use this verse to claim they are blessed today because God has favored them by placing them in a prosperous country. If their interpretation is correct, it can only mean God has purposely given the Hajis of the poverty-stricken regions the short end of the stick.

I choose to call it luck, or better yet, "a good outcome" from decisions made by others long before my birth which allowed me to be born in a particular city and then raised by the parents who loved me. My forefathers freely chose to live where they saw best—not because there was a God directing them to one continent or city over another. Remember, you're only reading this book because my birth father visited Las Vegas from another country and had a random sexual encounter with my birth mother. It's kind of hard to believe God sent him to the US for the purpose of creating me and blessing me with a life in the Western world.

If we compare our Western lifestyles to those of children dying from starvation in poverty-stricken nations and then claim that we are blessed to live here rather than there, then we charge God with favoritism. So many Christians flippantly use the term "blessed" when referring to good outcomes and even for their possessions. But what do they really mean when they say they are blessed? What are people who make these claims subtly telling us, and what do the less fortunate think of these claims?

We all have an insatiable desire to feel special. That desire is magnified when we apply it to favorable outcomes that may seem to have been fashioned by the Creator. As we discussed in the last chapter, some Christians subliminally believe their obedience and virtuous deeds have earned them blessings from an active God. They think, "If I'm good, I'm more deserving of blessings. When I'm bad, I don't deserve as much."

When Christians receive something tangible or have a specific favorable life experience, they are apt to tell others they are blessed. Some Christians consider material possessions as blessings, while others apply the label to the simple joys in life. When a Christian declares they are blessed, they're normally not simply referring to Jesus taking their place on the cross.

The term "blessed" can certainly mean different things to different people. Most Christians use this word to infer their blessings have come to them individually by the direct hand of God. Do you see the subtlety in this? There are some who are bold enough to say, "God provided this for me," or "God planned and saw to it I received that." But most don't explicitly say it that way. Most Christians just say, "I am blessed."

It's up to the listener to determine whether the claimant means to give God the credit for directly providing their "blessing," that God has shown them favor. I despise the word "blessing" because it is almost exclusively used for the sole purpose of letting others know the claimant is special to God and has earned favor with him. Many Christians avoid the word "luck" because it is random and excludes a supernatural provider with cause. Christians use the word "blessed" because they want to believe they have been the target for good fortune with God as their provider.

A few years ago, I stumbled across a blog titled, "The Accidental Missionary", authored by Scott Dannemiller. Scott and his wife Gabby spent a year in Guatemala as Christian missionaries, and they seem to be good examples of how Jesus would want us to live. Scott currently makes his living traveling the country, talking to people about how to think and communicate better, to leave the world better than they found it. I encourage the reader to check out his blog. He has what I think are Jesus-like interpretations on Scripture and how we should all consider honoring God with our lives.

Scott wrote a blog post titled, "The One Thing that Christians Need to Stop Saying." His thoughts convey nearly all that needs to be said about what it really means to be "blessed" and why Christians need to be careful with their public and even private thoughts regarding the notion of godly blessings. When you finish reading his message here, you may want to reconsider what "blessed" is.

The One Thing Christians Should Stop Saying[39]

I was on the phone with a good friend the other day. After covering important topics, like disparaging each other's mothers and retelling semi-factual tales from our college days, our conversation turned to the mundane.

"So, how's work going?" he asked.

For those of you who don't know, I make money by teaching leadership skills and helping people learn to get along in corporate America. My wife says it's all a clever disguise so I can get up in front of large groups and tell stories.

I plead the fifth.

I answered my buddy's question with, "Definitely feeling blessed. Last year was the best year yet for my business. And it looks like this year will be just as busy."

The words rolled off my tongue without a second thought. Like reciting the Pledge of Allegiance or placing my usual lunch order at McDonald's.

But it was a lie.

Now, before you start taking up a collection for the "Feed the Dannemillers" fund, allow me to explain. Based on last year's quest to go twelve months without buying anything, you may have the impression that our family is subsisting on Ramen noodles and free chips and salsa at the local Mexican restaurant. Not to worry, we are not in dire straits.

---

39.   Scott Dannemiller, "The One Thing Christians Should Stop Saying," Huffpost, updated April 29, 2014, https://www.huffingtonpost.com/scott-dannemiller/christians-should-stop-saying_b_4868963.html. Retrieved August 2015. Used by permission.

Last year was the best year yet for my business. Things are looking busy in 2014. But that is not a blessing. I've noticed a trend among Christians, myself included, and it troubles me. Our rote response to material windfalls is to call ourselves blessed. Like the "amen" at the end of a prayer.

"This new car is such a blessing."

"Finally closed on the house. Feeling blessed."

"Just got back from a mission trip. Realizing how blessed we are here in this country."

On the surface, the phrase seems harmless. Faithful even. Why wouldn't I want to give God the glory for everything I have? Isn't that the right thing to do?

No.

As I reflected on my "feeling blessed" comment, two thoughts came to mind. I realize I'm splitting hairs here, creating an argument over semantics. But bear with me, because I believe it is critically important. It's one of those things we can't see because it's so culturally ingrained that it has become normal.

But it has to stop. And here's why.

First, when I say that my material fortune is the result of God's blessing, it reduces The Almighty to some sort of sky-bound, wish-granting fairy who spends his days randomly bestowing cars and cash upon his followers. I can't help but draw parallels to how I handed out M&Ms to my own kids when they followed my directions and chose to poop in the toilet rather than in their pants. Sure, God wants us to continually seek his will, and it's for our own good. But positive reinforcement?

God is not a behavioral psychologist.

Second, and more importantly, calling myself blessed because of material good fortune is just plain *wrong*. For starters, it can be offensive to the hundreds of millions of Christians in the world who live on less than $1 per day. You read that right. Hundreds of millions who receive a single-digit dollar "blessing" per day.

During our year in Guatemala, Gabby and I witnessed first-hand the damage done by the theology of prosperity, where faithful people scraping by to feed their families were simply told they must not be faithful enough. If they were, God would pull them out of their nightmare. Just try harder, and God will show favor.

The problem? Nowhere in Scripture are we promised worldly ease in return for our pledge of faith. In fact, the most devout saints from the Bible usually died penniless, receiving a one-way ticket to prison or death by torture.

I'll take door number three, please.

If we're looking for the definition of blessing, Jesus spells it out clearly.

Now when he saw the crowds, he went up on a mountainside and sat down. His disciples came to him, and he began to teach them, saying:

> "Blessed are the poor in spirit,
> for theirs is the kingdom of heaven.
>
> "Blessed are those who mourn,
> for they will be comforted.
>
> "Blessed are the meek,
> for they will inherit the Earth.
>
> "Blessed are those who hunger and thirst after righteousness,
> for they will be filled.
>
> "Blessed are the merciful,
> for they shall be shown mercy.
>
> "Blessed are the pure in heart,
> for they will see God.

"Blessed are the peacemakers,

for they will be called the sons of God.

"Blessed are those who are persecuted because

of righteousness,

for theirs is the kingdom of heaven.

"Blessed are you when people insult you, persecute you and falsely say all kinds of evil against you because of me. Rejoice and be glad, because great is your reward in heaven, for in the same way they persecuted the prophets who were before you." (Matthew 5:1–12)

I have a sneaking suspicion verses 12a, 12b, and 12c were omitted from the text. That's where the disciples responded by saying,

12a Waitest thou for one second, Lord. What about "blessed art thou comfortable," or 12b "blessed art thou which havest good jobs, a modest house in the suburbs, and a yearly vacation to the Florida Gulf Coast?"

12c And Jesus said unto them, "Apologies, my brothers, but those did not maketh the cut."

So, there it is. Written in red. Plain as day. Even still, we ignore it all when we hijack the word "blessed" to make it fit neatly into our modern American ideals, creating a cosmic lottery where every sincere prayer buys us another scratch-off ticket. In the process, we stand the risk of alienating those we are hoping to bring to the faith.

And we have to stop playing that game.

The truth is, I have no idea why I was born where I was or why I have the opportunity I have. It's beyond comprehension. But I certainly don't believe God has chosen me above others because of the veracity of my prayers or the depth of my faith. God can't be directly handing out blessings my way based solely on my merit. Still, if I take advantage of the opportunities set before me, a comfortable life may come my way. It's not guaranteed. But if it does happen, I don't believe Jesus will call me blessed.

He will call me "burdened."

He will ask,

"What will you do with it?"

"Will you use it for yourself?"

"Will you use it to help?"

"Will you hold it close for comfort?"

"Will you share it?"

So many hard choices. So few easy answers.

So, my prayer today is that I understand my true blessing. It's not my house. Or my job. Or my standard of living.

No.

My blessing is this. I know a God who gives hope to the hopeless. I know a God who loves the unlovable. I know a God who comforts the sorrowful. And I know a God who has planted this same power within me. Within all of us.

And for this blessing, may our response always be, "Use me."

There were thousands of comments listed below this blog post and a few of them happened to be from me. I'll spare you my comments and provide a few of the comments from others I consider misguided at best.

Comment: You said in this article, "The truth is, I have no idea why I was born where I was or why I have the opportunity I have. It's beyond comprehension." We most certainly do know why we are born where we are born! The Scripture cannot be clearer and more precise about this issue, (Acts 17:26) NIV, "From one man he made all the nations, that they should inhabit the whole Earth; and he marked out their appointed times in history and the boundaries of their lands."

Comment: That means you "spiritualize" every instance where Jesus literally says, "Whatsoever things ye desire when ye pray, believe that ye receive them and ye shall have them" or "If you believe you will receive whatever you ask for in prayer" or "Ask anything in my name and I will do it" or "Everyone who asks receives." God is not a worldly ATM, but he has shown in the ministry of Jesus that we may ask for ANY good thing (not out of greed or selfishness or immorality) and we will receive it, if we believe. Jesus gave a very "unspiritual" example of this when he cursed the fig tree and said we could do the same "if we believe." I take Jesus to mean what he says all the time, not selectively based on someone else's theological opinion. Read God's Word and believe it—period—if you want to see the miraculous become common in your life.

Comment: I would like to warn against the slippery slope of using words like "random" in relation to God and suffering. If these things happen by random, it can be implied that God does not control them or cannot control them. If God does not control them, we can conclude that God is uninterested in our well-being, which is Biblically false (Jer. 29:11 and Rom. 8:28). If God cannot control them, we have stripped him of his omnipotence, which is also biblically false (Gen. 18:14 and Jer. 32:17). Saying that things happen by random can have greater theological consequences than it first appears.

Comment: I also believe God blesses people in different ways. To say that a good financial standing, success, or even wealth is not from God is nonsense. He gave you the skills, the drive, the job, and anything else for those material blessings to happen, and for you to say they are not blessings from God, again, rob him of glory.

Comment: Dumb luck isn't part of our Christian belief, so if God is numbering the hairs on our very head, I'm certain that he also ordained where we'd be born. It seems that you are confusing two words: blessing and favor. God does not bless us because he favors us. The blessings come as part of his plan to show his love.

Comment: Okay, I get the desire to avoid the prosperity gospel, and I'm completely with you on that. There is great danger in that theology, and I respect and encourage your desire to stay away from it. However, material blessing is from God, and he blesses those as he chooses. Your assertion that "My place of birth, my opportunities, and my good fortune are not a result of God's choosing. It's dumb luck" completely negates God's sovereignty; the fact that he has the power to do what he wants, and he will do whatever he chooses to.

Comment: I completely understand what you are saying. However, I do not at all agree with your claim, "My place of birth, my opportunities, and my good fortune are not a result of God's choosing. It's dumb luck." I don't believe anything is due to luck or chance. God is sovereign, and he is in control of EVERYTHING. I thought this was really a great article until I read that statement. I was about to recommend the article, but I won't recommend anything that gives credit to dumb luck.

Comment: According to this article, my home isn't a blessing from God? So, then I earned [it] myself? I don't agree with that. I would consider my home a gift, or a blessing from God. Just because there are people less fortunate doesn't mean what I have been given isn't a gift. If that is the case then God shouldn't allow me to be blessed with sight, because there are blind people in the world, and that wouldn't be fair to them.

You may have noticed two of the commentors used Scripture to refute the author's "dumb luck" argument regarding where we are born, from Acts

17:26. This simply reflects how Christians continue to refute reality as they hang on to their misguided interpretations of Scripture.

Another commenter agreed with the biblical authors' false notion that God creates every human and he is responsible for creating those with sight and those who are born blind. Another commentor stated, "He gave you the skills, the drive, the job, and anything else for those material blessings to happen" which is in line with Rick Warren's false claim that God genetically and specifically designed each of us with different skill sets as part of our "SHAPE".

Many people continue believing the biblical authors' theories that God creates each individual with their specific inherent and physical traits. And since they believe he created each of us individually, that must imply he knows how many hairs we have on our scalps. They think, if the words or concepts are in the Bible, then they must be true.

To me, these lines of thought illustrate that many Christians today don't think for themselves. They just want to follow and defend Scriptures to the bitter end, even ones completely at odds with sound reasoning and with unmistakable evidence to the contrary. We've already disproven the biblical notion that God designs and creates each of us in a hands-on way. Remember, our common reality needs to be our measuring standard, not acceptance of every Scripture.

One of the commenters concluded that the "dumb luck" argument of the author would negate God's sovereignty (God can be in control of anything). But that would only be true if we knew God was currently intervening—as the acts of Jesus showed through Scripture when he was here. If I'm right and God has suspended intervention, then God's Sovereignty is still intact. God's voluntary suspension of miracles does not negate his sovereignty.

Follow me on this: assume for the moment God decided he would not be involved in the matters of this Earth after Jesus ascended and he has entrusted us to run this world. Those who love him would do their best to live by his standards and serve others as he asked them to do. They could feel blessed and live their life in gratitude for what Jesus did with hope for an eternity with him. Evil people and even people that are not followers of Jesus would continue to make life decisions that may or may not be in line with how Jesus has asked us to live.

In a world like this, there would still be deadly tornadoes, hurricanes, earthquakes, car accidents, and disease. A horrific event like the Holocaust could have taken place and thousands of people could be at risk to die from starvation daily. A viral pandemic could kill four million humans.

A young mother of three young children could suffer and die from breast cancer. Women could still be raped, and a million children could be aborted annually. Children could still be born with Down syndrome or autism. Good things could happen to bad people and bad things could happen to good people. Systemic racism could run rampant.

In a world like this, prayers, even unselfish prayers, would never be answered affirmatively. Those that appear to have been answered favorably would have a logical explanation and be labeled a mere coincidence. Apparent "answered" prayers would simply have occurred synchronously with the natural events that would have come to fruition absent prayer. Prayers not answered the way we hoped for would simply be because God decided to allow his world to run its course. No one would need to give some God-ordained mysterious reason we will never be able to understand for unanswered prayer. If people chose to perpetuate the notion that God was providing them specific favored blessings, we would know their claims were false because we began with the assumption that God suspended the supernatural after the era of Jesus.

Does the world I've just described sound familiar to you? Our "blessings" should not be based on our circumstantial good life outcomes. Our common reality should be that we are blessed because of God's amazing grace and not because God is selectively providing to the favored few.

So, what should we really mean when we use the term, "blessed"? One way we receive blessings in our lives is by honoring God's protective laws. In other words, when we follow these laws and / or the principles that define those laws, we are not as likely to suffer negative natural consequences which can be considered a "blessing."

Again, this is not to say that those who abide by all of God's laws are less likely to be tragically killed or contract a lethal virus. It's simply more likely that such a way of life will minimize the pitfalls that would undoubtedly come our way otherwise. Note the significant difference between what I have suggested as a catalyst for blessing and the standard Christian suggestion that God's hands are the root cause for our favor.

Of course, all of our universe is a blessing. In a general sense, we are all blessed because of God's initial creation. Few Christians would deny that everything we receive in this world is a blessing because God created all of it. Can we say that we are blessed when we observe the beauty and majesty of the planet and universe in which we live and experience all of it? I do.

Step back and consider that we can all say we are blessed to have a God who took our place on that horrific cross, and there is no condemnation for those who accept it. We are all blessed because we don't have to carry our past sins like an anvil on our backs for the remainder of our lives.

Can we feel blessed when we help our fellow man in his time of need with no expectation for reciprocation? Can we be blessed by showing and receiving love while we're here? I'm all over it.

One of the commenters on Scott's blog from above made the following statements which completely resonate with my position.

> *I don't really see material objects as a meaningful blessing. Blessings come, instead, in intangibles: a sense of peace, a revelation of grace, or the awareness of a God who loved us enough to die for us. This perception moves blessings out of the world's hoardable, "mine not yours" economy, and puts blessings back in God's economy, where immaterial riches are available to all, regardless of our human scaled rank in the world.*

His statement shouts truth to me. And I implore all readers to consider that the pious acts of claiming blessing from an active God of favor who acts on behalf of the supposed recipient needs to be minimized at all cost. How can any one of us know that God has provided any of these other types of "favor blessings" individually? But the main reason to stop is simple: to stop damaging Christians and non-Christians alike who do not experience the same blessings as others claim to receive.

Consider the following scenario: Let's say you're in remission from some form of cancer after receiving prayer and medical treatment, and you have convinced yourself that God was supernaturally involved in your recovery. You believe you have been "blessed" by God. Months later, you visit your close Christian friends at a pediatric hospital only moments after they've watched their five-year-old son succumb to leukemia. Your friends seem inconsolable and are sobbing with grief-filled hearts. Do you believe God would support you announcing to your friends during your visit that he blessed you by miraculously healing your cancer months earlier? Would God support you making that claim in the presence of those same friends a year later? I hope your answer is "No!" If that's your position, then why would it be ok for you to think or ever publicly (by mouth or through social media) announce at any time God was responsible for eradicating your cancer in any forum? If it's not ok to make that announcement in front of others who are suffering and who didn't receive a miraculous blessing, then why would it be ok to publicly make a claim like that at any time? At some point, your favored "blessing" claim is sure to fall on the ears of someone less fortunate / "blessed".

Since Jesus asked his followers to pray in the privacy of their bedrooms and not publicly, why shouldn't we apply the same principle to these godly favor claims? Even if one is convinced God has acted specifically for them, why would they need to claim it publicly? If they are making sure God knows they recognize his favor, why can't the recognition to God be made privately? If it is to show others how special they are to God, there's not much to say about that.

Does God want us to hurt others? What's it like for a married couple whose child is suffering from a disease, to hear another couple say that God has blessed them with healthy children? We're not discussing the outer bounds like comparing a person who buys a new Rolls Royce and to a child starving in the African desert as I type. I'm referring to situations like a man in a Bible study claiming a godly blessing because his son is now free from drug addiction after prayerful requests to the Almighty, while another small group member in the same room contemplates and agonizes over why her Christian daughter died in a car accident a year earlier.

It honestly makes my skin crawl to hear any claim of favor. None of us deserves any more favor from God than any other human. Until Christians grasp this concept, our religion as a whole will continue to alienate itself into an inconsequential faith.

People are looking for a real God. It's hard enough for many to believe in an invisible God who, if he exists, has clearly hidden himself from all of us. And they don't need and won't accept a "magic" God who mysteriously sneaks around behind the scenes defying our common realities, altering the intentions, actions, or the courses of favored people's lives. Or a God who causes or allows certain events to occur with some premeditated intention or plan, who "uses" those situations to teach us something or to provide blessings to the select few. Deviating from our common realities and attempting to claim these interventive activities come from God only further alienates the unblessed and the non-believer.

Are we to think favored blessing claims will draw non-believers closer to considering a loving God who died for them? I've had agnostic friends tell me they don't if there is a God, but they know with certainty, if God exists, he is not giving to some who claim favor and not others. For them, that type of God cannot be real, and those who believe they receive from him in that way live in pretend-world.

I hope I have convinced you now the harm of using words, phrases, and sentences that lead others to believe that God is showing us individual favor. We shouldn't need to tell others that God is actively blessing us to validate our Christianity. We should let our lives reflect the love of God, and we should acknowledge our blessing solely from God's amazing grace.

[24] Examining "God Did It!"

WE'VE ALREADY DISCUSSED A FEW CLAIMS REGARDING God's current miraculous actions that I am convinced are false. I'd like to dig into some of the irrational and illogical thinking girding these claims. I'll provide many examples of these claims in this chapter and let you decide if godly intervention is the best explanation for each outcome.

Many Christians make daily claims about what God is actively doing in their lives or in the lives of others as a direct result of their prayers, while others argue that, as fallible human beings, we are unable to use human logic to discern the same. While it's true we are fallible and flawed in many ways, each of us relies on logic to function in every aspect of our lives. We use it to make important decisions, including which religion we should follow, and in most ways, it allows for and perpetuates our survival. God clearly instilled the capability to use reason and logic into his first two human masterpieces, and we have all inherited those traits, albeit some more than others. Our common realities are based on observation, reason, and logic, and they must be our measuring rod for truth. Again, if we can't depend on the truth of our common realities, our lives will be filled with even greater cognitive dissonance and confusion.

I don't believe God is illogical. The Bible tells us we are made in his image, and I'm yet uncertain that "his image" relates to only our physicality. Perhaps "his image" also refers to how we are able to reason, use logic, discern justice, or offer love to others. If God made this planet and the first human creation, the miraculous events that occurred to produce our universe and its first inhabitants defy logical reasoning. But there is order to what God has made, logical, universal laws governing our universe.

Our understanding of gravity is logical. The laws of physics are rational and include many ordered unchanging constants that God wove into his creation. If God is fair and just, then we must also expect that he respects and honors reason and logic. Most Christians use reason and logic to believe in the existence of God and many of the timeless truths included in the biblical canon. However, I believe some followers of Jesus make claims of favor which are outside the limits of clear and sound reasoning.

Observation of Reality

Before we go any further, I would like to discuss something from the scientific world I once participated in. It wasn't until my third year in college that I decided to become a physicist. In all my lower division science classes during my first two years, I wasn't really being taught any theory but only handed formulas to solve specific problems. That never satisfied me.

I wanted to know how those formulas were derived and what theoretical processes were involved in developing them. Perhaps this foreshadowed my inability to simply accept things that were told to me. I couldn't just take things on faith. It seemed I really needed to know the causes behind the effects for everything knowable. So, I decided to declare physics as my major and gutted my way through that complicated process until I finally received my degree.

In general terms, physics is the study of the universe and the causes behind the effects of all that takes place. It's the intense dissecting of the laws of nature—which, to me, are the laws that God instilled within our universe from the time of creation. Man studies physics attempting to observe these God-created laws and to formulate mathematical equations that describe the events that occur within time and space.

In a way similar to arriving at the existence of God, by observation and mathematical theory, man has derived his knowledge of the God-given laws of nature, not by current supernatural events. Unless a specific supernatural event is consistently being observed, we are unable to quantify any working theories. Physics measures reality and has no interest in studying miracles, because miracles, if they occur at all, are certainly not measurable with any consistency. We develop theories and equations to describe God's laws of nature and devise testing procedures to verify or refute them. One cannot study physics without being a skeptic. It's essentially a requirement. It requires deep thinking, critical examination, as well as a willingness to alter one's theory when it doesn't agree with the measurable observation of reality.

What refutes science? The answer is "better science." What doesn't refute science? Our feelings, our religion, our favorite politician, and certainly not our opinions after watching a couple of YouTube videos. Science is the study of reality, and that reality will not change based on our ability to stomach it.

Shouldn't all of us, Christians, agnostics, and atheists alike, care about truth and reality? Shouldn't we all think deeply about certain matters before we claim to believe anything? When we simply leave important matters up to faith, don't we shortcut the work required to draw conclusions which shouldn't be based on our religious backgrounds or determined by our geography or our heritage? Can any of us afford to make a mistake in these theological matters, especially with such high stakes? The concept of a place like hell should certainly be a high-stakes proposition for anyone.

I've been accused of being a curious skeptic because I'm always looking for alternative explanations to life's events that may better explain the causes behind those events. I'm always searching for other factors that may have influenced the life events I've been exposed to. I have a lot of questions, and I'm not apt to just take the first proposed theory as fact. I've certainly had many theories I once considered rock solid go up in flames when a better theory came along explaining a specific event with better accuracy. I don't take it personally when I'm wrong. I'm happy to do whatever it takes to make the theory fit reality.

I'm always curious about how this universe operates, and I don't feel odd because of it. Physicist Neil deGrasse Tyson once said, "No one is dumb who is curious. The people who don't ask questions remain clueless throughout their lives." Dr. Tyson is also the one who said, "The good thing about science is that it's true whether or not you believe in it."

The late astrophysicist Carl Sagan also said something very profound during one of his last interviews with noted journalist Charlie Rose: "Science is more than a body of knowledge. It is a way of thinking; a way of skeptically interrogating the universe with a fine understanding of human fallibility. If we are not able to ask skeptical questions to interrogate those who tell us that something is true, to be skeptical of those in authority, then we are up for grabs for the next charlatan (political or religious) who comes rambling along."

Towards Substantive Critical Thinking

As we have already discussed, most people don't really choose their religion. It's chosen for them by their parents. There are some who rebel against their family's religious preference and convert to a different religion or become agnostic or atheistic. But most of us worship the God of our predecessors. So, most people do not investigate the truth or reliability of other religions and therefore they only have a general skepticism towards other faith-based systems. Since they've never really investigated other faiths, they can't really approach other faiths with specific skeptical arguments against them.

However, there are many Christians who are skeptical behind the scenes of their own religion. They have doubts about the validity of certain passages within the Christian Bible or the current miracle claims made by others. But as I've mentioned, most won't discuss their doubts since doing so would reveal they're not "all in" with their faith.

So, let's discuss some other irrational claims purported by Christians who continue to perpetuate how God may be actively involved in their daily lives. I found one of the most irrational posts on a social media site several years ago that continues to make the rounds from time to time. The post itself made me shake my head with disgust, but it was the comments from others that really floored me. The post begins with a picture of the standard Caucasian Jesus clothed in his white robe, wearing sandals, and sitting next to a young adult who is dressed in the casual clothes of our time on a park bench with a few trees in their background. In this fictitious setting, Jesus seems to be leaning toward the young adult as if he's offering comfort and counsel. The dialogue is between Jesus and the young male adult (referred to as "Me" below).

The post beneath the picture goes like this:

ME: God, can I ask you a question?

JESUS: Sure.

ME: Promise you won't get mad. . .

JESUS: I promise.

ME: Why did you let so much stuff happen to me today?

JESUS: What do you mean?

ME: Well, I woke up late.

JESUS: Yes. . .

ME: My car took forever to start.

JESUS: Okay. . .

ME: At lunch they made my sandwich wrong, and I had to wait.

JESUS: Humm. . .

ME: On the way home, my phone went DEAD, just as I picked up a call.

JESUS: All right. . .

ME: And to top it all off, when I got home, I just wanted to soak my feet in my new foot massager and relax. But it wouldn't work!!! Nothing went right today! Why did you do that?

JESUS: Let me see, the death angel was at your bed this morning and I had to send one of My Angels to battle him for your life. I let you sleep through that.

ME: (humbled) Oh...

JESUS: I didn't let your car start because there was a drunk driver on your route that would have hit you if you were on the road.

ME: (ashamed)

JESUS: The first person who made your sandwich today was sick, and I didn't want you to catch what they had; I knew you couldn't afford to miss work.

ME: (embarrassed) Okay.

JESUS: Your phone went dead because the person that was calling was going to give false witness about what you said on that call, I didn't even let you talk to them so you would be covered.

ME: (softly) I see, God.

JESUS: Oh, and that foot massager, it had a short that was going to throw out all of the power in your house tonight. I didn't think you wanted to be in the dark.

ME: I'm sorry, God.

JESUS: Don't be sorry, just learn to trust Me.... in All things, the good and the bad.

ME: I will trust you.

JESUS: And don't doubt that my plan for your day is always better than your plan.

ME: I won't God. And let me just tell you God, thank you for everything today.

JESUS: You're welcome, child. It was just another day being your God,
and I love looking after My children. . .

REPOST if you Believe in HIM. Worth posting.

The following responses are just a snippet of the over one million comments representing the general theme of most:

Comment: It just goes to show that, not all bad things that happen
to us are considered bad luck... sometimes they are even blessings in
disguise. We just need look at the other positive side...

Comment: Amen. We may not understand his plans, but HIS plans
are always better than ours.

Comment: What an amazing God we serve. Let's give him the highest praise.

Comment: God is good all the time.

Comment: Amen.

Comment: I was so touched while reading this story and I realized
that everything good or bad really has a reason. :-) thank God:-)

Comment: A few years ago, I had to drive from Louisiana to
Virginia. Long drive. At some point in the middle of nowhere, I
REALLY needed a bathroom and NEEDED a cup of coffee even
more so! In the middle of nowhere. . . here is a Starbucks. I thought
thank you GOD!!!! When I got back in my truck and started heading
down the highway, I hear on the radio of a fatal wreck at mm. . . I
don't remember. Anyway, I realized it was about 20 miles ahead of
the Starbucks in the middle of nowhere. . . And in the 20 minutes

it took to get coffee and use the bathroom. . . kept me OUT of that pileup! Say what you will, but GOD was really working hard that day. I drove through that same area a couple weeks later.... No Starbucks, nothing. I feel sorry for those who don't believe and remember how horrible my life was when I kicked GOD out. He came back into my life that day!

Comment: This happened to me, a friend of mine's car broke down while at my house. While we were sorting her car out, there was a massive car crash on the motorway. Not only were people terribly injured but also other motorway users were stuck in traffic for hours in hot weather. You can call it the universe, coincidence or whatever, but I believe it to be God looking after us.

Comment: Everything happens for a reason. I was kicked off from my previous job cuz my officemate did something behind my back. They even canceled my visa right away even though I had a 1-month notice to work and couldn't find other work. I didn't fight for it cuz I'm not a fighter. I just gave it all to God. In just 2 weeks, God provided me a better job with good working hours and a lot of holidays and a very nice boss. I just got my bonus too. Thank you, Lord!

And on the other side, where I've been speaking from:

Comment: The people you should explain God's love to are not here. They are dead. Tell them about God's plan. Tell them about your story where God helped you avoid a traffic accident. Tell them they starve "for a reason". Explain how "God is good all the time". Tell them to say "Amen".

Comment: My 39-year-old daughter just passed away from breast cancer. Left 2 children and a husband and a family that loved her very much. She suffered for over a year! I wore my knees out praying for God to help her. And she only got worse. I am not saying there is no God, I am just wondering how he chooses who gets to suffer, and who doesn't. And why???

There are so many crazy levels of delusion going on in this post and subsequent comments I almost don't know where to start. I was astounded at the more than 1.5 million likes and nearly 1 million comments at the time I first discovered this. Interestingly, there were a few assumed atheists hammering this post, and in my opinion, rightfully so. There was also an honest comment (the last one above) from a woman trying to reconcile the reality of losing her suffering daughter with her once-held preconceived notion of an all-loving, caring, and now apparent selective favor-providing God.

I want to briefly focus on the comment made by the presumed atheist from above: "The people you should explain God's love to are not here. They are dead. Tell them about God's plan. Tell them about your story where God helped you avoid a traffic accident. Tell them they starve 'for a reason.' Explain how 'God is good all the time.' Tell them to say 'Amen.'" Can you see the anger and frustration coming from this commenter's sympathetic heart? This person was clearly assessing the obvious injustice between the author's post of godly favoritism, sometimes in petty matters, with those that were not shown the same measure of favor.

Christians assume atheists are evil because they won't acknowledge the existence of God. They also assume atheists are incapable of showing empathy, but I know that's a false premise. You can't convince me atheists don't donate to or participate with charitable organizations. In fact, atheists are probably more likely to participate or donate to charitable causes because they know sending "thoughts and prayers" or waiting on God for help will accomplish nothing.

If you're looking for one of the reasons why there are people who will never accept the God of the Christian Bible, you need to look no further than the post and comments listed above. I'll never understand how anyone could be gullible enough to believe there is any truth in this way of thinking. For those currently outside of the Christian community who engage in critical thinking, they would never want to their name or reputation be associated with the word "Christian" because of posts and comments like this. I consider myself a Christian of some sort, and I'm embarrassed to have my name associated with the people who think this way. It is beyond me that any rational person could ever find truth in any of it. Yet, there were all of those "likes" and all the comments supporting its basis for truth. It's enough to drive the "seeker" away from ever checking out the Christian faith and deepens the stake in the ground for those already alienated.

This kind of irrational thinking leads me to believe that many people don't use reasoning or have critical thinking capabilities. They want a God like this, so they are constantly looking for what appears to be mysterious, favorable coincidental events, then claim them as truth to justify God is looking out for them. This seems like a form of egotism and narcissism to think this way, but too many Christians won't see it any other way.

They huddle up on Sundays in their mutually reinforcing echo chambers with likeminded people who continue to perpetuate this way of thinking, and they all influence each other with these types of claims. They have placed themselves under the fictitious notion that God is constantly providing a hedge of protection around them. To them, there is nothing random about the events that go on in their lives. Every one of their life events has been preplanned or is being assessed and favorably executed by the Almighty. When their plans conflict with God's plans, his plans win out because he cares so much more for them than others who are so much less fortunate.

Yes, they will admit that seemingly bad things happen to them (good people). But these "bad" things are allowed or even orchestrated by God to teach them a lesson or to provide something better in the future, as any good earthly parent would do. But where is their free will, logic, and reasoning? It's as if these people have turned off their minds and have succumbed to the puppet master who is pulling all the strings behind the scenes, and they are compelled to believe it. I see malleable minds which would be willing to sign up for any religious belief system they were ever exposed to. This isn't a childlike faith as described in the Bible. It's a lazy and misguided type of faith that can lead to a very emotionally destructive path for those who continue to think and believe this way.

I'm merely trying to highlight the incongruency of a favor-giving God and his supposed actions in light of the world's suffering. For people who sign up for this falsehood, they are mindlessly believing that all the unknown mysteries of life are God manipulating circumstances for their well-being. Each and every one of the people who claim to believe in this kind of God should be required to spoon feed the Hajis of this world for the remainder of their lives. Anyone who has the guts to think or make these claims publicly should be willing to do it face to face with those who are suffering immeasurably.

Why Do Bad Things Happen to Good People?

Dr. James Dobson, for whom I have profound respect for in most areas of his ministry, authored a book titled *When God Doesn't Make Sense*.[40] Dobson opens his book with a story about a young man named Chuck Frye who just graduated with his undergraduate degree and was headed to medical school. Later, Frye decided he wanted to take his medical knowledge to the missionary fields and treat the poor and needy who would otherwise suffer and die.

Chuck wasn't just planning to physically treat these people for their illnesses. His ultimate plan was to share the good news of the gospel to those who had never heard about God's amazing grace. That sure seemed like a noble and honorable mission to me. Unfortunately, despite fervent prayers of his family and friends, Frye died of leukemia shortly after starting medical school. Dobson then asks the question, "How can we make any sense of this incomprehensible act of God?"

---

40. James Dobson, *When God Doesn't Make Sense* (Carol Stream, IL: Tyndale House, 1993).

You and I both know that these sorts of "incomprehensible acts of God" occur by the thousands every day, like when my fourteen-year-old baseball teammate died from a massive heart attack on the diamond. How can we make sense of that with a loving God who is supposedly active? Consider the Sandy Hook Elementary school shooting in December of 2012. I know all humans have flaws and are not without sin, but how can any of us look at the children who were senselessly killed at Sandy Hook and claim that they were not innocent or "good"? And why would Dobson suggest that Frye's death was an act of God? Is it because Dobson thinks God orchestrated his death or is responsible because he did nothing to cure Frye?

After events like these, we are all forced to ask ourselves, "Why do bad things happen to good people?" If God loves us and answers our prayers, how could he allow these horrific things to happen to anyone? And what about the biblical authors who suggested people who remained obedient to God would receive their just rewards? Why would he ignore their prayers or the prayers of their loved ones?

As we previously discussed, believers and non-believers succumb to cancer and deadly traffic accidents at the same rate per capita. Hurricanes and tornados do not differentiate between believers or non-believers. Ironically, tornadoes mostly occur in the Bible Belt of the Midwest and Southeast. Lipid bilayer molecules don't seem to care whether they attach to the inner walls of arteries that supply blood to the hearts of believers or non-believers. Viral pandemics are not repelled by the faithful.

Whether God exists or not, these statistics do not lie. This should confirm for all of us that there is not a God who is actively looking out for or placing any hedge of protection around believers (good people) any more than non-believers (not-so-good people?). This is what the author of Ecclesiastics suggested, reflected by statistical data on morbidity. It should be our common reality.

Irrational Panacea

But this irrefutable data does not stop today's Christians from taking biblical Scriptures out of context and attempting to apply them to their lives today. Even if some of these Bible verses had merit during the biblical era, they are certainly not true for us today. In March of 2020, as the Covid-19 virus was beginning to spread rampantly in the US, I found Christians posting the following Scriptures from Psalm 91:6–12 NLT on their social media timelines:

Coronavirus Encouragement

Do not dread the disease that stalks in darkness, nor the disaster that strikes at midday. Though a thousand fall at your side, though ten thousand are dying around you, these evils will not touch you. Just open your eyes, and see how the wicked are punished.

If you make the Lord your refuge, if you make the Most High your shelter, no evil will conquer you; *no plague will come near your home.* For he will order his angels to *protect you* wherever you go. They will hold you up with their hands, so you won't even hurt your foot on a stone.

Yet Christians (good people?) were being infected at the same rates as non-believers—living and dying in the same proportions they were statistically represented in our society. That virus was an equal opportunity infector and killer—never caring whether one was a believer or a non-believer. If there was any truth to today's application to those verses, Christians could have volunteered to help care for hospital patients suffering from the virus without wearing protective gear.

I didn't see any Christians trying that. I saw them fervently washing their hands, socially distancing themselves from others, wearing facemasks, and sheltering in place as recommended by the CDC. God was not sending spiritual angels to protect or care for anyone. This is yet another false premise from antiquity that Christians tried to apply to our era.

Irrational thinking that God looks out for Christians more than others confounds them when confronted with the reality of everyday events that include bad things happening to "good" Christian people. My pastor's wife was diagnosed with breast cancer about eight years ago, and she told me she was surprised by how many church members seemed shocked that God would allow a pastor's wife to contract cancer.

Many say, "ignorance is bliss," and maybe there's some truth to that statement for some people. For me, it's no way to live one's life. When one believes God is orchestrating the events of people's lives in some way, it removes our responsibility and eventually limits our desire to provide help.

Thoughts, Actions, and Belief Systems

There are many people who will interpret events in their lives as if God was not only behind those events but that he might also be leading them in a direction they may never have logically considered. If they believe in God's "leading" more than their logical interpretation of a certain situation, logic and reason will most likely succumb to their feelings. I think we can all agree that this can be dangerous for not only the misguided believer but others who are in their immediate circle—especially their children.

Mahatma Gandhi once said: "Your beliefs become your thoughts, your thoughts become your words, your words become your actions, your actions become your habits, your habits become your values, your values become your destiny."

Normally, this saying is an instruction to establish one's life on moral beliefs. When they do, it can positively affect their thoughts, words, actions, habits, values, and, finally, their destinies. The converse is also true. Without a moral belief system, our destinies are likely to include suffering.

Let's redirect this teaching away from the application and reference to morality and immorality most often used. I'd like to apply this saying to Christians who have a belief system that includes an active God who is selectively granting favors to the chosen few. When people choose to believe a favor-giving God is working behind the scenes to help them, they reflect this notion with their words, actions, and habits. Their values are not affected by these intervention belief systems, nor are their overall eternal destinies. Christians don't have heaven or hell riding on their active godly intervention belief systems. But often, when the all-loving and all-caring God of their universe doesn't act in a way they prayed for, even though their requesting prayers are what most of us would consider unselfish, it can rock their world. Their emotional destinies balanced on their original belief that God would actively look out for them.

There are millions on this planet who ask themselves, why would God allow this, or why did God cause that? Why would God reject my humble prayer—even when it was on behalf of a loved one or friend? We can discard bewildering questions like these by simply recognizing God is not acting in our era. It's critical we establish our thoughts and lives on reality. When we choose to ignore reality, we put our emotional stability at risk. A friend of mine once said, "When I argue with reality, I always lose—but only 100 percent of the time."

Here's yet another prayer posted on social media promoting the common thinking that God pulls the strings behind the scenes so each of us has better lives:

God, thank you for the closed doors. Thank you for not allowing me to settle for second best. God, every time I thought I was being rejected from something good, you were redirecting me to something better. God, I pray that you will give me peace when frustration creeps in. I pray you will give me strength to press on when I'm told, "no." God, thank you for teaching me that "no" is just a step to a bigger and better "yes." Amen.

If a Christian who just committed suicide could speak, would they be able to cite the words of that prayer? Where did their godly peace run off to during their "closed doors"? At first glance, such an optimistic prayer seems wonderful. But what happens when tragedy strikes and we're left in a pile of rubble—without the possibility of a "better 'YES'" showing up? I'm all for having a positive attitude but never at the expense of refuting reality.

Most Christians perceive God as an entity located in the heavens, constantly monitoring and assessing every thought, circumstance, and action of every human. They also errantly believe he's constantly looking ahead and either allowing events to play out or intervening in places where he needs to. They live in a world where God alters people's thoughts, intentions, or actions—ensuring they stay on a course that will lead to the best outcomes for them and the entirety of humanity.

They continue to believe this false premise even when the evidence laid before them clearly shows the effects of randomness and the direct consequences of our freewilled decisions. I can't count the times I've heard Christians say that "God uses. . ." Christians believe God uses specific circumstances for the betterment of everyone. If a life situation seems bad to a Christian, they will claim God is "using" that circumstance for their betterment—as if to say God has caused or allowed a specific circumstance as part of his plan. Perhaps he's trying to teach them a lesson, or maybe he's working things out to ensure the Christian will end up with a better outcome.

God doesn't need to orchestrate or "use" circumstances, nor is he doing so. The world's natural order presents all of us with challenging life circumstances, and God is neither creating those circumstances nor employing them for some mysterious purpose. When we face challenging times, we can choose to irrationally react or to use those difficult circumstances to align ourselves with the principles of Jesus to learn and grow. Life naturally brings these difficult situations our way. They are not from a God who is purposefully causing and "using" them for some ulterior motive. Wearing supernatural rose-colored glasses will not refute our common realities.

Many of us have also heard the popular Christian rhyme, "If God brings you to it, he will bring you through it." What is the implication of a saying like this? Not simply that God will provide aid in a time of crisis. We all know many Christians believe that. This little sentence subtly implies that God himself leads one into a crisis. If this is how it works in the real world, then I'm not sure about the validity of free will. And, if God was really directing his creation into the path of bad circumstances, then I guess I should expect him to bail us out. To me, misguided Christians give this as a supernatural reason explaining God's involvement with our personal problems, even though no one can prove or know God did it. We only use it to make ourselves believe God controls our circumstances—even the difficult ones. But not to worry. We're well cared for, because he will get us through them.

PART 8:

GOD OF

REFUGE

[25] God-Ordained Quirks

A CLOSE CHRISTIAN FRIEND OF MINE RECENTLY TOLD me a story regarding some comments his wife made during a phone conversation they were having. His wife is a Christian marriage and family counselor, and they were communicating by phone off and on throughout the morning over some major issue they were having with their teenage son. She made the following comments to him while she was at her office, "My next client had to cancel his appointment with me because he was awake all night throwing up. I guess God knew we needed some extra time today to sort through how we're going to handle this issue with our son."

My friend (her husband) replied, "Are you saying God caused your client to get sick so he could give us some extra time to sort through our family issues?"

She paused for a moment, then replied, "Well, no, I guess not."

This story doesn't sound like much, but to me, it has preprogrammed delusion written all over it. My friend's wife's gratitude for the extra hour not having to counsel her client made her feel the need to give credit to God.

Here again, we have someone who not only has invented a reason as to why she was afforded favor, but she involved a "Reason-er" for providing it. She said this with no shred of evidence for its validity. She wanted to have a God who was looking out for her. It was only when her husband asked her to examine her reasoning that she realized the folly of invoking a God who would bring misery to someone else for her favor.

This is the kind of subtle method many Christians use to convince themselves and others that God is good and looks out for (some of) us. If my friend had not challenged his wife about her subtle comment, she may have never reconsidered her faulty line of reasoning and left another supernatural act from God chalked up on her "favored" scoreboard.

Again, I think it's important to discuss these kinds of subtle remarks and imperative to challenge people who make them. If we don't, people like my friend's wife will continue to perpetuate faulty reasoning regarding God's character, which isn't good for any of us—including God. I wonder if she would have felt comfortable sharing her initial misguided reasoning with her client. What would he have thought?

There's one other explanation I have for why people want to give credit to God for the good events that occur in their lives. It's not only to let others know that they are worshiping the "correct" God who specifically looks out for them. Potentially, in the mind of the supposed recipient, if God had done something favorable for them and they failed to give him credit, what would God think about their lack of gratitude? Perhaps he won't be so willing to help them with their next crisis.

Preferential Parking Spaces

I really hate providing this next purported favor claim, but I just can't help myself. I have tried to stay away from Joel Osteen's prosperity gospel here because I didn't want the reader to think this book was only targeting the extreme favor-claimers of his kind. This excerpt was taken from one of Joel Osteen's sermons, and you can decide for yourself it has any merit. As petty as this example may seem, there are still Christians who believe God operates this way.

> One time Victoria and I were taking our children to the zoo. It was about 10:00 in the morning. We didn't think anybody would be there. But when we arrived, the place was packed. We didn't realize it was

spring break and all the children were out of school. The parking lot was so backed up with traffic. People were everywhere. We drove around and around the parking area, up and down, back and forth. Couldn't find any place.

Just as we were about to leave, I did what I'm asking you to do. Under my breath I said, "Lord, thank you for your favor. Thank you for helping us find a parking spot so we can have fun with our children." This is not a magic formula. I was simply acknowledging God. The Scripture says, "When you acknowledge God, he will crown your efforts with success." A couple of minutes later, just like it was perfectly on cue, as I was driving around, this car backed out. We were able to pull in. My first words were, "Lord, thank you for your favor."

When something good happens, recognize it's the favor of God, and then learn to thank him for it. At the office, all of the sudden you have a good idea. It comes out of nowhere. "Lord, thank you for your favor." At the mall you find what you want on sale. At lunch you bump into somebody you've been wanting to meet. Those aren't lucky breaks. Those aren't coincidences. That's the favor of God. If you will recognize it and thank God for it, you'll see more of his favor.

I know many Christians may doubt this was God's activity because it deals with such a trivial matter. Having to walk another five or ten minutes wasn't going to keep the Osteens from enjoying their day at the zoo. But these same Christians may be willing to believe miracle stories from others who claim God has healed them from a terminal disease or saved them in a car accident. It seems many Christians have a threshold of seriousness that needs to be met before giving credence to a specific favor claim. I sincerely hope the Hajis of this world are never exposed to this story.

Healed by God or Science?

In August of 2014, there were two US citizens working in Liberia during an outbreak of the Ebola virus. One of them was a Christian doctor named Kent Brantly who was treating many diseased patients, even those who contracted the Ebola virus. Both he and a fellow Christian nurse who worked beside him contracted the virus and became gravely ill. When they were stable enough, a special quarantined plane was sent from the US to pick them up separately to return them to Emory Hospital in Atlanta, Georgia.

A few years prior to Dr. Brantly's Ebola encounter, a Canadian company had been fervently developing a serum that would cure certain Ebola strains. This company only tested their serum on monkeys and discovered it produced a 99% cure rate. Since it had never been tested on humans, the FDA had not yet approved it. But Dr. Brantly and his nurse were allotted the small quantities of the serum that existed. In fact, there was technically only enough of the serum produced for one dose. Dr. Brantly received 75% of the dose whereas his nurse only received 25%. I'm not sure how one would ethically allot those doses, but that's how they were distributed. At that time, no one in Africa had received any percentage of that new serum.

After receiving the experimental drug, and staying quarantined for more than two weeks, both Dr. Brantly and his nurse were deemed completely cured from the virus and released from the hospital. In a press conference upon his release, Dr. Brantly stated the following: "Today is a miraculous day. I serve a God who answers prayers. I want to express my deep and sincere gratitude to Samaritan's Purse (the missionary foundation he was part of), Emory Hospital, and all of the people involved in my treatment and care." He went on to say, "Above all, I am forever thankful to God for sparing my life."

Not once during his press conference did he explicitly mention the 1,300 African people who previously died from that exact same strain of virus he claimed God saved him from. I'm sure we're not going to hear from those 1,300 people. We're not going to hear stories about how many people prayed for their healing, and yet the apparent answer from God was, "No!". If we do, it will only be from the delusional who will claim that God said "no" to their loved ones for some special reason only God knows.

Dr. Brantly is a doctor of medical science. He attempted to heal his Ebola infected patients using science, and yet most, if not all, died. Dr. Brantly was given an experimental drug after returning to the US, and by all medical accounts, that drug is the sole reason that both he and his nurse lived to talk about it. Do you find it perplexing that both he and the nurse lived after receiving that experimental drug, but the other 1,300 left behind in Liberia who did not receive the same drug, died? It's not perplexing for any critical thinker. They received the drug, and they lived. Those who didn't receive the drug died. How did Dr. Brantly have the audacity to claim it was a miracle or that God was active in both his and his nurse's recoveries, while 1,300 others died?

Even when scientific evidence stares in the face of a Christian medical doctor—evidence that could be understood by an uneducated janitor—he still credited God. Well, one might say, "The doctor really means he's thanking God for leading or guiding the researchers to invent this new drug, and therefore it was God who is responsible for saving him." But what evidence do we have to suggest that God led the researchers to a cure? Who among us will be the first person to tell the family members of the 1,300 who perished that God's drug developmental timing seemed to be in favor of the doctor and nurse and those who may follow, but it just wasn't in time for their family members?

This miracle claim really begs an even bigger question. If God had anything to do with either the discovery of the new drug or even healing Dr. Brantly independent of that drug, why would God allow Dr. Brantly or the other 1,300 people to contract the disease in the first place? After all, when you think along the same lines as people like Dr. Brantly, that God heals, why not ask yourself why he even caused or allowed the disease to exist or infect Dr. Brantly and the others who died? Is there really a God who sits back and allows diseases to infect people, then later decides to step in and provide care for the select few?

There was another Ebola case a few weeks later, but this time it was the first in the US. A Liberian man named Thomas Duncan traveled from Liberia to Texas where he began to show signs of the disease. He was cared for my multiple nurses within a Texas hospital but later died from the disease. It turns out that Dr. Brantly mentioned above, who had been given the serum, could now donate his blood carrying the antibodies to others who were infected. This was possible, if and only if, the others who were infected had his blood type. Unfortunately, Mr. Duncan did not have the same blood type as Dr. Brantly or his nurse.

Due to the lack of proper isolation equipment at the Texas hospital Mr. Duncan was treated at, two other nurses contracted the virus from Mr. Duncan. Nurse Nina Pham was diagnosed with the virus within two weeks of caring for Mr. Duncan. As it turned out, Ms. Pham's blood type matched Dr. Brantley's, so she was able to receive his antibody-rich blood in the form of a transfusion. Ms. Pham was completely cured of the disease within two weeks.

But here's what's interesting. Who did Ms. Pham credit for her complete recovery? Well, of course it was God. Here's what she had to say at her press conference in October of 2014.

> "I feel fortunate and blessed to be standing here today, I would first and foremost like to thank God, my family, and my friends. Throughout this ordeal, I have put my trust in God and my medical team. I believe in the power of prayer because I know so many people all over the world have been praying for me." She continued, "I join you in prayer now for the recovery of others."[41]

41. Fox10 News, "Nina Pham, Free of Ebola, Speaks during Press conference," YouTube, October 24, 2014, https://www.youtube.com/watch?v=fraeLlGIa7A. Retrieved June 2015.

Ms. Pham also stated the same over her twitter account, and the atheists' responses—or maybe people like me who believe that God does not act when we pray—were overwhelming.[42] They went like this:

— But the power of science is the only reason she's alive!

— How about some credit for science, which saved your life?

— Sorry to be cynical, but Nina Pham just credited "the power of prayer" for helping her become Ebola-free. Yeah. . . That's what it was.

— Nina Pham needs to thank science not prayer. She's spitting in the face of the medical community that worked hard to save her life.

— I guess the Africans don't pray hard enough?

— Nina Pham says that prayer is central to her recovery. Evidently the African nations that are stricken are prayer-free zones.

— Maybe find a new profession if you're a nurse who thinks prayer cures diseases.

What do you think is the truth here? What does your common sense and reasoning mind tell you about all of this? Was medical science or God responsible for her recovery? If you say, "It could be both," then what shall we ascertain from the thousands of Africans who had been prayed for and did not receive a medicinal solution as did Dr. Brantly and nurse Pham? They all perished. If God had anything to do with nurse Pham's recovery, then the only other logical conclusion is that God didn't either hear, listen, or respond to the prayers of the thousands of Africans with Ebola who died prior to Ms. Pham's prayers and treatment (the death toll in Africa by this time was over 10,000). The only difference between Ms. Pham and the now 10,000 or so

42. Steve Straub, "Ebola Free Nurse Nina Pham Thanks God for Her Recovery; Outraged Atheists React in Vile Manner," The Federalist Papers, October 25, 2014, https://thefederalistpapers.org/us/ebola-free-nurse-nina-pham-thanks-god-for-her-recovery-outraged-atheists-react-in-vile-manner-2. Retrieved June 2015.

Africans who died was that she received antibody treatment (developed by scientific methods) and the others did not. There's nothing supernatural or mysterious about any of this. As three of three who received the treatment survived and none who had only prayer, science alone shows the advantage.

We'll just have to chalk up Dr. Brantly's and nurse Pham's claims as false. These are statements by people who were grateful to be alive. They felt elated to be cured and needed to give thanks to something or someone. For them, that someone was the Almighty, and it's better to insinuate they have been shown favor by God in some mysterious way than to give the proper credit to the scientists in Canada who developed the antidote. In the meantime, they were implicitly telling the world that their physical lives mattered more to God than the 10,000 who died in Africa from the very same disease.

I wish I had the opportunity to interview both Dr. Brantly and nurse Pham. I want to ask them point-blank, "What do you think the African family members of those who died after only receiving prayer but no serum or antibody treatment would have to say after hearing your claims that God was in any way responsible for your recovery?"

This story that included Ms. Pham's favor of God claim was reported on in the Political Insider website,[43] evidently a pro-"active God" site. Here are the comments from the author of this article from that website:

— The pathetic thing about this is, it is clear this hard-working nurse counted on her faith and the power of prayer to get her through such a time of tragedy. She put her life on the line trying to cure a patient and was infected herself. Considering how easily she could have died within days, it's not unreasonable to think a higher power assisted in her speedy recovery.

— Atheists will stop at nothing to smear those who believe in God. From insulting this nurse's intelligence to assuming that anyone

43. Content removed from https://thepoliticalinsider.com/nurse-cured-ebola-thanks-god-atheists-furious/. Retrieved June 2015.

in the medical profession can't believe in biblical truths, militant atheists will stop at nothing to promote their anti-American views.

— Please share this story if you support Nina Pham's praising God and thanking her medical team for saving her life.

Obviously, the author of this website thinks it's not unreasonable for anyone to think God assisted Nurse Pham's speedy recovery.

I cannot understand it.

Perhaps I have this all this wrong, and God has already told us who is responsible for all the good and bad that occurs on this Earth. Remember? Isaiah, speaking on behalf of God to the Jewish nation: "'I form the light and create darkness, | I bring prosperity and create disaster; | I, the Lord, do all these things'" (Isaiah 45:7).

According to the author of Isaiah, God causes both prosperity and disaster. When he wants to give us good stuff, he does it with his active hand. When he wants to knock the crap out of any of us, he sends a natural disaster, virus, or manipulates our circumstances to put us down. The prophet Isaiah supposedly received this information from God, and he relayed this information to the Jewish people of his time. Apparently the Jews believed it, because it's reflected many times over in all their Scriptures (our Old Testament). But it shocks me that today's Christians continue to believe theories generated by the unenlightened authors of the Hebrew Scriptures still apply today.

[26] Acts of God

LET'S TURN TO ANOTHER EXAMPLE OF GOD'S ALLEGED actions which occurred on April 27, 2014. FamilyLife, headquartered in Arkansas, broadcasts a daily radio program dedicated to Christian families. One of their employees, Rob Tittle, and all his family were victims of a tornado that night. It killed Rob and two of his daughters, but his wife Kerry and their seven other children survived. The following story was written by the FamilyLife founder, Dennis Rainey (emphasis added by me):[44]

April 28th, 2014

Rob Tittle, a FamilyLife staff member and kindred spirit warrior for the family, died last night in the tornado that crushed parts of central Arkansas. Two of his daughters—Tori, age 20, and Rebekah, 14—were among the 15 killed in the storm.

Rob, 48, and his wife, Kerry, had watched the sky grow dark and ominous and were shepherding their nine children under a stairwell when the tornado disintegrated their home. Rob was doing what a man does—putting his family first and trying to get two of his daughters to safety—when the twister hit.

All that is left is a grim gray slab of concrete.

---

44.   Dennis Rainey, "The Lord Gives, the Lord Takes Away," FamilyLife, April 24, 2014, https://www.familylife.com/articles/topics/life-issues/challenges/death-and-dying/the-lord-gives-the-lord-takes-away/. Retrieved June 2015.

The Tittles' 19-year-old daughter posted this on Facebook from a friend's house: ". . . my mom, and my six brothers/sisters are alright. We have lost three of our family. . . Dad, Tori and Rebekah, prayers would be appreciated. The house is gone stripped from the foundation. The Lord Gives and *the Lord Takes away*, blessed be the Name of the Lord."

Minutes later and less than 10 miles away, Barbara (Dennis Rainey's wife) and I peeked out from under the stairs as the storm passed in front of our home. It tends to get your attention when the TV weatherman says the tornado is bearing down on your street! We could see the wall cloud crossing a lake, less than two miles away.

Thankfully the twister missed our home, but it did chew through the property of another staff couple, Dan and Nancy Butkowski. Their house suffered roof and window damage and the tornado scattered more than 100 trees like matchsticks.

Unfortunately, that wasn't the end for our staff. The tornado swept across the Arkansas River and smashed into the small community of Mayflower (population 2,312) where another staff couple, Dan and Kristin, lost their home and their two cars.

With about 10 minutes' warning, they were able to see the tornado approaching across the river and moved their six children and four pets into the master bedroom closet, which was constructed as a tornado safe room.

At the last minute, Dan closed the door as the family prayed and held onto each other through the terrifying storm. When it was over, after checking to see that everyone was okay, they were unable to open the door until neighbors, whose homes were also badly damaged or destroyed, quickly arrived with help. An overturned pick-up truck stood on its side just a foot from their safe room wall.

Facing the very real possibility of meeting the Savior that night, Dan challenged his children to be sure they had received God's salvation through Jesus Christ. While the family is grateful beyond words for *God's protection*, they are grieving with their community as recovery begins.

This is a time of extreme emotions here at FamilyLife. We mourn the loss of a good man and coworker and his two daughters, and at the same time we celebrate the survival of so many children and family members. The news could have been much worse. We are "giving thanks always and for everything" (Ephesians 5:20).

Can you see the delusion Dennis Rainey perpetuated to his believing audience? On one hand, he is mourning the loss of his staff member and his two daughters. On the other hand, he celebrates the miraculous protection that God supposedly provided for those who did survive. Mr. Rainey is telling us there was a divine reason behind who lived and who died that night— yet we'll never be able to understand it.

God's reasoning for allowing some to die and some to live were not just random events to Mr. Rainey. There was an active God who was pulling the strings for the survivors but not for those who were crushed in their homes. Can you attempt to give a good theological explanation as to why our God would purposely see to it that a father and two of his daughters were removed from this Earth and from their remaining family members? Can there really be a master plan or purpose for God to be responsible for taking a husband and father and two of his children? Is this how God works all things for the good of those who love him (Roman 8:28)?

Ironically, the other staff member's family with six children survived because they were relocated to a known tornado-safe room purposely built by the owner. Yet, after the tornado passed, this family was "grateful beyond words for *God's protection*." Really? What did Rob's wife and seven surviving children think after hearing this family say God protected them in their tornado safe room?

Then there's the coping proclamation that one of Rob's surviving daughters posted to her Facebook account. According to the FamilyLife quotation, her post read as follows: "The Lord gives, and the Lord takes away, blessed be the name of the Lord." I understand this girl was only nineteen years old, but her Bible verse recitation confirmed she also believes God is the "taker" of every life. We don't just die of disease, famine, tornadoes, auto accidents, or because our arteries leading to our hearts are blocked with plaque. To her, when someone dies, it's at the direct hand of the Creator (he gives and takes). So, based on the belief system instilled in her by her parents (from passages like we have discussed from Isaiah and Job), I can understand how she can view God as a "taker." Once again, how do people living in the twenty-first century continue to apply and perpetuate Bronze-Age thinking to explain tragedy?

Unfortunately, Dennis Rainey's radio cohost, Bob Lepine, had more to add to this tragedy during his radio broadcast the next day. The next broadcast, "God of The Whirlwind," offered Rainey and Lepine attempting to explain the reason for removing Rob and his two daughters from this Earth. Lepine said the following: "God says 'Rob's time is in my hands.' Last night, the tornado was God's target to take Rob home. Rob was looking for protection in his house, but God said No. It's time for Rob and his girls to pass through the veil."

I think Mr. Lepine mistakenly stated that, "The tornado was God's target." I believe he meant, "God used the tornado to target Rob and his two daughters to take them home." His quote doesn't really make any sense because the tornado itself could not be a target. To Mr. Lepine, Rob and his two daughters had to be the target for that tornado because God declared from the heavens those three family members would die that very night. As we all know, when we shoot at a target, we normally take aim at it. If we follow Mr. Lepine's logic, God was the one aiming, and he accurately collected the three family members he wanted to take.

But what if God had nothing to do with any of this tragedy? If he was not involved, what would God think about Mr. Lepine's claim? In your heart of hearts, deep in your reasoning minds, wouldn't you agree that God had nothing to do with either of those things? Yet Christians like Rainey and Lepine continue to perpetuate delusional explanations for random tragic events. To these Christian radio hosts, there must be a supernatural reason behind every event that occurs on this Earth—both good and bad. God isn't just in control by way of sitting on his perch. God orchestrates tornadoes, then uses his giant steering wheel in the sky to target and kill whomever he desires.

Lepine needs a "logical" reason to explain why this family was devastated yet provides primitive, illogical reasoning. There is no possible way he can validate his claims. It is true that natural disasters have been referred to as "acts of God" by the insurance industry for years. I believe that terminology goes back many centuries. It came from primitive men who thought God controlled when the clouds would produce rain for crops. They believed God's wrath caused the withholding of rain to create droughts for the disobedient.

In this modern era, apparently not all of humankind has moved past that way of thinking. Do any of us really believe that there were no rainbows until after the flood Noah survived, even if water and sunlight were present before that time? Are we to believe that the people of the Earth did not need the sun and rain to exist? Do you still believe rainbows were only sent by God as the Hebrew Scriptures tell us, as a reminder that he will never flood the Earth again? We all know that rainbows are an effect caused by the refraction of sunlight through the water molecules that are present during a rainstorm.

On the FamilyLife website the next day, there was a photo of the entire Tittle family prior to the tornado. The caption underneath the photo read, "The LORD is near the brokenhearted, and saves those who are crushed in spirit" Psalm 34:18. The note below read:

> *Miraculously,* Kerry and the other 7 children survived with relatively few injuries. Please pray for Kerry and the children as they deal with

this loss on many fronts. Pray for comfort, for healing, for strength, and for trust in God when the events of their lives are beyond understanding. God promises in Isaiah 41:10, "I will strengthen you, surely I will help you, surely I will uphold you with my righteous hand." We don't always know what God is doing, but we can be assured that he is working all things together for the good of those who love him and who have been called according to his purpose in Christ (Romans 8:28).

What could make Mr. Rainey think these verses or our prayers will entice God to supernaturally offer any comfort to the remaining Tittle family? We are all convinced the Tittle family was calling out to God to save them before the tornado ripped through their house. Apparently, Mr. Rainey asked his radio audience to pray for God to honor his supposed word to offer comfort and healing to the Tittle family, regardless of the fact that Rob and his two daughters were not physically saved after prayerfully calling on God. Again, Mr. Rainey is applying an OT verse (Isaiah 41:10) that was not written to or for us, but for the Jewish nation at that time and place. And I seriously doubt God was providing strength and holding up anyone with his righteous hand during the OT era. We should not trust God will save or protect us from disasters or offer us comfort in the aftermath. Our comfort should come from believing he has our back *in the end*, and we certainly shouldn't be crediting him for causing death.

You should also note that Mr. Rainey and others like him always try to use a plethora of Scriptures to either explain why something bad happened or to offer comfort to the downtrodden. If you consider this way of thinking just one man's opinion, you would be mistaken. The problem is, Mr. Rainey and others like him preaching from pulpits and leading small group Bible studies perpetuate these opinions and influence people to believe in a God who acts like this. Millions hear Mr. Rainey daily through the Christian radio stations airing his programs throughout the world. Every listener has the ability to accept or reject his messages. However, most of his sheep-like followers accept his reasoning because it seems unlikely that a prominent pastor like this could have flawed theological arguments. It's also not likely his listeners will discredit any of Mr. Rainey claims because he's using the ancient authors' interpretations of life events (the Bible) that most Christians believe cannot have errors.

[27] Acts of Men

YOU'LL SEE SOMETHING VERY SIMILAR IN THE NEXT
example regarding the Sandy Hook school shooting. But we should never
use Scriptures to provide reasoning for events like these. We should be using
evidentiary common reality to explain them because that will explain the
event completely—even random and chaotic events.

Let's turn our attention to the Sandy Hook Elementary school shooting
in Connecticut that occurred in December of 2012. Twenty young children
and six school staff members were senselessly killed by a deranged young
adult who, on some level, had been diagnosed with some measure of autism.
Our nation, in shock, tuned in to the news to learn the horrific details.
Although you are certainly free to contemplate the reason for God's inactivity in this tragic event, hopefully you'll reasonably conclude the God who
afforded us our free will has no choice but to allow the events of this Earth
to run their course.

This story will focus on another Christian pastor's meritless supernatural claims that probably caused even greater anguish for the grieving family
members of those killed that day[45]:

> "Only one child made it out alive of the first-grade classroom at
> Sandy Hook Elementary School last week—by fooling the gun-
> man into thinking that she was dead," the family's pastor says. The

---

45.   Philip Caulfield, "'Mommy, I'm Okay, but All My Friends Are Dead,'" *New York
       Daily News*, December 18, 2012, https://www.nydailynews.com/news/national/
       first-grader-survived-playing-dead-article-1.1221997. Retrieved December 2012.

Reverend Jim Solomon, who was speaking at an interfaith vigil for the Connecticut shooting victims Dec. 16th, 2012, in Newton, Conn., said the girl "has wisdom beyond her years." The little girl, who is 6-1/2 years old but hasn't otherwise been identified, "ran out of the school building covered in blood from head to toe, and the first words she said to her mom when she got outside was, 'Mommy, I'm OK, but all of my friends are dead,'" the Reverend Jim Solomon, pastor of Newton, Conn., told ABC News in a report that aired Sunday. "Of those that were left in the classroom of the first graders, she was the lone survivor," Solomon said. (Law enforcement officials and witnesses say that seven pupils survived in a second classroom by hiding in a closet.)

"*Somehow, in that moment, by God's grace she was able to act as if she was already deceased,*" said Reverend Solomon, who spoke at the community interfaith vigil Sunday night on the same program as President Barack Obama.

Solomon went on to say, "*That the little girl couldn't have survived outside of divine intervention.*" (Emphasis mine.)

Well, here we are again. We have another pastor making a miracle claim with absolutely no validation possible. He's labeled God as a favor provider for one child which can only appear unfair to the family members who lost their loved ones that day.

I could hardly fathom the claims of Rev. Solomon, and so I took to the "pen." I emailed him through his church's website three days after the shooting with the following:

Pastor Solomon, if you really said the following: "Solomon said the little girl couldn't have survived outside of divine intervention." I hope you have the courage to say that face to face to the families of the 25 others killed that day. How could you suggest that God showed favoritism to the little girl who played dead over the other

19 children who died? I hope the press misquoted you because, if that's what you believe, perhaps you shouldn't be teaching others about God's character or his supposed actions.

To my surprise, I received the following email reply from Rev. Solomon later that night:

Dear Jeff,

Unfortunately, the media hasn't shown "the rest of my story" regarding those children, all precious and dearly loved, who didn't have the opportunity to "play dead." Perhaps they were too good for this world and as another friend of mine has said, "heaven keeps getting better." I've ignored the media since many things are being taken out of context. I'm close friends with those who lost their children and have been for years and they all know as I've said since the day some of those children were born that I think each of those children were precious, wise, insightful, and beautiful gifts to us from God (James 1:17) and were tragically taken away from us (tragic for us, not them, as they are in a much better place) and they will live on with us in our hearts. At the same time, I am feeling very judged and condemned by people who don't even know me constantly critiquing a few words shared apart from their complete context by me while my two young daughters weep over people misunderstanding me as they've been very loved by me.

God's receiving those children into his hands is divine intervention and sovereignty (Psalm 139:16) and love (Romans 8:31–39) too. Please pray for the parents and siblings and other loved ones who remain and please encourage people not to be so judgmental of other's hearts or minds based on a few words uttered from their mouths while they themselves are personally grieving. We live here. We love one another. The rest of the country and the world do not have personal relationships with these precious people and so we respectfully ask you all to "back off" and give us some space and time to heal (Matthew 7:1–6).

Under God's Mercy,
Jim

Upon reading Rev. Solomon's response, I sent the following reply, and as expected, he never wrote back.

Reverend Solomon,

First, thank you for taking your precious time to reply to my message.

I understand that you and your community are devastated, and I know people like yourself in the clergy are giving your all to care and comfort those whose lives have been crushed by this tragedy.

I am a Christian of another sect. I'm convinced there is a God and likewise convinced that God is not active in this world. People like you and I are active on God's behalf because of what Jesus did on that cross. People intervene on God's behalf which is much different than God intervening on this Earth on our behalf.

If you're saying the press misquoted you, then I am sorry for my comments. If you're saying you did not suggest that God was involved with this little girl's survival, then I'm begging you to forgive me.

The problem arises for me if and only if you actually said and meant "that little girl couldn't have survived outside of God's intervention". If those were your words, and that's what you meant, then I'm not sure any contextual references on your part will make any difference in this matter.

I'm so exhausted with plane crash survivors claiming that God saved them while the other dead passengers weren't shown the same favor. I'm tired of hearing from Christian cancer patients in remission who've received medical treatment and claim their prayers along with others' prayers were answered by a God who showed them favor.

In my heart of hearts, these divine intervention claims are not fair to God. They're also not fair to those less fortunate including the family members in your community who have lost their loved ones in this shooting. The worst part of claims like these is they make the families of those who died think they were less qualified to receive the same favor and feel abandoned by him.

Rev. Solomon, with all due respect, none of us can know with any certainty if God has miraculously intervened in any circumstance. Since we cannot know, none of us should make claims that we do know. It's reckless.

Respectfully yours
Jeff

Please understand my position here. I was grieving for the children who died and the devastating consequences for their families. Even today, I think about those grieving parents and what it must be like to sit in their children's empty bedrooms while staring at their photos. How do these parents not constantly wonder what their children were thinking and how afraid they must have been when the gunman began shooting? I understand people like Rev. Solomon were trying their best to cope with this tragedy and that he was giving everything he had to comfort the families who lost their children. This isn't about me being calloused or cold towards anyone who was involved in this tragedy.

My problem is with those like Rev. Solomon who intentionally or unintentionally spread a message of a God playing favorites. His comments continue to coerce Christians, and maybe even himself, to believe that God was still doing good things—at least for the little girl who, through godly intervention, played dead and survived. Lay people and certainly people in the clergy need to be very careful about their miracle claims. There's no truth in Rev. Solomon's claim, and nothing good can come from it.

Reverend Solomon tried to use biblical Scripture (as did Dennis Rainey before) to provide an explanation as to why those people were slaughtered. If you go back and reread Rev. Solomon's reply, you should notice other misguided coping claims.

He suggests, as his friend puts it, "*The children that were killed might have been too good for this world*," and "*Heaven just keeps getting better.*" This can't be true on any level, but I'm sure it was his attempt to make the families who lost their children feel better. But would it? I sure would like to know if that's something the Reverend would be willing to directly suggest to the families of those deceased children.

The Reverend is trying to make sense of these senseless killings with a cosmic theistic reason. If we take the Reverend's position, specifically that these children needed to go to heaven because they were too good, then we are forced to believe God orchestrated and arranged their meeting with him that day. In other words, God must have directed the shooter to kill only those 20 children and 6 staff members. "Too good" will not satisfy the grieving families left behind, and in all honesty, no one for that matter.

I watched a documentary that included some of the grieving parents' thoughts regarding that horrific event. One of the parents, David Wheeler, who lost his son Benjamin, made the following statement: "If you look at any catastrophic event, there will be places where if that person had turned left instead of right, events would not have unfolded the way they did. But that's life. That's the chaos of the universe. And I previously found a certain amount of beauty in that chaos. And now the challenge is to continue to see the beauty in that chaos, because now the chaos has hurt me."

Mr. Wheeler's comments reaffirmed for me that the events of this Earth are not being controlled by God. If one of the parents who lost their child had randomly scheduled a dentist appointment for that child on that day, their child would be alive. If the gunman had randomly decided to enter a different hallway, different children on that campus would have died that morning. These events occur all around us and have logical explanations, even if they are random and chaotic at times.

Cause and effect direct this world. God had nothing to do with seeing those children were killed that day, and he did nothing to stop it. They didn't die because they were too good to be here. He didn't cause the one little girl to play dead. They died because a mentally disturbed young adult went over the edge and used deadly force. God didn't take them, and he certainly didn't orchestrate that event. It was by the free will of the killer and by no other reason. There's our answer. There's nothing divine about that answer either. It's real and true, even if it doesn't sit well with those who wish a divine reasoner had some mysterious unknown motive or purpose for it to occur.

God's Will Equates to Our Free Will

One of the very few good things I discovered during the Sandy Hook tragedy came directly from Robbie Parker, the father of six-year-old Emilie Parker who died that day. I'm pretty sure Mr. Parker and his family are of the Mormon faith, and truthfully, to me it doesn't really matter which faith background he represents. What he had to say was nothing short of a perfect forgiving and loving truth, and it will stay with me for the rest of my life. It's exactly how I think Jesus would have responded and dealt with an issue like this if Jesus himself was the father of a child who was senselessly killed. I want to believe I could act like Mr. Parker if I were ever in a position like his, but I'm not sure my love runs that deep.

The night of the shootings, only hours after Robbie Parker learned of his daughter's death, he gave an interview to news cameras outside his church. He said, "I don't know how to get through something like this. My wife and I don't understand how to process all of this. We find strength in our religion and in our faith, family, and friends."

He went on to say, "It's a horrific tragedy and I want everyone to know our hearts and prayers go out to the other families that have lost their children. This includes the family of the shooter. I can't imagine how hard this experience must be for them, and I want them to know that our family's love and support goes out to you as well."

Robbie Parker continued, "*I know God can't take away free will and would have been unable to stop the Sandy Hook shooting.*" While the gunman used his free will to take innocent lives, Parker said he planned to use his free will in a positive way. He said, "I'm not mad, because I have my free will to use this event to do whatever I can to make sure my wife and my other daughters are taken care of. And if there's anything I can do to help anyone at any time at any place, I'm free to do that."

Wow! How can a father who just lost his little six-year-old daughter have sympathetic feelings towards the gunman's family only hours after discovering she was dead? I can't be certain Mr. Parker was really expressing what he was feeling, but if he was, it reflects the same kind of love Jesus had for the Pharisees and the Romans who nailed him to his cross. This was a display of true love, and I applaud Mr. Parker for his exemplary behavior, which appeared to come straight from his Jesus-filled grieving heart. He used that "space" between stimulus and response to offer an answer as he assessed the situation through the lens of Jesus. Mr. Parker also confirmed the truth regarding God's ordination of our free will and his position to allow everything to run its course on this Earth.

As I mentioned previously, it's important to differentiate between God's desires and God's will. One may think differentiating between those two terms is only a matter of semantics, but I disagree. When the Bible and Christians refer to God's will, it is always in reference to what God caused or allowed to occur. For Christians, his will includes his assessments, oversights, or active control. For Christians "his will" is not simply God's passive preferences for outcomes he might have hoped would occur. The outcomes that God hopes for (his desires) through our freewilled choices are not always in sync with our decisions. And I will continue to argue God's will is our free will and the natural random events that occur on our planet.

If God is fair and just and has a deep-seated love for his creation, it could not have been his desire for that gunman to kill those teachers and children. But it must have been his will (the gunman's choice). If it wasn't his will, we could have expected God to intervene and stop it. But if God's will is to allow and accept all the events created by our freewilled choices, then his will must be our will. I cannot find another way to see this, and it completely explains the reasons for the chaotic events occurring on this planet. The best explanation cannot be that God is favoring and intervening for the select few, while suffering chaos decimates so many in our world.

[28] The Favored Christian Athlete

Most of those who follow sports have become accustomed to hearing Christian athletes give their customary postgame interviews that at some point include the comment, "I just want to thank my Lord and savior Jesus Christ . . ." Sometimes we even hear the extension, "for this victory." Or sometimes we hear the extension, "because without him, none of this would be possible for me." I've witnessed countless baseball players pointing their fingers to the sky as they cross home plate after hitting a homerun—thanking God for his favor.

Countless Christian athletes over the years have proclaimed their faith when the big stage has been available to them. A former famous football star, Tim Tebow, seemed to stop at nothing to get the word out that not only was Jesus his Lord and savior but God was Tim's inspiration for every part of his life. He became famous for his pregame prayer pose, known as Tebowing. On the sideline near one end zone and away from his teammates, he knelt on one knee with his bicep flexed and his fist under his chin, as he prayed before each game. It became a pregame spectacle in the stadiums, and every TV and phone camera focused on him.

Christians loved to see Tim "Tebowing," but it bothered me deeply. To me, Tim was doing exactly what the Bible says Jesus asked us to not do. "And when you pray, do not be like the hypocrites, for they love to pray standing in the synagogues and on the street corners to be seen by others. Truly I tell you, they have received their reward in full. But when you pray, go into your room, close the door and pray to your Father, who is unseen'" (Matthew 6:5–6). I can't be certain that Tim's motive was to be seen by others so that they would know the depth of his faith, but why couldn't Tim have "Tebowed" at his hotel or even in the locker room before the game? Don't get me wrong. Tim is a great example of how we should all be serving God in so many other areas of our lives. But why did he need to "Tebow" in front of the 70,000 fans and the millions watching on TV?

In December of 2015, The Michigan State Spartans played the Iowa Hawkeyes for a chance to make the collegiate football playoffs. Michigan State beat Iowa 16–13 and after the game, their coach, Mark Dantonio, was asked how it was that his team was able to win. He said, "I have thought that this team was special. I think quite honestly that we have God's favor. I know I'm going to get criticized for that, but I think we do."

I wasn't shocked to hear the coach's declaration because it's become commonplace. But just how quick can one lose God's favor? The following week The University of Alabama destroyed Michigan State 38–0 in the first playoff game. I never saw coach Dantonio publicly interviewed after their loss, but I sure would have liked to know where God's favor ran off to.

Russell Wilson, currently the starting quarterback for the Seattle Seahawks, is yet another famous NFL player to proclaim his faith on the big stage. He continually proclaims publicly that God is great, just as Tim Tebow did during his NFL career. He claims that God has inspired him to be who he is because of what God means to him.

In February of 2015, when Wilson and his Seahawks played the New England Patriots in the Super Bowl, things didn't go well. He led his team to the one-yard line with just seconds left. The Seahawks only needed to score a touchdown and they would have won two consecutive championships. Everyone was certain the Seahawks would run the ball, but Wilson threw a pass at the goal line that was intercepted by the Patriots and the game was over. It was a tough way to lose a Super Bowl, but it turns out, Russell Wilson provided divine reasoning behind the outcome.

In 2012, three years prior, Wilson was introduced to a former San Diego Charger player Miles McPherson who was the pastor of a church in San Diego. They met at a prayer breakfast, became good friends and at one point, the pastor asked Wilson if he would be willing to speak on stage at his church.

In July 2015, Wilson spoke at McPherson's church and the video of their exchange can be found on YouTube.[46] In front of a packed church, Wilson took a selfie with the pastor and settled into an armchair. From the stage, Wilson recalls the heartbreaking moments of his team's loss in the Super Bowl months earlier, that as he walked off the field after throwing that game losing interception, Jesus told him that he'd sent the interception. Wilson said Jesus wanted to test his faith to see if he would doubt him. Wilson also said Jesus sent the interception so that he could show the world he would remain devoted to God.

Wilson said this not with arrogance but with the casual matter-of-factness that only someone speaking to fellow believers can pull off. "There's a silver lining" Wilson told McPherson and the church. "Jesus is so amazing."

Many of the commenters on YouTube praised Wilson for his bold faith, but not everyone was along for the same ride. One of the commenters posted the following:

> I question if there is a god now. My sister is 31 years old has had stage 4 breast cancer, brain cancer and skin cancer. She was diagnosed at the age of 27 and never did drugs or alcohol and has made sure she is the best mother to her kids. Our parents neglected us when we were young . . . she is a mother of 3 kids, one who is autistic. My autistic nephew has the biggest heart and has a deep bond with my sister. Now please "GOD" tell me what plan involves my sister having to suffer all this pain and her kids having to watch their mother go through this pain and suffering? And most importantly to have their

---

46.   Rock Church, "Rock Church—Russell Wilson Q&A w/ Pastor Miles," July 9, 2015, https://www.youtube.com/watch?v=-rrsg3Js_tQ. Retrieved July 2015.

mother taken from them? I'm sure other families have gone through this, and I'd like to speak for them as well . . . where are you at, GOD?

This poor emotionally suffering commenter could not reconcile a God who alters the flight paths of footballs with a God who sat idle as he fervently prayed for his suffering sister. This is what intervention claims do to those less fortunate whose prayers are not answered like others declare. And just how devastating it must have been to hear God altered the flight path of a football to test Wilson, while his sister suffered with a terminal illness and God never showed up.

After a playoff game against the Green Bay packers, Wilson once claimed that God caused his four interceptions during that game because God wanted to make their win against the Packers more dramatic.

At the time, Russell Wilson was only in his mid-twenties. He wasn't experienced enough to know his claims were false. He wasn't, and probably still isn't aware of the emotional damage he inflicted on those less fortunate—like the suffering person commenting above. They too have prayed in vain to God for something way more important than a drama-filled football game and yet received nothing. I would like to ask Mr. Wilson if he would accompany me to a children's hospital of his choice and make those same "testing" claims to the Christian parents who have just lost their child to cancer.

PART 9:

RELATIONSHIPS, FOREKNOWLEDGE, AND CONCLUSIONS

[29] The Personal Relationship

ARE CHRISTIANS BEING TRUTHFUL WHEN THEY CLAIM
God communicates with them? Or are they possibly misattributing the
source of their feelings during prayer? If our God communicates in the way
that so many Christians attest, I wish I could understand how to have him
participate with me in that manner.

I would like more than a one-way form of communication—as seems
to be the case with my prayers. Over the thousands of times I prayed for
answers, not once did I ever hear or feel a response from him. Many of my
Christian friends claim they have a personal relationship with Jesus that
includes reciprocal communication. I can't seem to find or interpret these
godly indicators or "signs" that others claim to experience. I want a close God
like others claim to have, but I seem to have a distant God.

Silence from the Heavens

People have said to me, "Well, Jeff, you're just not trying to find God hard
enough." "You're not tuning into the right frequency." "You're too distracted."
"If you spent as much time alone with God and communing with him as
you do on your phone or watching TV, you might just find a God who will
communicate with you."

I have spent my share of "quiet times" away from all distractions over
a period of many years while communicating my one-way prayers to God.
I've meditated on "his Word" and begged him to communicate with me. If
he's communicated with me in any way, I must have been too ignorant to

recognize it. I'm a Jesus-follower who never considered this whole "personal relationship" with some imaginary being as something foolish.

I wanted what so many claimed to have, and when I was open to believing in godly communication, my inability to hear from him hurt me deeply. I have not found the phrase "personal relationship" anywhere in our collection of sixty-six books. Nowhere. Is this just another man-made attempt to paint a picture that God is an active participant in our daily lives?

As it turns out, there is another person who I assume had more faith than I have who also struggled with having a personal relationship with God during her lifetime. The Catholic nun Mother Teresa, renowned for her benevolent service, sacrificially committed herself to loving people during their last moments of life. However, most are unaware she said that she didn't understand how to have a personal relationship with God.

She struggled with multiple facets of her faith at times and even went to the extreme of doubting the existence of God. In the book *Come Be My Light*, the author Brian Kolodiejchuk compiled twenty-two letters written by Mother Teresa revealing her deep longing to experience God.[47] Shortly after beginning her work in the slums of Calcutta, she wrote: "Where is my faith? Even deep down there is nothing but emptiness and darkness. If there be a God—please forgive me."

In letters eight years later, she was expressing "such deep longing for God," adding she felt "repulsed, empty, no faith, no love, no zeal." Her smile to the world from her familiar weather-beaten face was a "mask" or a "cloak" she said. "What do I labor for? If there be a God, there can be no soul. If there be no soul then, Jesus, you also are not true."

Mother Teresa died in 1997 and the Catholic church beatified her, recognizing her as one who can posthumously intercede via prayer on behalf of others. Yet she felt abandoned by God from the very start of the work that

---

47.   Brian Kolodiejchuk, *Mother Teresa: Come Be My Light* (New York: Doubleday Crown Publishing, 2007).

made her a global icon in the way of servanthood. Her doubts persisted until her death.

"I am told that God lives in me—and yet the reality of darkness and coldness and emptiness is so great that nothing touches my soul," she wrote at one point. "I want God with all the power of my soul—and yet between us there is a terrible separation." On another occasion she wrote, "I feel just that terrible pain of loss, of God not wanting me, of God not being God, of God not really existing."

She wrote the following to her spiritual advisor, Michael van der Peet, in 1979 shortly before she received her Nobel peace prize: "Jesus has a very special love for you. As for me, the silence and emptiness are so great that I look and do not see, listen and do not hear. The tongue moves but does not speak."

When I first read about her doubts, it did make me feel as if I were not alone. And it immediately made me question the validity of claims others make that God communicates with them. I thought, "If God didn't speak to Mother Teresa, who else qualifies?" I also remember wondering, "How could someone so devoted to God, who served in the most sacrificial way, not only struggle with God's continual silence but, at times, question his existence?" My own experience, coupled with hearing Mother Teresa's story, has led me to suspect most, if not all, godly communication claims are perpetuated by Christians who want them to be true.

Christian Peer Pressure

In my experience, when a small group Bible study member hears another member make claims of godly communication, it seems to drive other members to make similar claims in the future. I'm not saying these people are competing on a superficial level to one-up fellow believers. It's more likely they feel more "spiritually qualified" by claiming to receive godly messages. I've been involved with many small groups of Christians sharing their "God messages." When someone within the group seems to continually receive messages from the Lord, it's not long after that some of the others follow suit.

It is unfortunate that Pastor Rick Warren was never able to give Mother Teresa his advice on how to hear from God. According to Pastor Warren, "When you get that desperate, you're going to hear from God." Or maybe people like Mother Teresa and like me haven't really been desperate enough. Here's another excerpt from Rick Warren's Purpose Driven Connection daily email, dated December 9, 2013.

You Have to Want to Hear from God[48]

"You will search again for the LORD your God. And if you search for him with all your heart and soul, you will find him." (Deuteronomy 4:29 NLT)

You're not going to hear God unless you really, really want it. I'm not saying it's an option. I'm not saying it would be nice. It is a necessity!

God won't tell you about his dream for your life if he knows you'll want to debate it. God doesn't tell you what he put you on Earth to do just so you can say, "Let me think about it."

No! It's got to be a necessity. You have to say, "I've got to know why I'm here. I've got to know what you want me to do with my life. *I've got to hear your voice.* I've got to have your vision."

King David wrote in the book of Psalms, "My God, I want to do what you want," and "What I want most of all and at all times is to honor your laws" (Psalm 40:8 NCV; Psalm 119:20 CEV).

David was passionate in his declaration that what he wanted most of all was to honor God. Being obedient and following God were not options for him. It was the only thing David wanted to do.

---

48.   Rick Warren, "You Have to Want to Hear from God," Pastor Rick's Daily Hope, April 11, 2018, https://www.oneplace.com/ministries/daily-hope/read/devotionals/daily-hope-with-rick-warren/you-have-to-want-to-hear-from-god-daily-hope-with-rick-warren-april-11-2018-11790035.html. Emphasis mine.

He used words for seeking God like, "I long for it," "I crave it," "I hunger for it," and "I'm like a deer panting for water."

When you get that desperate, you're going to hear from God.

A lot of people talk to God, but they never hear from God. For them, prayer is a monologue. But you can't have a relationship when it is wrapped up in a monologue from you. What if I had married my wife and talked to her, but she never talked to me? That's not a relationship. You've got to have a conversation. Just as important as talking to God in prayer is listening to God and letting him talk to you. How does that happen? First, you've got to want it more than anything else.

Deuteronomy 4:29 says, "You will search again for the Lord your God. And if you search for him with all your heart and soul, you will find him" (NLT). *It's guaranteed!*

According to Pastor Warren, if we really want to hear from God, all we need to do is want it bad enough and be willing to listen to him. That has not worked for me and apparently never for Mother Teresa either. Maybe others truly have this kind of two-way relationship with him, and that's why they are sold out to the premise that he is active. But, since I consider myself no better nor worse than other humans on this Earth, I'm extremely skeptical God actively communicates with anyone. If he does, who would need to extend faith in his existence?

Think about what Pastor Warren is saying. He suggests there are conditions required to receive godly communication. Apparently, we need to jump through some desperation hoops to qualify for it. Are we to believe that the same God who loves us without bounds and suffered on a cross to prove it disconnects his cosmic phone line between us until we cross some unknown threshold of desperation to consider communicating with us?

Forms of Godly Direction

God is not communicating with us by audibly speaking to us or manipulating our circumstances. When we turn our backs on the moral laws of God, the natural consequences of our sin can speak to us loud and clear. When people get to the end of their ropes after continually making bad life choices, many hit rock bottom.

My choice to gamble drove me to that place. It's in that place where natural consequences drive people to change. I've heard many times, "When we get to the end of ourselves, we get to the beginning of God." When consequences take us to a place of quiet desperation, many of us turn to what is good and right—away from destructive choices.

But consequences or our change of heart shouldn't be perceived as godly communication. These are not the same as what many Christians consider "communication," hearing God's voice or experiencing feelings they attribute to God during prayer. God's laws and principles were put in place from the beginning of time for our protection. If we ignore those laws and violate godly principles, the natural consequences themselves cause grave danger and can speak to us.

The pastor of my church tells me that God's primary form of communication to us is through the Bible. He doesn't rule out that God speaks audibly to us, albeit he seems to suggest that if it does happen, it's not very often. My pastor affirms God's usual form of active communication occurs through his Word, and it convicts our hearts.

This premise seems very strange to me, because in my mind, the Bible is a one-way source of information via man's interpretation of what its authors wrote. It's a guide for us to understand the events that have been tied to God's character and how we should live our lives. It is a source that attempts to describe God and his historical relationships with mankind. I understand gathering knowledge from the Bible and applying it to my life, but this is not like having a live conversation with another person. It's certainly not the same primary way Rick Warren claims God communicates with us.

Direction from the Bible

To me, reading the Bible is not active two-way communication any more than reading a health textbook from the 1920s to learn about hygiene and health care and apply it to my life. The author of that old health textbook would not be actively communicating with me as I read it today. I would be gathering information from what he wrote years ago and analyzing the information in light of what we know about health now. I couldn't ask the author questions and have any further dialogue with him about what he wrote because he would have already passed on.

This is exactly what we have with the biblical authors from antiquity. I also may or may not be willing to apply some of that old health book information to my life. If God is communicating with us only through the biblical text, then I do not consider that as active two-way communication. I can't have a relationship with textual information.

One-Way Communication

I mentioned earlier that I am in the communications business. I won't hold it against you for breaking out in laughter after reading the next sentence. I have been in the "pager"—yes pager like a "beeper"—business since 1987.

If you are old enough to recall, nearly all paging devices ever made communicated only one-way. Before cell phones became affordable, you could call someone's pager number, then enter your callback number on the phone pad and wait for their callback from a home or payphone. Or you could call an answering service, speak to a live operator, and they would send a text message to more sophisticated pagers capable of receiving alphanumeric characters. If you asked the pager recipient a question in that text, they most likely had to call you back either on your landline or your cell phone—if you had one. Nearly all pagers are a simple one-way form of communication.

For me, when communing with God, it's as if I have paged him thousands of one-way messages over the years, but he doesn't have a way to respond. There are no callbacks or responses. I don't know how to have a relationship with anyone who refuses to respond back to me. Yet Rick Warren claims we all just need to desperately want to hear from him, and then and only then will he speak up.

For many, this inability to receive communication from God creates doubts regarding even God's existence. These doubts become even more intense when they are exposed to other Christians who continually claim that God has spoken to them. Non-believers consider those who say "the Lord spoke to me" completely delusional. Hearing such claims will not cause them to consider God.

Mother Teresa also seemed to have doubts about God's existence because she was unable to hear from him. It's one thing to rely on ancient texts and a God who remains hidden and another thing to realize we are supposedly being placed on his "pay no mind" list because he doesn't communicate with some of us as he purportedly does with others.

Relationship Building

When we communicate, we actively share our thoughts with one another in a two-way form of communication. First, I say something to you. You acknowledge that you have understood what I have said, and then you speak your thoughts to me. I ask you a question, and you answer. Two-way communication builds up our human personal relationships. I do not understand how to have an "active" personal relationship with anyone or anything in its absence.

Even my dog communicates with me better than God. When she rolls over on her back and moves her front paws back and forth, she is telling me that she wants me to rub her underside. When she's hungry, she sits in front of me and barks. When she wants to go outside, she stands at the backdoor and either barks or scratches the bottom section of the door. When I ask her, "Do you want a Milk Bone?" she gets very excited and audibly barks at me. I need to spell the word "walk" because, if I say the word, she runs towards the front door waiting for me to put her leash on.

My wife has seen and heard my frustration with God's inactivity. In a similar way to Pastor Warren's example from above, she one day asked, "How do you think it makes God feel that you don't pray (she meant requesting prayer) or communicate with him?" She went on to say, "How would you feel if your son chose not to speak to you?"

I answered her simply and truthfully. First, I explained that I do pray to God but no longer in the form of requests. I explained to her that as a "good" father, I would do whatever it took to have a relationship with my son—even if he was rebellious. No circumstance or my son's unwillingness to desire my love would keep me from trying to communicate with him. Unlike my God, I would reach out and speak to my son. I would reach out and hug my son and actively show and communicate my love for him.

God seems to be unwilling to do that with me. I'm not only referring to the last twenty years of my struggle. The heavens were silent even during the seven years prior to that when I considered God active. My wife's example was perfect for me. It reaffirmed to me that personal relationships require "active" two-way communication—just as Pastor Warren suggests it should be.

So, I have concluded that the people who say God speaks to them are either untruthful or self-deceived. The alternative I cannot fathom: God is purposely showing them favor over those like me who have neither heard nor felt God communicating.

When people make statements like, "God spoke to my heart today," or "God reminded me," I don't believe that really happened. Our consciences speak to us—not an active God who is sending communicative signals.

When one has aligned themselves with the principles of God, their thoughts about specific matters will most likely align themselves with his higher standards that will direct them through their life experiences. When their thoughts are centered on God, reasoning in all life experiences should follow. That's not God talking. That's our consciences aligning with God.

[30] God's Foreknowledge

THERE ARE SCRIPTURAL ARGUMENTS THAT CAN BE MADE for and against God's foreknowledge. An overwhelming number of biblical passages back up traditional Christians' claims of God's omniscience—that he knows the past, present, and the future. But, in line with the many arguments I have made previously, these biblical foreknowledge claims likely only reflect man's attempts to characterize God's attributes in their own understanding, statements made by the biblical authors who knew no more about godly attributes than we know today.

Another sect of Christianity, open theism, uses other less frequently cited Scriptures to make the case that God does not know the future. Although biblical prophecies appear to have come true in most cases, and traditional Christians use this to claim God knows the future, open theists claim that most of these biblical prophecies were conditional.

In the many prophecies from the Hebrew Scriptures, God tells his people through his prophets, "If you do this, then I will do that." The final future actions by God are predetermined by God based on the conditional choices made by humans. Analogously, you might tell your son you will take his car away for a week if he stays out past his curfew tonight. You don't foreknow what choice he will make regarding his curfew, but if he did violate your condition, you will enforce your restriction. Your prediction regarding the consequences of his actions would come true, but it was based on your son's choice. It would have nothing to do with your foreknowledge of his future actions.

Arguing for Limited Knowledge

There are many conflicting theological arguments regarding what God knows and when he knows it. The open theists suggest that God has allowed his creation to determine the majority, if not all, of the future. God knows only what can be known, and the future is open to our human decisions. The future is not reality yet, and therefore God cannot know what we will decide to do, thus he cannot know the future. If open theology is correct, it could refute the notion that God intervenes because he knows what needs to be accomplished for the betterment of mankind.

Open theists believe God has given his creatures libertarian free will. This type of free will allows everyone to freely make a certain choice or the opposite of that choice. For example, all of us are free to accept God or to reject him. Someone may choose to attend college while others choose to enter the work force immediately after high school.

Traditional Christianity purports that God is omnipotent, omnipresent, and omniscient. "Omnipotence" refers to God's limitless power. He is not subject to physical limitations as humans are, and he has power over all the physical elements of the universe. God's power is infinite. But we shouldn't take this to the nth degree. Many traditional Christians use the term omnipotent to refer to a God who controls everything, rather than simply God's *ability* to control certain earthly events. Omnipotence does not mean that God controls each thought and action that occurs on this Earth.

Open theists argue that God has limitations centered in logic. They suggest God can't create round squares, make a rock too heavy for him to lift, or make 2+2=5. In other words, even though God has extreme power, he cannot, and therefore does not, violate the principles of logic that he instilled within his creation.

"Omnipresence" suggests that God is present everywhere and also infers that God is capable of being everywhere at any time. His divine presence encompasses the whole of the universe. There is no location where he is not present. This should not be confused with pantheism, which suggests that God is synonymous with the material universe itself. Instead, omnipresence suggests that God is distinct from the universe but inhabits all of it. The question we need to ponder with this godly attribute is, Does God inhabit the future?

"Omniscience" for traditional Christianity suggests that *nothing takes him by surprise*. His knowledge is total. He knows all that there is to know and all that can be known and can simultaneously observe all of time—including the future.

Let's examine the attribute of omniscience, that God knows and has known everything that has and will happen in our universe. Because traditional Christianity bases much of its theology—and therefore, its actions—specifically on claims of divine intervention around this specific godly attribute, we must examine it. This theology asserts that God acts to control the future, since he purportedly knows how earthly events can work in conjunction with his plans and for the betterment of mankind.

Yet, there are many Scriptures that open theists use to argue that God does not know the future. For example, when considering Israel's wickedness, Jeremiah presumes to declare on God's behalf, "*Nor did it enter my mind that [the people of Israel] should do this abomination*" (Jeremiah 32:35 ESV, emphasis mine). If God really knows the future, how could he possibly have been quoted saying that he had no idea how his people would act?

In the book of Jonah, God threatens the city of Nineveh with destruction and then decides against it when the people of Nineveh repent and turn from their evil ways (Jonah 3:10). If God knows the future and he had preplanned to destroy Nineveh, how could it be possible for God to change his mind? These passages imply that God's actions are not set in stone with foreknowledge, so they are subject to the conditional, freewilled actions of humans.

Before God chose to flood the Earth because of man's wickedness, the author, said to be Moses, wrote, "The LORD regretted that he had made human beings on the earth, and his heart was deeply troubled" (Genesis

6:6). The more accurate Hebrew translation for the word "regretted" would be "repented." But in either case, how is it that God could be in a regretful or repenting position if he already knew that man would become so wicked?

In the story of Abraham and Isaac, after Abraham was ready to follow God's order to kill his son, God purportedly said through an angel, "'Do not lay a hand on the boy,' he said. 'Do not do anything to him. *Now I know* that you fear God, because you have not withheld from me your son, your only son'" (Genesis 22:12, emphasis mine). How can we claim that God knows the future when God uses this unusual challenge to discover Abraham's fear and obedience?

In Jeremiah 7:31 God reportedly said, "They have built the high places of Topheth in the Valley of Ben Hinnom to burn their sons and daughters in the fire—something I did not command, *nor did it enter my mind*" (emphasis mine). Again, how can we try to explain how God could have foreknowledge, and yet he is quoted as saying that something never entered his mind?

In these cases, traditional Christians refute verses which they argue are simply anthropomorphic terms used by the biblical authors and not what God was thinking or feeling. (Hmm . . . where have we heard that explanation?) But, if they refute the actual words of the authors making claims about God's lack of knowledge, how can Christians then confidently assume correct literal interpretations of every other Scripture contained in the Bible? Doesn't this contradiction refute other biblical claims that suggest God does know the future?

Scholars, theologians, and sometimes everyday Christians read biblical Scriptures scrutinizing every word and premise and, in many instances, take them literally to mean exactly what has been translated. This clear double standard has been a theme throughout this book. I hope you are now at least aware of the dichotomy.

The biblical authors used human words to try to describe the attributes of God, and they did this throughout the Bible. This makes me skeptical about the trustworthiness of many Scriptures and explains why I question whether all were inspired by God. Perhaps they were just man's attempt to describe God's attributes and activity. I very carefully assess every quoted verse written by all the biblical authors. I also look at how modern followers of Christ use and attempt to apply those words and principles today. Is our canon of Scripture really the "gospel truth," all of what God wanted placed in a sacred book to direct us to him, or could it be laced with authors' personal thoughts and opinions or even faulty premises?

Traditional Christian theologians who believe in godly foreknowledge rely on verses like the following to claim that God does know the future:

You know what I am going to say
    even *before* I say it, LORD.
You saw me *before* I was born.
    Every day of my life was recorded in your book.
Every moment was laid out
    before a single day had passed. (Psalm 139:4, 16 NLT, emphasis mine)

For me, these two verses, and even the verses that don't support godly foreknowledge listed above, are simply the results of what we'd expect from uneducated men living 3,000 years ago applying what they understood regarding God's attributes. They didn't really know what God knew in advance any more than we do today. We have added logic to this subject in an attempt to reason out the unfathomable.

Let's consider the following: What if on the day that your child was born, he or she came out of the womb holding a recording of every action of your child throughout every second of their life, concluding with their death. It would also contain the audio of all your child's thoughts for every second of their life. You could play the video at normal speed, or you could advance it to any period of your child's life. Would you watch it? If so, would you be tempted to watch all of it?

If any of us had the courage to watch a video like this, I think most of us would immediately look down at the status bar to check the total length of our child's life in years. What would life be like for parents if they knew exactly everything their child would do, every thought they would have, every good or bad experience they would go through, all before they lived it? I've asked a few of my friends about this when we discuss God's foreknowledge whether they would want to watch a video like that. All of them have told me they'd simply discard the recording. Why? They wouldn't want to spoil the anticipation of what's to come, good or bad. They also wouldn't want to know if their child might succumb to a premature death by disease or accident.

Knowing every detail of the entire life of our children would ruin our own life's experience. There would be nothing to look forward to with anticipation or we might be overcome with horror for the negative events we know in advance. I wouldn't want to know, and I wonder if God really wants to foreknow all outcomes. Yes, these are just my human feelings and thoughts that I am superimposing onto the character of our Creator— just as I believe the biblical authors did.

[31] Why This Matters

I KNOW THIS HAS BEEN A BUMPY RIDE FOR THOSE OF YOU
who began this journey believing that God currently intervenes in the affairs
of man. I'm sure some have felt on their heels, continually being challenged
on beliefs and desires held for the majority of their lives. My premises must
have seemed negative and pessimistic because I postulate that the Bible is
not perfect and describe a God who seems indifferent to our worldly needs.

I doubt I've moved too many from their positions on this matter, and I
know it's because they would never allow themselves to accept a God like that.
Many seem resistant to remove the miracle card from their wallets because
they would feel insecure. And yet, the only answer intervention believers have
for the horrific suffering of others is, "God's ways are higher than our ways."

I also trust many have made it to the end of my treatise who started it
feeling abandoned by God during portions of their lives. I hope I have provided them with a pathway to reconcile their reality with the known essentials
of the Christian faith. Hopefully you have been able to realize that you can
live a life that honors God, Christ, and others without believing in a *perfect*
Bible and overextending faith to an intervening God. If any of these confused
or hurting Christians have ever considered abandoning their faith or actually
done so, I hope I've encouraged them to hold on to God in a way that removes
the mysterious and centers them in the reality of God's forgiving grace.

I also aimed to educate non-believers who have considered Christians
delusional. Beliefs in an invisible God, seemingly farfetched stories from the
Bible, and current miracle claims cause many to discount faith founded on

Jesus. I hope they will measure the more realistic and logical pathway that I have presented to at least consider God.

I have written this book with sincere conviction that current intervention-believing Christians should consider the damage they are causing by perpetuating their miracle claims—even if they sincerely believe in God's current earthly activity. Think about others less fortunate who never receive the miraculous favors you lay claim to, and please, do not publicly wave the favor flag.

In order not to cause one another to stumble, I humbly suggest they should keep perceived answered prayer between themselves and God in the same way that Jesus asked us to make our prayers in the privacy of a closet. If we really believe that God would never want our actions to hurt anyone less fortunate, wouldn't he prefer private praise to him for our perceived individual blessings rather than collateral damage to others?

We discussed how blessing claims may lead other Christians within earshot to establish *expectations* for God to provide for them. If they hear that Johnny received a job after prayerful request, they are apt to think God may act on their behalf when a more serious life event comes their way.

Favor / blessing claims can *damage* the faith of other God-loving Christians who never seem to have their prayers answered affirmatively. When less fortunate believers sense God's provisions for others but not themselves, this may cause them to question God's love for them. If Cindy receives a new house and claims she was blessed by the hand of God, and another Christian prays for their loved one's cancer to be eradicated, yet it is not, wouldn't one wonder why they are not receiving these favors from the Almighty? These misunderstandings can cause God to appear unfair, unjust, or an imaginary construct.

Miraculous favor / blessing claims further alienate "seekers" or those more skeptical to ever consider God. Again, Jesus told us in Matthew 28:19, "'Therefore go and make disciples of all nations.'" If Christians really want to reach non-believers, current claims of supernatural intervention will kill that opportunity with those more skeptical.

Christians in the past centuries may have been persuaded by these tactics because those generations lived in greater ignorance. They won't affect those in the twenty-first century and beyond. Some non-believers are willing to consider an authentic God only as reflected in the realities of this natural world, and the natural world that non-believers and Christians like me live in does not include miraculous intervention. If it does, Christians will have no choice other than to admit that God plays favorites.

In one of my favorite movies, *City Slickers*, an old burly trail boss cowboy named Curly, played by Jack Palance, rides his horse in the wilderness next to Mitch, a man suffering a midlife crisis from New York City, played by Billy Crystal. After Mitch explains his difficult life circumstances to Curly, job and marriage problems, their exchange is as follows:

CURLY: Do you know that the secret of life is?

MITCH: No, what?

CURLY: *Holds up his hand with his index finger indicating the number one and says,* "One thing. It's just one thing. You stick to that and everything else don't mean $hit."

MITCH: "That's great, but what's the one thing?"

CURLY: "That's what you gotta figure out"

Here's what I've figured out for myself and what I'm encouraging others to consider. That "one thing" for all of us should be God's forgiving, gracious love. That one thing is not answered prayers for physical healing or material possessions. That one thing is not supernatural relief for our personal problems. Once we faithfully center our lives only on the miracle of our redemption from sin, the need for godly intervention or anything else for that matter "don't mean $hit." Our difficult circumstances, shortcomings, or desires for supernatural relief become meaningless.

When one feels secure in believing their past has been removed, there is nothing more freeing in life. There are no earthly substitutes for that kind of freedom, and the gratitude that flows within us will be our greatest motivator to honor God and love others for the rest of our life.

If you can mindfully ingest and apply the words of Jesus to your life, you'll realize they are true and the best way to live. His principles can resonate in your soul in a way that will bring meaning and purpose to life. In doing so, you can stretch your arms out wide, look up to the sky, and in gratitude, bask in his amazing forgiving grace! Center your life on *only* that; do not hope for current godly intervention. If it turns out there's a prize (heaven) at the end of your race (life)—then even better.

If you're a fellow Christian, what does it really matter if you and I arrive at the same destination (accepting and basking in God's grace) even though one of us refutes current miracles while another believes they continue to occur? The one who continues to believe and perpetuate that God is selectively favoring some but not others will need to answer that for themselves. They will need to reconcile that notion with the obvious evidence that suggests otherwise, and more importantly, with other less fortunate God-honoring people.

We need to let go of the premise that God will supernaturally offer any favors for our benefit. God's ultimate favor has already come to all of us through Jesus. We don't need godly intervention to live a full and abundant life, and we risk our peace when we extend our faith in a God who provides favor. We only need a sacrificial mentor who has provided truths to live by and set us free from the bondage of our past. I hope I have successfully pointed you to these essential common realities throughout the body of this book.

Epilogue

I HAVE TRIED THROUGHOUT THIS BOOK TO CONVEY JUST how difficult my journey to freedom and authenticity has been—a lonely, meandering road that at times had me dangling on the cliff's edge of complete disbelief. I have felt like an outcast in Christian circles when few around me outwardly doubted God's present-day activity as I have. For the most part, I was convinced their refusal to agree with my arguments centered more in their desire to have an active God than their refusal to consider reasoning.

I take some solace knowing others think as I do, even if they won't publicly acknowledge it. Most Christians will never allow themselves to reside where God doesn't supernaturally help anyone. However, when I contemplate my belief system and compare it with our common realities, it takes me to a place of confidence and a place of intellectual and emotional equilibrium.

I'm not getting the active, favor-providing God I once hoped for, but the trade-off is worth it. I am free from the cognitive dissonance I once experienced. I have decided living in logical and reasonable reality rather than in false hope is well worth the price of isolation. My universe makes sense to me now, and God's amazing grace has even greater meaning to me.

However, God's amazing grace alone hasn't helped every life circumstance. My journey has negatively affected my wife and our relationship. It's extremely difficult acknowledging what I thought I believed about God's intervention even before I met her is not what I believe today. I have hurt and greatly disappointed her because we no longer share this core value. There were many times earlier in our marriage when we collectively went to God in prayer asking him for help. Today, she does not have that same person in her corner—her husband and supposed closest confidant who once prayed with her for godly relief.

There have been multiple family health crises during my theological struggle when I knew she needed a requesting prayer partner, but I just could not cross that line. I still carry guilt over this issue because I love her dearly. Yet to her, it must seem as if I don't care. But how could I consider making prayerful requests when doing so would be completely contrary to everything I now believe?

"Fake it until you make it" can't be a plausible option—I'd already tried that for many years. I'm also fairly certain my wife would have rejected my overtures during our courting years if my theology regarding godly activity had been what it is today. I have thought many times, as I'm sure she has, that this is the kind of issue that could excuse divorce.

I'm aware that all people change over time in many ways. It's not like I've completely rejected God. I am a follower of Jesus. However, my wife and seemingly all Christians want to believe there's a God who cares enough about all of us that he would be willing to help us by altering our circumstances for the better. I once believed in that same kind of God. I once prayed to a God like that. I used to prayerfully make requests to the Almighty with her, but I cannot bring myself to do that anymore.

To my wife, I am so sorry for the ways this issue has hurt our marriage, and I hope you will find it in your heart to forgive me. Maybe you already have, or maybe you will before your time on this Earth comes to an end. I am truly sorry for any pain or embarrassment I have caused you. This change on my part has not been fair to you, and I know it has been extremely devastating. All of this is on me, and I know that I have hurt you beyond measure.

I never thought in my early years I would someday conclude that God is inactive, and yet today I can see it no other way. For so many years I tried with all my might to reconcile my Christian actions and beliefs to what reality was telling me, but I just could not continue pretending. I want you to know that

I don't think of you as delusional or dumb. I see your adherence to believing in an intervening God, just as I do in others, as something grounded in your human desire for a divine helper ingrained in you since childhood.

To my two amazing children, I also humbly ask for your forgiveness. I never want you to think for one moment that I harbor any disappointment because you have continued in many ways on the path I raised you to follow. I don't desire that you change any of your core beliefs just to agree with me about any of this. It also hurts me to my inner core that I am unable to participate with you in requesting prayer.

I spent many hours at your bedsides reading Christian devotionals and praying with you to a God that I wanted to believe was active. I led premeal prayers with you at our dinner table every night and even prayed for safety before every road trip. I cherish those times and our many late-night discussions when you became older.

You both love and honor God with all you have, and you both will make this world a much better place, whether God is active or not. You both have become amazing individuals who I'm convinced God takes great pride in. I carry that same level of pride for both of you within me.